YOUR PERSONAL HOROSCOPE 2018

JOSEPH POLANSKY

YOUR PERSONAL HOROSCOPE 2018

Month-by-month
forecast for every sign

Thorsons

Thorsons
An imprint of HarperCollins*Publishers*
1 London Bridge Street
London SE1 9GF

www.harpercollins.co.uk

First published by Thorsons 2017

1 3 5 7 9 10 8 6 4 2

A catalogue record for this book is
available from the British Library

ISBN 978-0-00-823938-1

Printed and bound in the United States of America by
LSC Communications

Find out more about HarperCollins and the environment at
www.harpercollins.co.uk/green

The author is grateful to the people of STAR ★ DATA, who truly fathered this book and without whom it could not have been written.

Contents

Introduction

Welcome to the fascinating and intricate world of astrology!

For thousands of years the movements of the planets and other heavenly bodies have intrigued the best minds of every generation. Life holds no greater challenge or joy than this: knowledge of ourselves and the universe we live in. Astrology is one of the keys to this knowledge.

Your Personal Horoscope 2018 gives you the fruits of astrological wisdom. In addition to general guidance on your character and the basic trends of your life, it shows you how to take advantage of planetary influences so you can make the most of the year ahead.

The section on each sign includes a Personality Profile, a look at general trends for 2018, and in-depth month-by-month forecasts. The Glossary (*page 5*) explains some of the astrological terms you may be unfamiliar with.

One of the many helpful features of this book is the 'Best' and 'Most Stressful' days listed at the beginning of each monthly forecast. Read these sections to learn which days in each month will be good overall, good for money, and good for love. Mark them on your calendar – these will be your best days. Similarly, make a note of the days that will be most stressful for you. It is best to avoid booking important meetings or taking major decisions on these days, as well as on those days when important planets in your horoscope are retrograde (moving backwards through the zodiac).

The Major Trends section for your sign lists those days when your vitality is strong or weak, or when relationships with your co-workers or loved ones may need a bit more effort on your part. If you are going through a difficult time, take a look at the colour, metal, gem and scent listed in the 'At a Glance' section of your Personality Profile. Wearing a piece of jewellery that contains your metal and/or gem will strengthen your vitality, just as wearing clothes or decorating your room or office in the colour ruled by your sign, drinking teas made from the herbs ruled by your sign or wearing the scents associated with your sign will sustain you.

Another important virtue of this book is that it will help you to know not only yourself but those around you: your friends, co-workers, partners and/or children. Reading the Personality Profile and forecasts for their signs will provide you with an insight into their behaviour that you won't get anywhere else. You will know when to be more tolerant of them and when they are liable to be difficult or irritable.

In this edition we have included foot reflexology charts as part of the health section. So many health problems could perhaps be avoided or alleviated if we understood which organs were most vulnerable and what we could do to protect them. Though there are many natural and drug-free ways to strengthen vulnerable organs, these charts show a valid way to proceed. The vulnerable organs for the year ahead are clearly marked in the charts. It's very good to massage the whole foot on a regular basis, as the feet contain reflexes to the entire body. Try to pay special attention to the specific areas marked in the charts. If this is done diligently, health problems can be avoided. And even if they can't be completely avoided, their impact can be softened considerably.

I consider you – the reader – my personal client. By studying your Solar Horoscope I gain an awareness of what is going on in your life – what you are feeling and striving for and the challenges you face. I then do my best to address these concerns. Consider this book the next best thing to having your own personal astrologer!

It is my sincere hope that *Your Personal Horoscope 2018* will enhance the quality of your life, make things easier, illuminate the way forward, banish obscurities and make you more aware of your personal connection to the universe. Understood properly and used wisely, astrology is a great guide to knowing yourself, the people around you and the events in your life – but remember that what you do with these insights – the final result – is up to you.

A Note on the 'New Zodiac'

Recently an article was published that postulated two things: the discovery of a new constellation – Ophiuchus – making a thirteenth constellation in the heavens and thus a thirteenth sign, and the statement that because the Earth has shifted relative to the constellations in the past few thousand years, all the signs have shifted backwards by one sign. This has caused much consternation, and I have received a stream of letters, emails and phone calls from people saying things like: 'I don't want to be a Taurus, I'm happy being a Gemini', 'What's my real sign?' or 'Now that I finally understand myself, I'm not who I think I am!'

All of this is 'much ado about nothing'. The article has some partial truth to it. Yes, in two thousand years the planets have shifted relative to the constellations in the heavens. This is old news. We know this and Hindu astrologers take this into account when casting charts. This shift doesn't affect Western astrologers in North America and Europe. We use what is called a 'tropical' zodiac. This zodiac has nothing to do with the constellations in the heavens. They have the same names, but that's about it. The tropical zodiac is based on the Earth's revolution around the Sun. Imagine the circle that this orbit makes, then divide this circle by twelve and you have our zodiac. The Spring Equinox is always 0 degrees (Aries), and the Autumn Equinox is always 0 degrees Libra (180 degrees from 0 Aries). At one time a few thousand years ago, these tropical signs coincided with the actual constellations; they were pretty much interchangeable, and it didn't matter what zodiac you used. But in the course of thousands of years the planets have shifted relative to these constellations. Here in the West it doesn't affect our practice one iota. You are still the sign you always were.

In North America and Europe there is a clear distinction between an astrological sign and a constellation in the heavens. This issue is more of a problem for Hindu astrologers. Their zodiac is based on the actual constellations – this is called the 'sidereal' zodiac. And Hindu astrologers have been accounting for this shift all the time. They keep close tabs on it. In two thousand years there is a shift of 23 degrees, and they subtract this from the Western calculations. So in their system many a Gemini would be a Taurus and this is true for all the signs. This is nothing new – it is all known and accounted for, so there is no bombshell here.

The so-called thirteenth constellation, Ophiuchus, is also not a problem for the Western astrologer. As we mentioned, our zodiac has nothing to do with the constellations. It could be more of a problem for the Hindus, but my feeling is that it's not a problem for them either. What these astronomers are calling a new constellation was probably considered a part of one of the existing constellations. I don't know this as a fact, but I presume it is so intuitively. I'm sure we will soon be getting articles by Hindu astrologers explaining this.

Glossary of
Astrological Terms

Ascendant

We experience day and night because the Earth rotates on its axis once every 24 hours. It is because of this rotation that the Sun, Moon and planets seem to rise and set. The zodiac is a fixed belt (imaginary, but very real in spiritual terms) around the Earth. As the Earth rotates, the different signs of the zodiac seem to the observer to rise on the horizon. During a 24-hour period every sign of the zodiac will pass this horizon point at some time or another. The sign that is at the horizon point at any given time is called the Ascendant, or rising sign. The Ascendant is the sign denoting a person's self-image, body and self-concept – the personal ego, as opposed to the spiritual ego indicated by a person's Sun sign.

Aspects

Aspects are the angular relationships between planets, the way in which one planet stimulates or influences another. If a planet makes a harmonious aspect (connection) to another, it tends to stimulate that planet in a positive and helpful way. If, however, it makes a stressful aspect to another planet, this disrupts that planet's normal influence.

Astrological Qualities

There are three astrological qualities: *cardinal, fixed* and *mutable*. Each of the 12 signs of the zodiac falls into one of these three categories.

Cardinal Signs
Aries, Cancer, Libra and Capricorn
The cardinal quality is the active, initiating principle. Those born
under these four signs are good at starting new projects.

Fixed Signs
Taurus, Leo, Scorpio and Aquarius
Fixed qualities include stability, persistence, endurance and
perfectionism. People born under these four signs are good at
seeing things through.

Mutable Signs
Gemini, Virgo, Sagittarius and Pisces
Mutable qualities are adaptability, changeability and balance. Those
born under these four signs are creative, if not always practical.

Direct Motion

When the planets move forward through the zodiac – as they normally
do – they are said to be going 'direct'.

Grand Square

A Grand Square differs from a normal Square (usually two planets
separated by 90 degrees) in that four or more planets are involved.
When you look at the pattern in a chart you will see a whole and
complete square. This, though stressful, usually denotes a new manifestation in the life. There is much work and balancing involved in the
manifestation.

Grand Trine

A Grand Trine differs from a normal Trine (where two planets are 120 degrees apart) in that three or more planets are involved. When you look at this pattern in a chart, it takes the form of a complete triangle – a Grand Trine. Usually (but not always) it occurs in one of the four elements: Fire, Earth, Air or Water. Thus the particular element in which it occurs will be highlighted. A Grand Trine in Water is not the same as a Grand Trine in Air or Fire, etc. This is a very fortunate and happy aspect, and quite rare.

Houses

There are 12 signs of the zodiac and 12 houses of experience. The 12 signs are personality types and ways in which a given planet expresses itself; the 12 houses show 'where' in your life this expression takes place. Each house has a different area of interest. A house can become potent and important – a house of power – in different ways: if it contains the Sun, the Moon or the 'ruler' of your chart; if it contains more than one planet; or if the ruler of that house is receiving unusual stimulation from other planets.

1st House
Personal Image and Sensual Delights

2nd House
Money/Finance

3rd House
Communication and Intellectual Interests

4th House
Home and Family

5th House
Children, Fun, Games, Creativity, Speculations and Love Affairs

6th House
Health and Work

7th House
Love, Marriage and Social Activities

8th House
Transformation and Regeneration

9th House
Religion, Foreign Travel, Higher Education and Philosophy

10th House
Career

11th House
Friends, Group Activities and Fondest Wishes

12th House
Spirituality

Karma

Karma is the law of cause and effect which governs all phenomena.
We are all where we find ourselves because of karma – because of
actions we have performed in the past. The universe is such a balanced
instrument that any act immediately sets corrective forces into motion
– karma.

Long-term Planets

The planets that take a long time to move through a sign show the long-term trends in a given area of life. They are important for forecasting the prolonged view of things. Because these planets stay in one sign for so long, there are periods in the year when the faster-moving (short-term) planets will join them, further activating and enhancing the importance of a given house.

Jupiter
stays in a sign for about 1 year

Saturn
2½ years

Uranus
7 years

Neptune
14 years

Pluto
15 to 30 years

Lunar

Relating to the Moon. See also 'Phases of the Moon', below.

Natal

Literally means 'birth'. In astrology this term is used to distinguish between planetary positions that occurred at the time of a person's birth (natal) and those that are current (transiting). For example, Natal Sun refers to where the Sun was when you were born; transiting Sun refers to where the Sun's position is currently at any given moment – which usually doesn't coincide with your birth, or Natal, Sun.

Out of Bounds

The planets move through the zodiac at various angles relative to the celestial equator (if you were to draw an imaginary extension of the Earth's equator out into the universe, you would have an illustration of this celestial equator). The Sun – being the most dominant and powerful influence in the Solar system – is the measure astrologers use as a standard. The Sun never goes more than approximately 23 degrees north or south of the celestial equator. At the winter solstice the Sun reaches its maximum southern angle of orbit (declination); at the summer solstice it reaches its maximum northern angle. Any time a planet exceeds this Solar boundary – and occasionally planets do – it is said to be 'out of bounds'. This means that the planet exceeds or tres-passes into strange territory – beyond the limits allowed by the Sun, the ruler of the Solar system. The planet in this condition becomes more emphasized and exceeds its authority, becoming an important influence in the forecast.

Phases of the Moon

After the full Moon, the Moon seems to shrink in size (as perceived from the Earth), gradually growing smaller until it is virtually invisible to the naked eye – at the time of the next new Moon. This is called the waning Moon phase, or the waning Moon.

After the new Moon, the Moon gradually gets bigger in size (as perceived from the Earth) until it reaches its maximum size at the time of the full Moon. This period is called the waxing Moon phase, or waxing Moon.

Retrogrades

The planets move around the Sun at different speeds. Mercury and Venus move much faster than the Earth, while Mars, Jupiter, Saturn, Uranus, Neptune and Pluto move more slowly. Thus there are times when, relative to the Earth, the planets appear to be going backwards. In reality they are always going forward, but relative to our vantage point on Earth they seem to go backwards through the zodiac for a period of time. This is called 'retrograde' motion and tends to weaken the normal influence of a given planet.

Short-term Planets

The fast-moving planets move so quickly through a sign that their effects are generally of a short-term nature. They reflect the immediate, day-to-day trends in a horoscope.

Moon
stays in a sign for only 2½ days

Mercury
20 to 30 days

Sun
30 days

Venus
approximately 1 month

Mars
approximately 2 months

T-square

A T-square differs from a Grand Square (see above) in that it is not a complete square. If you look at the pattern in a chart it appears as 'half a complete square', resembling the T-square tools used by architects and designers. If you cut a complete square in half, diagonally, you have a T-square. Many astrologers consider this more stressful than a Grand Square, as it creates tension that is difficult to resolve. T-squares bring learning experiences.

Transits

This term refers to the movements or motions of the planets at any given time. Astrologers use the word 'transit' to make the distinction between a birth, or Natal, planet (see 'Natal', above) and the planet's current movement in the heavens. For example, if at your birth Saturn was in the sign of Cancer in your 8th house, but is now moving through your 3rd house, it is said to be 'transiting' your 3rd house. Transits are one of the main tools with which astrologers forecast trends.

YOUR PERSONAL HOROSCOPE 2018

Aries

THE RAM

Birthdays from
21st March to
20th April

Personality Profile

ARIES AT A GLANCE

Element – Fire

Ruling Planet – Mars
  Career Planet – Saturn
  Love Planet – Venus
  Money Planet – Venus
  Planet of Fun, Entertainment, Creativity and Speculations – Sun
  Planet of Health and Work – Mercury
  Planet of Home and Family Life – Moon
  Planet of Spirituality – Neptune
  Planet of Travel, Education, Religion and Philosophy – Jupiter

Colours – carmine, red, scarlet

Colours that promote love, romance and social harmony – green, jade
  green

Colour that promotes earning power – green

Gem – amethyst

Metals – iron, steel

Scent – honeysuckle

Quality – cardinal (= activity)

Quality most needed for balance – caution

Strongest virtues – abundant physical energy, courage, honesty, independence, self-reliance

Deepest need – action

Characteristics to avoid – haste, impetuousness, over-aggression, rashness

Signs of greatest overall compatibility – Leo, Sagittarius

Signs of greatest overall incompatibility – Cancer, Libra, Capricorn

Sign most helpful to career – Capricorn

Sign most helpful for emotional support – Cancer

Sign most helpful financially – Taurus

Sign best for marriage and/or partnerships – Libra

Sign most helpful for creative projects – Leo

Best Sign to have fun with – Leo

Signs most helpful in spiritual matters – Sagittarius, Pisces

Best day of the week – Tuesday

Understanding an Aries

Aries is the activist *par excellence* of the zodiac. The Aries need for action is almost an addiction, and those who do not really understand the Aries personality would probably use this hard word to describe it. In reality 'action' is the essence of the Aries psychology – the more direct, blunt and to-the-point the action, the better. When you think about it, this is the ideal psychological makeup for the warrior, the pioneer, the athlete or the manager.

Aries likes to get things done, and in their passion and zeal often lose sight of the consequences for themselves and others. Yes, they often try to be diplomatic and tactful, but it is hard for them. When they do so they feel that they are being dishonest and phoney. It is hard for them even to understand the mindset of the diplomat, the consensus builder, the front office executive. These people are involved in endless meetings, discussions, talks and negotiations – all of which seem a great waste of time when there is so much work to be done, so many real achievements to be gained. An Aries can understand, once it is explained, that talk and negotiations – the social graces – lead ultimately to better, more effective actions. The interesting thing is that an Aries is rarely malicious or spiteful – even when waging war. Aries people fight without hate for their opponents. To them it is all good-natured fun, a grand adventure, a game.

When confronted with a problem many people will say, 'Well, let's think about it, let's analyse the situation.' But not an Aries. An Aries will think, 'Something must be done. Let's get on with it.' Of course neither response is the total answer. Sometimes action is called for, sometimes cool thought. But an Aries tends to err on the side of action.

Action and thought are radically different principles. Physical activity is the use of brute force. Thinking and deliberating require one not to use force – to be still. It is not good for the athlete to be deliberating the next move; this will only slow down his or her reaction time. The athlete must act instinctively and instantly. This is how Aries people tend to behave in life. They are quick, instinctive decision-makers and their decisions tend to be translated into action almost immediately. When their intuition is sharp and well tuned, their actions are powerful and successful. When their intuition is off, their actions can be disastrous.

Do not think this will scare an Aries. Just as a good warrior knows that in the course of combat he or she might acquire a few wounds, so too does an Aries realize – somewhere deep down – that in the course of being true to yourself you might get embroiled in a disaster or two. It is all part of the game. An Aries feels strong enough to weather any storm.

There are many Aries people who are intellectual. They make powerful and creative thinkers. But even in this realm they tend to be pioneers – outspoken and blunt. These types of Aries tend to elevate (or sublimate) their desire for physical combat in favour of intellectual, mental combat. And they are indeed powerful.

In general, Aries people have a faith in themselves that others could learn from. This basic, rock-solid faith carries them through the most tumultuous situations of life. Their courage and self-confidence make them natural leaders. Their leadership is more by way of example than by actually controlling others.

Finance

Aries people often excel as builders or estate agents. Money in and of itself is not as important as are other things – action, adventure, sport, etc. They are motivated by the need to support and be well-thought-of by their partners. Money as a way of attaining pleasure is another important motivation. Aries function best in their own businesses or as managers of their own departments within a large business or corporation. The fewer orders they have to take from higher up, the better. They also function better out in the field rather than behind a desk.

Aries people are hard workers with a lot of endurance; they can earn large sums of money due to the strength of their sheer physical energy.

Venus is their money planet, which means that Aries need to develop more of the social graces in order to realize their full earning potential. Just getting the job done – which is what an Aries excels at – is not enough to create financial success. The co-operation of others needs to be attained. Customers, clients and co-workers need to be made to feel comfortable; many people need to be treated properly in order for success to happen. When Aries people develop these abilities – or hire someone to do this for them – their financial potential is unlimited.

Career and Public Image

One would think that a pioneering type would want to break with the social and political conventions of society. But this is not so with the Aries-born. They are pioneers within conventional limits, in the sense that they like to start their own businesses within an established industry.

Capricorn is on the 10th house of career cusp of Aries' solar horoscope. Saturn is the planet that rules their life's work and professional aspirations. This tells us some interesting things about the Aries character. First off, it shows that, in order for Aries people to reach their full career potential, they need to develop some qualities that are a bit alien to their basic nature: they need to become better administrators and organizers; they need to be able to handle details better and to take a long-range view of their projects and their careers in general. No one can beat an Aries when it comes to achieving short-range objectives, but a career is long term, built over time. You cannot take a 'quickie' approach to it.

Some Aries people find it difficult to stick with a project until the end. Since they get bored quickly and are in constant pursuit of new adventures, they prefer to pass an old project or task on to somebody else in order to start something new. Those Aries who learn how to put off the search for something new until the old is completed will achieve great success in their careers and professional lives.

In general, Aries people like society to judge them on their own merits, on their real and actual achievements. A reputation acquired by 'hype' feels false to them.

Love and Relationships

In marriage and partnerships Aries like those who are more passive, gentle, tactful and diplomatic – people who have the social grace and skills they sometimes lack. Our partners always represent a hidden part of ourselves – a self that we cannot express personally.

An Aries tends to go after what he or she likes aggressively. The tendency is to jump into relationships and marriages. This is especially true if Venus is in Aries as well as the Sun. If an Aries likes you, he or she will have a hard time taking no for an answer; many attempts will be made to sweep you off your feet.

Though Aries can be exasperating in relationships – especially if they are not understood by their partners – they are never consciously or wilfully cruel or malicious. It is just that they are so independent and sure of themselves that they find it almost impossible to see somebody else's viewpoint or position. This is why an Aries needs as a partner someone with lots of social graces.

On the plus side, an Aries is honest, someone you can lean on, someone with whom you will always know where you stand. What he or she lacks in diplomacy is made up for in integrity.

Home and Domestic Life

An Aries is of course the ruler at home – the Boss. The male will tend to delegate domestic matters to the female. The female Aries will want to rule the roost. Both tend to be handy round the house. Both like large families and both believe in the sanctity and importance of the family. An Aries is a good family person, although he or she does not especially like being at home a lot, preferring instead to be roaming about.

Considering that they are by nature so combative and wilful, Aries people can be surprisingly soft, gentle and even vulnerable with their children and partners. The sign of Cancer, ruled by the Moon, is on the cusp of their solar 4th house of home and family. When the Moon is well aspected – under favourable influences – in the birth chart, an Aries will be tender towards the family and will want a family life that is nurturing and supportive. Aries likes to come home after a hard day on the battlefield of life to the understanding arms of their partner and the unconditional love and support of their family. An Aries feels that there is enough 'war' out in the world – and he or she enjoys participating in that. But when Aries comes home, comfort and nurturing are what's needed.

Horoscope for 2018

Major Trends

Some of the long-term major planets are shifting this year. They will make sure that you don't get too fixed in your ways. Saturn changed signs at the end of 2017. Most of you – especially those of you born late in the sign of Aries in April – haven't felt this yet, but you will feel it more next year. Saturn will be in Capricorn, your 10th house, for the next two years, which will make the year ahead a very strong career year. It's the kind of year where you succeed by sheer merit and for no other reason. Therefore strive for excellence in all that you do. More on this later.

The other important headline is Uranus's move out of your sign – where he's been for the last seven years – into Taurus. This is not yet the full-blown transit but a 'shot across the bows', an announcement of things to come. After seven years of redefining yourself and experimenting with your image, you seem to have settled on something that works for you. You've learned to deal with sudden personal changes. Now, you will learn to deal with sudden financial changes. The financial life is becoming very exciting – very adventurous – just as you like it. This move will also start to stabilize your love life. More details later.

Jupiter has been in Scorpio, your 8th house, since October 2017 and he will be here into November of the year ahead. This indicates the prosperity of partners or the current love interest. Often it shows inheritance, but hopefully no one has to die. It shows good fortune in tax and estate issues and an ability to pay off debt. It also favours projects involving personal transformation. For many of you, depending on your age, it indicates a sexually active kind of year. Again, more details later.

On November 8 Jupiter will move into Sagittarius and into a beautiful aspect with you. He will bring more travel, more money and more optimism. He will bring good news for those applying to colleges or universities – and for those already enrolled in these places, he brings success in studies. But first, you have to pay your dues of hard work and striving for excellence.

Neptune has been in your spiritual 12th house for many years now, and he will be there for many more. So the spiritual life is important, and growing. Those of you on a spiritual path will see much progress this year for Jupiter in Scorpio is making very nice aspects to Neptune.

Two important planets in your chart – Mars, the ruler of your Horoscope, and Venus, your love and financial planet – will make rare retrogrades this year. Unlike most of the other planets, these only move backwards once every two years. Mars will be retrograde from June 26 to August 27 and Venus from October 5 to November 16. Retrogrades are good times for reflection and review, rather than overt action, and we will deal further with this in the monthly reports.

Your most important interests this year will be your body and image (from January 1 to May 16 and from November 6 to December 31); finance (from May 16 to November 6); sex, occult studies, personal transformation and reinvention (until November 8); foreign travel, higher education, theology and philosophy (from November 8 onwards); career; and spirituality.

Your paths of greatest fulfilment this year are personal transformation and reinvention (until November 8); foreign travel, higher education, religion, philosophy and theology (from November 8 onwards); children, fun and creativity (from January 1 to November 17); and home and family (after November 17).

Health

(Please note that this is an astrological perspective on health and not a medical one. In days of yore there was no difference, both of these perspectives were identical. But now there could be quite a difference. For a medical perspective, please consult your doctor or health practitioner.)

Though Uranus leaving your sign is a good aspect for health, you still have two cosmic heavy hitters – Saturn and Pluto – in stressful alignment to you, so health still needs careful attention paid to it this year, even if you don't feel like it. The empty 6th house of health suggests that you're not paying enough attention.

Two long-term planets in stressful alignment will not of themselves cause disease, although if you have pre-existing conditions they can worsen now. But when the short-term planets join the party, this is when you become more vulnerable. So the times to watch are from January 1 to the 20th, June 21 to August 22, September 22 to October 23 and December 21 to the 31st. Try as much as possible to rest and relax more during those periods. If you can afford it, spend time in a health spa or book some massages. Let go of frivolities that waste your energy and focus only on essentials.

As our regular readers know, there is much that can be done to enhance the health and prevent problems from developing. Give more attention to the following – the vulnerable areas of your Horoscope (the reflex points are shown in the chart below):

- The heart has become important in recent years and is still important this year. Cultivate a healthy faith. Many spiritual healers affirm that worry is the root cause of heart problems: replace worry with faith.
- The head, face and scalp are always important for Aries. Regular scalp and face massage will not only strengthen these areas but the

Important foot reflexology points for the year ahead

Try to massage all of the foot on a regular basis – the top of the foot as well as the bottom – but pay extra attention to the points highlighted on the chart. When you massage, be aware of 'sore spots' as these need special attention. It's also a good idea to massage the ankles and below them.

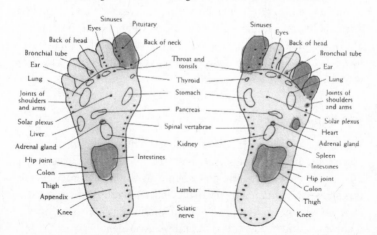

entire body as well, as there are reflexes and meridian lines there that run through the whole body.

- The musculature. It isn't necessary to be Arnold Schwarzenegger, just to have good muscle tone. Weak or flabby muscles can knock the spine and skeleton out of alignment, which will cause all kinds of other problems. What are often diagnosed as 'back' problems are really muscle problems. Vigorous exercise – appropriate to your stage of life – is advisable.
- The adrenals are also always important for Aries. More importantly, learn to control anger and fear, the two emotions that stress the adrenals.
- The small intestine is another important area for Aries, and the reflex points are shown above.

Mercury is your health planet, and he is a fast-moving – and often erratic – planet. Sometimes he moves very fast, sometimes he goes slowly, sometimes he goes backwards. It is no accident that the qualities of flexibility and changeability are attributed to Mercury. Your health regime should embody this kind of flexibility.

Because Mercury moves so fast, he will move through every sign and house of your Horoscope in a given year. Thus there are many short-term health trends that depend on where Mercury is (and the aspects he receives). These are best dealt with in the monthly reports.

Mercury will go retrograde three times this year – from March 23 to April 15; July 26 to August 19 and from November 17 to December 6. These are times to avoid making major changes to the diet or your health regime. Instead, do more research and homework during these periods.

Home and Family

This is not an especially strong home and family year; career seems much more important this year. Your 4th house is basically empty in 2018, with only short-term planets moving through there. Generally this shows the status quo prevailing. You seem more or less satisfied with your home and family situation and have no pressing need to make important changes. It is basically a good sign.

However, changes and upheavals will happen, but you will more or less react to them rather than be initiating anything new. For a start there are three solar eclipses this year. This is very unusual – generally there are only two in a year. This indicates dramas – life-changing kinds of events – in the lives of children or children figures in your life. The eclipses will also impact the overall finances of the family and especially of one of your parents or parent figures. One of the solar eclipses – the one on July 13 – actually occurs in your 4th house and this will impact strongly on the family. You will need to be more patient with them as passions seem to run high.

Two lunar eclipses (the usual number) will also affect the home and family, and we will discuss them more fully in the monthly reports.

Parents and parent figures in your life are having a stable home and family year. Likewise, siblings and sibling figures. Children, however, are likely to move, and it looks happy. If a parent or parent figure has been ailing, there is good news on the health front towards the end of the year. If he or she is not ailing, there are happy job opportunities coming. Grandchildren of appropriate age are prospering this year – especially after November – and can have multiple moves. This has been the story with them for some years now. They seem very unsettled and restless. Children or grandchildren of appropriate age (or those who play this role in your life) also seem more fertile than usual.

One of the parents or parent figures in your life is feeling older than his or her years and seems overly pessimistic. Everything looks black. They need to lighten up a bit. He or she seems to be taking on more responsibility, and this could be the cause.

This is not an especially great year for heavy duty house renovation or repairs. However, beautifying the home in cosmetic ways will go especially well from May 19 to July 23.

Finance and Career

A new financial era is just beginning in your life this year, and it will continue for at least seven more years. The financial life is about to become *very* exciting – very adventurous – just as you like things.

Uranus is making a major move into your 2nd money house on May 16, remaining there until November 8. This is going to produce many dramatic financial changes – changes of investments, of financial strategy and of thinking. If you've been dissatisfied with the way your finances have been going, you have to allow Uranus to shake things up a bit, so that the obstructions can be removed. His goal is to bring you to 'financial freedom', but this can't happen if you're stuck in old attitudes.

In general you tend to be a risk taker – the Aries nature is about overcoming fear and developing courage – and now you will be even more so. So what if some things don't work out as planned! As long as you maintain your fearless attitude, you've won. There's always tomorrow.

The old financial rule books – the collected financial wisdom of the experts – get thrown out this year (and for the next few years). You're going to learn what works for you through trial and error and experiment. You will explore new paths. Some, as we mentioned, might not work out – but others will. You will gain all kinds of insight into wealth, not written in any books. This is knowledge worth having.

Uranus in the money house suggests earning through the high-tech sector – a huge sector. It favours online activities and cutting-edge technologies (some not even invented yet). You will probably spend more on technology too, but it seems like a good investment.

Uranus favours start-ups – especially in the high-tech industries. These are interesting as jobs, investments or business ventures.

When Uranus is involved in finance anything can happen at any time. Opportunities can come in the darkest moments when you least expect it. Earnings can be more erratic too. The financial highs can exceed your wildest dreams, but the lows can also be ultra-low. It will be a good idea to set aside money from the good times to tide you over during the low times. The financial swings can be very extreme. One must learn not to fear either the heights or the depths. One must expect nothing, but be ready for anything.

Career, as we mentioned above, is very important this year. It has been important for many years, but now even more so than before. Saturn's move into your 10th house of career is the cause. This indicates that you are taking on more responsibility – always a sobering factor. Saturn will exert pressure on you, not a punitive pressure but a pressure designed to educate and organize. Under pressure, one is forced to stretch one's abilities, to find the best, most efficient way of doing something, to bring out the best that you have to offer. When Saturn is finished with you in two years' time you'll find that you can do a lot more than you ever believed.

This pressure can come in various ways. You can have a very demanding boss, or demanding clients and customers. Satisfying them is a challenge. Saturn in your career house shows a need for more management skills. Good management will enable you to handle all this. Many of you will be placed in managerial positions.

As we mentioned earlier, the year ahead is about succeeding through sheer merit and for no other reason. It is about being the best at what you do, without gimmicks or short cuts. You will see the positive results of this approach in 2019 and 2020, when you start to reach new career heights.

Love and Social Life

Last year was a banner love and social year. Many of you married in 2017, or met significant others. You seem more or less satisfied with the status quo this year. Your 7th house of love is not a house of power. Those of you involved with someone special will probably continue in that relationship. The unattached will most likely stay unattached. There is no cosmic pressure to make drastic changes.

In general, Uranus's move out of your sign is a positive move for love. People will find you less rebellious and more stable. A lot of your freedom-loving urges have been sated in the past seven years and you're more open to settling down.

Venus, a fast-moving planet, is your love planet. She is a good planet to have as this is her natural domain. In any given year, she will move through all the signs and houses of your Horoscope. Thus love opportunities can happen in many ways and through many people – it all depends on where Venus is and the aspects she receives. These short-term trends are best dealt with in the monthly reports.

Venus will make a rare (once in two years) retrograde movement from October 5 to November 16. Don't be too upset if a current relationship seems to go backwards instead of forwards, or seems tentative during this period. This is a time to review the love life and to plan positive improvements for the future. You can act on your plans when Venus starts moving forward again. (The same applies to financial matters too.)

Those of you working towards a second marriage will have very wonderful opportunities towards the end of the year – from November 8 onwards. Something serious is developing here. Those of you working towards your third marriage will have opportunities with people involved in your finances. Wealth seems an important romantic turn on. A business-type partnership can happen from May 16 to November 6. Those working on the fourth marriage have a quiet, stable year.

Married children or children figures will have their relationships tested this year. They have two eclipses in their house of love. (This would apply to serious relationships too.) Siblings and sibling figures will find love from November 8 onwards. Grandchildren (if you have them) have a status quo social year.

Self-Improvement

Neptune, the most spiritual of all the planets, and your personal spiritual planet, has been in Pisces for some years now and will remain there for many more years. However, Neptune is much stronger in his own sign and house than usual. Thus your spiritual urges – your idealism – are much stronger these days. Jupiter, your planet of religion and philosophy, will be making very nice aspects to Neptune for most of the year – until November 8. So there's a lot of spiritual growth happening. Your dream life is more active and your extrasensory perception is stronger. You're experiencing all kinds of 'synchronicities', meaningful coincidences, these days. It would be tempting to let go of the world and just focus on spiritual matters. But the power in your career house (and especially Saturn's presence there) forces you to be more 'worldly'. Somehow you have to be practical and idealistic at the same time, to marry these two urges, to make them cooperate with each other. Getting the right attitude to spirituality will be a big help. When understood correctly it is the most practical thing a person can do. It leads (usually indirectly) to practical, measurable results.

I heard a radio host recently, who mockingly asked: 'Can prayer fill potholes?' He invited callers to comment on it. Most said no. But this only shows a lack of understanding. Prayer might not directly fill a pothole (though it can), but it will definitely fill them 'indirectly' by creating the conditions and circumstances where they get filled in natural ways.

So the cosmos is calling you to learn to make the spiritual power practical in your worldly affairs.

With Uranus in your sign for the past seven years you have had to deal with issues of 'identity'. This is more important than psychology. Most of what passes for psychological problems are really problems of 'mis-identification'. Get the right perspective on identity and the psychological problem melts away. By now, after seven years, you understand this. Now and for the next seven years the lessons from Uranus are financial. They are about learning to be comfortable with financial change and insecurity, to take the changes in your stride and to make the changes benefit you. You have plenty of time to learn these lessons, but it's good to get started now.

Jupiter, as we mentioned, spends most of the year in your 8th house. This favours your efforts to reinvent yourself and give birth to the person you want to be – your ideal self. This can be hard work, but you have the support of the cosmos. To have more, you must 'be' more.

Month-by-month Forecasts

January

Best Days Overall: 3, 4, 12, 13, 14, 22, 23, 31
Most Stressful Days Overall: 1, 2, 8, 9, 15, 16, 29, 30
Best Days for Love: 5, 6, 8, 9, 15, 16, 27, 28
Best Days for Money: 5, 6, 15, 16, 25, 26, 27, 28
Best Days for Career: 5, 15, 16, 25

You begin your year with 90 per cent of the planets above the horizon and a super-charged 10th house of career. The entire year ahead is a strong career year, but right now you're in the strongest month of a strong year. Almost all the action this month is in your 10th house of career. The message? Focus on your career – handle that properly and everything else will fall into place. (The lower part of your chart will get stronger in four or five months' time, but it will never completely dominate your chart. This is a year to focus on your outer objectives.)

You're working hard. You're successful, but you're earning it the hard way – through work and real merit. Yes, social connections are helpful this month – especially until the 18th – but they can only open doors. Eventually you have to produce. So, your health needs watching this month as this is not your best health period. Until the 11th pay attention to the liver and thighs. After the 11th give more attention to the back, knees, teeth and bones. (Regular thigh massage will strengthen the lower back.) The most important thing, as always, is to make sure you get enough rest. Health will improve after the 20th, but it will still need watching.

Mars, the ruler of your Horoscope, spends most of the month in your 8th house. This is a great aspect for weight loss and detox regimes. Mars will travel with Jupiter from the 4th to the 9th. This is a very happy transit and brings financial expansion and perhaps a foreign trip. Women of appropriate age are much more fertile then.

There is a Lunar Eclipse at the end of the month on the 31st. It occurs in your 5th house and affects family and children. Children and children figures are having important life changes. Family members can be more temperamental, and often repairs are needed in the home. Be more patient with your family at this time. This eclipse sideswipes Venus, your love and financial planet. It is not a direct hit, more a glancing blow, and often shows important financial changes (perhaps scares) and a need for a course correction in love and finance.

February

Best Days Overall: 9, 10, 19, 27, 28
Most Stressful Days Overall: 4, 5, 11, 12, 25, 26
Best Days for Love: 4, 5, 16, 25, 26
Best Days for Money: 4, 5, 6, 7, 16, 17, 21, 22, 25, 26
Best Days for Career: 2, 11, 12, 21

A Solar Eclipse on the 15th appears to be a powerful one – it is not just the Sun that's getting eclipsed, but Mercury and Jupiter as well. Mars in your 9th house all month indicates an urge for travel (and many of you will have to), but it's not very advisable during this period. (Apart from the eclipse, Jupiter, your travel planet, is receiving stressful aspects.) If your journey is not strictly necessary, don't do it. If it is necessary, avoid the eclipse period if at all possible, and allow more time to get to and from your destination.

The Solar Eclipse occurs in your 11th house of friends, so friendships can get tested. Often, the testing it is not the fault of your relationships but because of dramas that are happening in the lives of your friends. Children of appropriate age (or children figures in your life) are having their love relationships tested. Single children can decide to tie the knot over the next six months. Drive more defensively during this period. Communication and technology equipment can become more temperamental now and some of it might need replacement or repair. Make sure your anti-virus software is up to date and that all your important computer files are safely backed up. Technology is wonderful when it works as it should, but when it doesn't, oh my! It's a horror! It's as if life stops.

Health and energy are much improved over last month, but the eclipse can cause a health scare or necessitate a change in your health regime – an important change. The job situation is also shaky for a while.

Both love and money go well until the 11th, but afterwards you will have to work harder for earnings. Perhaps you're not enjoying what you have to do to earn your money. It is as if you can't be bothered. If you put in the extra work you should prosper. Venus will be in her most powerful position from the 11th onwards – in the sign of Pisces. This indicates strong earning power (and social magnetism). Financial intuition is important now and, happily, it appears strong.

Love can be found in spiritual locales from the 11th onwards, and is idealistic and very tender. The beloved (or the people you meet) are likely to be more sensitive, more easily hurt, so be aware of your body language and voice tones.

March

Best Days Overall: 8, 9, 18, 19, 26, 27
Most Stressful Days Overall: 3, 4, 10, 11, 12, 24, 25, 31
Best Days for Love: 3, 4, 8, 18, 19, 26, 27, 31
Best Days for Money: 6, 7, 8, 15, 16, 17, 18, 19, 20, 21, 24, 25, 26, 27
Best Days for Career: 1, 10, 11, 12, 20, 29

Spring is the season of new beginnings. Astrologically speaking it is the best time of year to start new projects or launch new products into the world. This year, it is better than usual. The planetary momentum is overwhelmingly forward. From the 20th (the first day of spring) to the 23rd, 90 per cent of the planets are moving forward – so those three days are the best days for starting a new project. (The Moon will also be waxing then, an added plus.) However, if you can't start your project on those three days, the 20th to the 29th is also a good time (80 per cent of the planets will be moving forward).

Career is still active – especially from the 17th onwards – but the month ahead is a mostly spiritual-type month. It is a time for inner growth. It is a good time to focus on meditation, spiritual studies and charitable activities. Good to feed the 'inner you'. Those of you on the spiritual path will gain insights.

The month ahead looks very prosperous as well. Venus, your financial planet, crosses your Ascendant and enters your 1st house on March 6. This brings financial windfalls and happy opportunities. You look rich these days. You have that image. People see you that way. This aspect gives a wonderful feeling of being 'pursued' by money, rather than you having to pursue it.

Love, too, is happy. Venus does double duty in your Horoscope. She is both the love and financial planet. So love, like money, pursues you. Your existing spouse, partner or current love is more attentive and is trying to please you. He or she is totally on your side.

Mars crossing your Mid-heaven on the 17th indicates personal career success. You're above everyone in your world. You're recognized for who you are and for your achievements. People look up to you.

The month ahead is very hectic and fast paced, especially from the 20th onward. But happily you have the energy to handle it. You can enhance your health even further through foot massage and spiritual healing techniques until the 6th. After then, scalp massage and physical exercise will be good.

April

Best Days Overall: 4, 5, 6, 14, 15, 23, 24
Most Stressful Days Overall: 1, 7, 8, 21, 22, 27, 28
Best Days for Love: 1, 7, 8, 16, 17, 27, 28
Best Days for Money: 2, 3, 7, 8, 12, 13, 16, 17, 21, 22, 27, 29, 30
Best Days for Career: 7, 8, 16, 25

Last month on the 20th the planetary power reached its most Eastern position. You were in your most independent kind of period and this continues in the month ahead. With your 1st house so strong, you're having your way in life (only career responsibilities are limiting you now). If changes need to be made – if conditions are not to your liking – then change them; make them as you wish. You have the power to do this now. (Later on in the year it will be more difficult.)

You also entered one of your yearly personal pleasure peaks last month and this continues, until the 20th of this month. This is a time for exploring (and gratifying) all the pleasures of the body. It is a great period for getting the body and image in right shape, the way you want it to be.

This year's personal pleasure peak is different from those of past years. Yes, you want to have fun and indulge the body, but you also want to be successful in the world. Career pulls you one way while the fun-loving urges pull you another. With a little bit of creativity you can manage both. There are no rules as to how this is done. Every person finds their own solution.

Last month, the planetary power started to shift below the horizon. The lower half of the Horoscope (the night side) is as strong as it will ever be this year – 40 per cent (and sometimes 50 per cent) of the planets are there. However, the upper half is still very dominant so you still need to focus on the career, but you can allot a little more time to the home, family and your emotional well-being. This is not a big priority this year, but it can't be completely ignored. Sometimes people need less sleep than at other times, but they still need some sleep.

The month ahead looks prosperous. On the 20th, the Sun enters your 2nd, money house and stays there for the rest of the month ahead. You're in a period of peak earnings. There is luck in speculations (though please don't do this with your rent or food money) and money is earned in happy ways. You're enjoying your wealth. Children – depending on their age and stage in life – are either supportive in a material way or through inspiring you to earn more. Venus in the money house until the 24th is another good financial sign. Financial judgement is good. Conservative. (Though you should be careful of overspending on the 17th and 18th.)

Singles find love opportunities as they pursue their normal financial goals and perhaps with people involved in their finances.

May

Best Days Overall: 2, 3, 11, 12, 13, 20, 21, 29, 30
Most Stressful Days Overall: 4, 5, 18, 19, 24, 25, 31
Best Days for Love: 7, 8, 17, 24, 25, 26
Best Days for Money: 7, 8, 9, 10, 14, 15, 17, 18, 19, 26, 27
Best Days for Career: 4, 5, 14, 22, 31

Venus spends most of the month 'out of bounds' – from the 6th to the 31st. This shows that in finance and love, you're going beyond your normal sphere, outside your normal neighbourhood. You're thinking 'outside the box', which often brings just the right solution. It was the 'box' itself that was causing the problem in the first place.

You're still very much in a yearly financial peak until the 21st. So you're in a period of peak earnings. The New Moon of the 15th occurs in the money house, making it an excellent financial day. But more importantly, it will clarify the financial life as the month progresses – and well into next month. The information that you need to make a right decision is winging its way towards you.

Uranus, as we have already mentioned, makes a major move into your money house on the 16th, creating excitement and change. This transit is only the harbinger of things to come. It favours online activities. Your financial planet, Venus, will be in your 3rd house of communication until the 19th. This favours sales, marketing, advertising and PR activities. People need to know about your product or service. Good use of the media pays dividends too. On the 19th Venus will move into your 4th house, indicating earning through the family and family connections. Family support is good (and mutual). Financial intuition is strong. Venus opposes Saturn from the 25th to the 27th; earnings can be stalled for a few days, but this is a short-term problem. Indeed, the delays will make the final outcome even better.

Mars, the ruler of your Horoscope, has spent the past two months in your 10th house of career. You've been very successful during this period, and now you're ready to be more socially oriented. You're still focused on your career, but you're more sociable about it. You're there for your friends now, and are probably more popular.

Love, for singles, can be found in your neighbourhood – but not in your usual haunts. There are love opportunities in educational settings – at school functions, the library or bookstore or at lectures. You're attracted to those who have the gift of the gab and people who are easy to talk to. You like the 'smart people' these days. Later on, after the 19th, you'll crave emotional intimacy and emotional sharing. Love becomes a 'mood' issue. The challenge will be to get in the right mood – and get your partner in the right mood.

June

Best Days Overall: 8, 9, 16, 17, 25, 26
Most Stressful Days Overall: 1, 2, 14, 15, 20, 21, 22, 28, 29
Best Days for Love: 6, 7, 16, 20, 21, 22, 23, 24
Best Days for Money: 5, 6, 7, 10, 11, 14, 15, 16, 23, 24
Best Days for Career: 1, 2, 10, 18, 28, 29

You're in the midnight hour of your year and should be sleeping and letting the inner forces work. But your work in the world is important and you keep breaking your sleep to focus on it. Metaphorically this is the situation. It is the dead of night, but you keep getting up.

This month you face one of the classic challenges that many face. Home and family are important, but so is the career and outer activities. Each claims their due and you can't ignore either. Somehow or other you have to deal with both. Now you will lean one way, now the other – it's not easy.

Retrograde activity among the planets increases this month, and by the 26th half of the planets will be retrograde – almost the maximum for the year. (August 7–19 will see 60 per cent of the planets going backwards.) The pace of life slows down. For an action-oriented Aries, frustration is the main challenge at this time. You're a thoroughbred, built for speed, but now you're forced to walk (and sometimes backwards). Everything seems so slow, slow, slow! The good part of this is that one learns patience. Do what is possible each day and let the rest go.

Health and energy become more of an issue from the 21st onwards too. Be sure to get enough rest. You can enhance your health through arm and shoulder massage until the 12th. From the 12th to the 29th make sure to eat right, and keep the emotions harmonious and constructive. After the 29th give more attention to the heart.

Love is still found close to home until the 14th. Make sure to keep your mood right. Bad moods will destroy romantic moments and complicate the love life. There is more socializing at home and with the family until the 14th. Don't be surprised if an old flame (or someone who reminds you of an old flame) comes back into your life. There is a romantic opportunity with someone spiritual at the beginning of the month.

The urge to travel is very strong these days, but if it isn't necessary avoid it. Jupiter, who rules travel for you, is receiving good aspects, but he is retrograde. If you must travel during this period, allow more time to get to and from your destination. Insure your tickets, and do what you can to protect yourself against delays and glitches.

July

Best Days Overall: 5, 6, 14, 15, 22, 23, 24
Most Stressful Days Overall: 12, 13, 18, 19, 25, 26
Best Days for Love: 5, 6, 16, 18, 19, 25, 26
Best Days for Money: 1, 5, 6, 7, 8, 12, 13, 16, 20, 21, 25, 26, 27, 28, 29
Best Days for Career: 7, 8, 16, 25, 26

Mars, the ruler of your Horoscope, spends almost the whole month 'out of bounds'. This indicates that you're outside your normal sphere, from the 9th onwards. You're in an adventurous period, meeting new friends and perhaps getting involved with groups and group activities that are outside the norm for you. Adding to the adventure and the sense of 'being ready for anything' are two eclipses this month.

The Solar Eclipse of July 13 occurs in your 4th house of the home and family. All of you will feel this, but those of you born later in the sign of Aries (April 8 to April 15) will feel it strongest. You should be taking things easier anyway until the 22nd, but especially around the period of the eclipse. It looks like it will have a strong effect and will bring family dramas and shakeups. Family members are more temperamental at this time, and are experiencing life-changing events. Often, as our regular readers know, repairs are needed in the home. Hidden flaws tend to come to light under an eclipse's influence. Parents or parent figures are having their marriages tested. Children or children figures are making life-changing kinds of decisions (some can be quite normal, but for them it is life changing). They too should take a more relaxed schedule. The family finances – especially those of a parent or parent figure – need a course correction. Pluto is affected by this eclipse, so you could be involved in near-death kinds of experiences. Death (usually on a psychological level) touches you in some way.

The Lunar Eclipse of the 27th also impacts on the home and family – as every Lunar Eclipse does. So there is more of the same with the family as we've written above. This eclipse occurs in your 11th house of friends, so there are dramas – and perhaps crises – in the lives of friends. Friendships get tested, as do computers and high-tech equipment (often these need repair or replacement). This eclipse affects you strongly as Mars is impacted here. So reduce your schedule and avoid dangerous or stressful situations. Spend more quiet time at home. The impact on Mars shows a need to redefine yourself – how you think of yourself and how you want others to think about you. This will be a six-month process. This redefinition is basically a healthy thing: since we are always changing we should always be redefining ourselves. But here it is rather forced on you. The events caused by the eclipse force you into this process.

August

Best Days Overall: 1, 2, 3, 10, 11, 19, 20, 29, 30
Most Stressful Days Overall: 8, 9, 14, 15, 21, 22
Best Days for Love: 5, 14, 15, 24, 25
Best Days for Money: 4, 5, 8, 9, 14, 15, 16, 17, 24, 25, 26, 27, 31
Best Days for Career: 4, 12, 21, 22, 31

Just when you thought the disturbances of last month's eclipses were over, there is another one – the third Solar Eclipse of the year – to keep you on your toes. It is helpful to understand that eclipses are not 'punitive' (though it can feel that way). Their cosmic job is to clear the obstructions to your path in life, the obstructions to your good. And, they generally do a good job of it. It is also helpful to know that this is the last one for the current year.

Mars is still 'out of bounds' this month – for the entire month. So you are still outside your normal haunts, in unknown territory. So the adventure continues.

This Solar Eclipse of the 11th occurs in your 5th house and impacts more on the children or children figures in your life. Whatever changes were not made last month will be made now (and over the next six months). This eclipse has less of an effect on you than the previous ones. Your overall health and energy are much better this month, and no other major planets are affected by it. But it won't hurt to take it easier over this period – and that goes double for the children or children figures in your life. As we mentioned, many of the changes in their lives are normal – part of growing up. Sometimes they have their sexual awakenings; sometimes they go off to school or university. But for them these are life-changing events. Whatever the actual event – and there are many, many scenarios – it will cause them to redefine themselves, to change their image and their self-concept, to change (over the next six months) their wardrobe and how they present themselves to others. And those of you in the creative and artistic spheres re changing your creativity – you are making course corrections here.

Venus has her solstice this month – from the 5th to the 9th. She pauses in her latitudinal motion and then changes direction. This shows a pause in your love and financial life and then a change of direction. This is nothing to be feared. The direction you're to take will become very clear.

On the 22nd the Sun enters your 6th house of health and work. This indicates a nice financial period for your children (or children figures in your life). For you, it shows a focus on health and work. It is a favourable time for job seekers.

September

Best Days Overall: 7, 15, 16, 25, 26
Most Stressful Days Overall: 4, 5, 11, 12, 17, 18, 19
Best Days for Love: 2, 3, 11, 12, 13, 22, 23
Best Days for Money: 1, 2, 3, 4, 5, 13, 14, 22, 23, 24, 27, 28
Best Days for Career: 1, 8, 9, 17, 18, 19, 27

The planetary power is now at its maximum Western position for the year. Thus, the planetary energies (the short-term planets) are moving away from you and towards others. You still have plenty of personal independence – the Western, social sector is not dominant – but less so than usual. So, this is a time to be more adaptive to the conditions around you. It's not an especially good time to make changes – that will come later in the year. Rather, it is a time to cultivate your social skills. Your likeability will get you further than your personal efforts.

Your 6th house is still strong this month, until the 22nd. So this is a good time to do all those detail-oriented, boring tasks that need to be done. You have more energy for them. It is still a good financial period for the children or children figures in your life, and it is still good for hiring others or for finding a job – whatever the need happens to be.

On the 22nd, the Sun enters your 7th house of love and you begin a yearly love and social peak. The love and social life becomes more active. Singles are dating more and are more in the mood for love. (This is 90 per cent of romance: being in the mood, being interested.) Those already in relationships are more romantic within that relationship.

Finances are good this month (and will get even better next month). On the 9th Venus enters your 8th house of regeneration, and stays there for the rest of the month. She is moving ever closer to Jupiter, so earnings are expanding. Opportunities are coming. Your financial planet in the 8th house shows a need to prosper others – to put the financial interest of others ahead of your own. This, by the karmic law, will bring your own abundance to you. Venus in your 8th house (and in Scorpio) is good for paying off debt or for taking on loans – according to your need. It is good for getting financially healthier, eliminating unnecessary expenses. Good to go through your belongings and get rid of things that you don't use. Clear the decks to allow the greater good to come in. This planetary position also indicates good financial cooperation with your spouse, partner or current love interest. Financial intuition is excellent this month. Take heed of your dreams, and be alert to nature's signals in everyday life.

October

Best Days Overall: 4, 5, 12, 13, 14, 22, 23, 31
Most Stressful Days Overall: 2, 3, 8, 9, 15, 16, 29, 30
Best Days for Love: 2, 3, 8, 9, 10, 11, 20, 21, 29, 30
Best Days for Money: 2, 3, 10, 11, 20, 21, 25, 26, 29, 30
Best Days for Career: 6, 15, 16, 24, 25

You're still in a yearly love and social peak until the 23rd of this month, but love is much more complicated now. Venus, your love planet, starts to retrograde on the 5th and will be that way until November 16. So social confidence is not what it should be (or will be). You're going out more but don't seem certain as to what you want. Existing relationships can seem to go backwards instead of forwards. This is not a good time to be making important social decisions one way or another. Rather, this is a time to put this area under review and to gain mental and emotional clarity. See where things can be improved. Then, when Venus starts moving forward again next month, you can put your plans into action. The same is true in finances. Avoid major purchases or investments from the 5th onwards. Put your financial life under review. Your financial thinking is not realistic right now, although this will change next month.

Health and energy are not up to their usual standards this month, so, as always, the important thing is to get enough rest. High energy levels are the first defence against disease. Enhance the health in the ways mentioned in the yearly report. Until the 10th you can add hip massage to your regime. A herbal kidney cleanse might also be a good idea. After the 10th detox regimes become more effective, and sexual moderation is also important (especially from the 28th to the 30th). Happily, health and energy will improve after the 23rd.

In finance, like last month, it is good to keep the financial interest of others in mind – even to put it ahead of your own. And it is still good to 'detox' the possessions, to get rid of what isn't useful.

Mercury moves into your 8th house on the 10th and the Sun will follow on the 23rd. Venus and Jupiter are already there. So this is a strong house from the 23rd onwards. Your finances might be slow, but your spouse, partner or current love is picking up the slack. He or she is having a banner financial month (in fact the whole year has been good). Even though your financial planet is retrograde at the moment, this is a great period for tax and estate planning (if you are of appropriate age). It doesn't mean that you have to finalize anything, only start investigating and making plans. Tax efficiency seems very important on the financial level this year.

November

Best Days Overall: 1, 9, 10, 19, 20, 27, 28
Most Stressful Days Overall: 4, 5, 11, 12, 25, 26
Best Days for Love: 4, 5, 14, 15, 23, 24
Best Days for Money: 4, 5, 8, 14, 15, 19, 21, 23, 24, 22, 27
Best Days for Career: 2, 10, 11, 12, 21

On September 22 the short-term planets began to move from the bottom half of your Horoscope to the upper half. Now, 80 per cent (and 90 per cent, for half the month) of the planets are in the upper half of your chart – the sector of career and outer achievement. This is a huge, huge, percentage. Career has been the major focus since that time and the trend continues. You're in a very successful period now (and it will get even more successful next month). Doing right is more important than feeling right. You will feel in harmony when you've achieved your outer goals. You have the aspects of someone who is very career-driven these days. If moving the family and disrupting the home advances the career, you will do it. (There is probably a price to pay for this further down the road, but you don't seem to care.)

Health and energy are much better than last month. They could be better still, but Saturn won't move out of Capricorn for another year or so. However, they are at their optimum for the year. You can enhance the health further by giving more attention to the thighs and liver. Thigh massage will not only strengthen the liver, but the lower back as well.

Jupiter has been in your house of regeneration all year. On the 8th he makes a major move into your 9th house of education, thought and travel. This is a happy transit for you. First off it will bring prosperity for the coming year. It will bring success to the children and children figures of your life. Career is still going to be important, and you're still going to work hard, but you'll also find time to play – time to enjoy yourself. There is foreign travel in your future. Those of you at university should have success in your studies. Those of you applying to colleges will also have success. If you are involved in legal issues there is good fortune with them.

Venus will start to move forward again on the 16th, so both the love and financial life will start to be clear. Both the social and financial judgement will improve. Venus spends the month in your 7th house of love. Thus business partnerships or joint ventures (cooperative enterprises) will be happening. Your social grace is not only helpful romantically but on the financial level as well. Friends seem supportive: who you know is perhaps more important than how much you have.

December

Best Days Overall: 6, 7, 16, 17, 25, 26
Most Stressful Days Overall: 2, 3, 9, 10, 23, 24, 29, 30
Best Days for Love: 2, 3, 14, 15, 23, 24, 29, 30
Best Days for Money: 2, 3, 6, 14, 15, 16, 18, 19, 23, 24, 26
Best Days for Career: 8, 9, 10, 18, 27

On November 16, Mars moved into your 12th house of spirituality, and he will remain there for the month ahead. So you have strong spiritual interests now – more so than usual. Spiritual-type exercises, such as yoga, are very powerful for you now. Mars will be conjunct to Neptune from the 5th to the 7th and you can expect revelatory dreams and spiritual breakthroughs during that period. There will be a meeting with a guru or guru figure in your life.

For those of you looking for work, there is good news from the 20th to the 22nd. There could be travel involved in this job. If there have been health problems, good news concerning them comes at this time too.

Uranus moved back into your sign last month on the 6th. For those of you born later in Aries (April 19 to 21) it shows important changes in your life and in the lives of children and children figures. But the financial life gets a bit less hectic. This is, as we have mentioned, a short-lived aspect: Uranus will move back into your money house next year and will stay there for many more years to come. Finances are good this month. Venus is moving forward and on the 2nd she moves into your 8th house. You and your spouse, partner or current love are cooperating financially. If you have good ideas it is a good time to attract outside investors. This is a good period to make money for others and with other people's money. A good time to borrow or repay debt – according to your need. Good tax planning will pay off now too.

Love is about eroticism these days. It's the sexual magnetism that matters more than anything else. Love is intense and passionate, and problems can come from too much of a good thing – jealousy, etc. Love and social opportunities can happen at funerals, wakes or memorial services (most people find these morbid, but this month they aren't).

On the 21st the Sun crosses your Mid-heaven and enters your 10th house of career. You enter a yearly career peak. The focus has been on the career for many months of course, but now it is even more so. Your challenge now is to make it more fun – to have fun as you pursue your career goals.

A foreign trip this month wouldn't be a surprise.

Taurus

THE BULL

Birthdays from
21st April to
20th May

Personality Profile

TAURUS AT A GLANCE

Element – Earth

Ruling Planet – Venus
  Career Planet – Uranus
  Love Planet – Pluto
  Money Planet – Mercury
  Planet of Health and Work – Venus
  Planet of Home and Family Life – Sun
  Planet of Spirituality – Mars
  Planet of Travel, Education, Religion and Philosophy – Saturn

Colours – earth tones, green, orange, yellow

Colours that promote love, romance and social harmony – red-violet, violet

Colours that promote earning power – yellow, yellow-orange

Gems – coral, emerald

Metal – copper

Scents – bitter almond, rose, vanilla, violet

Quality – fixed (= stability)

Quality most needed for balance – flexibility

Strongest virtues – endurance, loyalty, patience, stability,
  a harmonious disposition

Deepest needs – comfort, material ease, wealth

Characteristics to avoid – rigidity, stubbornness, tendency to be overly
  possessive and materialistic

Signs of greatest overall compatibility – Virgo, Capricorn

Signs of greatest overall incompatibility – Leo, Scorpio, Aquarius

Sign most helpful to career – Aquarius

Sign most helpful for emotional support – Leo

Sign most helpful financially – Gemini

Sign best for marriage and/or partnerships – Scorpio

Sign most helpful for creative projects – Virgo

Best Sign to have fun with – Virgo

Signs most helpful in spiritual matters – Aries, Capricorn

Best day of the week – Friday

Understanding a Taurus

Taurus is the most earthy of all the Earth signs. If you understand that Earth is more than just a physical element, that it is a psychological attitude as well, you will get a better understanding of the Taurus personality.

A Taurus has all the power of action that an Aries has. But Taurus is not satisfied with action for its own sake. Their actions must be productive, practical and wealth-producing. If Taurus cannot see a practical value in an action they will not bother taking it.

Taurus's forte lies in their power to make real their own or other people's ideas. They are generally not very inventive but they can take another's invention and perfect it, making it more practical and useful. The same is true for all projects. Taurus is not especially keen on starting new projects, but once they get involved they bring things to completion. Taurus carries everything through. They are finishers and will go the distance, so long as no unavoidable calamity intervenes.

Many people find Taurus too stubborn, conservative, fixed and immovable. This is understandable, because Taurus dislikes change – in the environment or in their routine. They even dislike changing their minds! On the other hand, this is their virtue. It is not good for a wheel's axle to waver. The axle must be fixed, stable and unmovable. Taurus is the axle of society and the heavens. Without their stability and so-called stubbornness, the wheels of the world (and especially the wheels of commerce) would not turn.

Taurus loves routine. A routine, if it is good, has many virtues. It is a fixed – and, ideally, perfect – way of taking care of things. Mistakes can happen when spontaneity comes into the equation, and mistakes cause discomfort and uneasiness – something almost unacceptable to a Taurus. Meddling with Taurus's comfort and security is a sure way to irritate and anger them.

While an Aries loves speed, a Taurus likes things slow. They are slow thinkers – but do not make the mistake of assuming they lack intelligence. On the contrary, Taurus people are very intelligent. It is just that they like to chew on ideas, to deliberate and weigh them up.

Only after due deliberation is an idea accepted or a decision taken. Taurus is slow to anger – but once aroused, take care!

Finance

Taurus is very money-conscious. Wealth is more important to them than to many other signs. Wealth to a Taurus means comfort and security. Wealth means stability. Where some zodiac signs feel that they are spiritually rich if they have ideas, talents or skills, Taurus only feels wealth when they can see and touch it. Taurus's way of thinking is, 'What good is a talent if it has not been translated into a home, furniture, car and holidays?'

These are all reasons why Taurus excels in estate agency and agricultural industries. Usually a Taurus will end up owning land. They love to feel their connection to the Earth. Material wealth began with agriculture, the tilling of the soil. Owning a piece of land was humanity's earliest form of wealth: Taurus still feels that primeval connection.

It is in the pursuit of wealth that Taurus develops intellectual and communication ability. Also, in this pursuit Taurus is forced to develop some flexibility. It is in the quest for wealth that they learn the practical value of the intellect and come to admire it. If it were not for the search for wealth and material things, Taurus people might not try to reach a higher intellect.

Some Taurus people are 'born lucky' – the type who win any gamble or speculation. This luck is due to other factors in their horoscope; it is not part of their essential nature. By nature they are not gamblers. They are hard workers and like to earn what they get. Taurus's innate conservatism makes them abhor unnecessary risks in finance and in other areas of their lives.

Career and Public Image

Being essentially down-to-earth people, simple and uncomplicated, Taurus tends to look up to those who are original, unconventional and inventive. Taurus people like their bosses to be creative and original – since they themselves are content to perfect their superiors' brainwaves. They admire people who have a wider social or political consciousness and they feel that someday (when they have all the comfort and security they need) they too would like to be involved in these big issues.

In business affairs Taurus can be very shrewd – and that makes them valuable to their employers. They are never lazy; they enjoy working and getting good results. Taurus does not like taking unnecessary risks and they do well in positions of authority, which makes them good managers and supervisors. Their managerial skills are reinforced by their natural talents for organization and handling details, their patience and thoroughness. As mentioned, through their connection with the earth, Taurus people also do well in farming and agriculture.

In general a Taurus will choose money and earning power over public esteem and prestige. A position that pays more – though it has less prestige – is preferred to a position with a lot of prestige but lower earnings. Many other signs do not feel this way, but a Taurus does, especially if there is nothing in his or her personal birth chart that modifies this. Taurus will pursue glory and prestige only if it can be shown that these things have a direct and immediate impact on their wallet.

Love and Relationships

In love, the Taurus-born likes to have and to hold. They are the marrying kind. They like commitment and they like the terms of a relationship to be clearly defined. More importantly, Taurus likes to be faithful to one lover, and they expect that lover to reciprocate this fidelity. When this doesn't happen, their whole world comes crashing down. When they are in love Taurus people are loyal, but they are also very possessive. They are capable of great fits of jealousy if they are hurt in love.

Taurus is satisfied with the simple things in a relationship. If you are involved romantically with a Taurus there is no need for lavish entertainments and constant courtship. Give them enough love, food and comfortable shelter and they will be quite content to stay home and enjoy your company. They will be loyal to you for life. Make a Taurus feel comfortable and – above all – secure in the relationship, and you will rarely have a problem.

In love, Taurus can sometimes make the mistake of trying to control their partners, which can cause great pain on both sides. The reasoning behind their actions is basically simple: Taurus people feel a sense of ownership over their partners and will want to make changes that will increase their own general comfort and security. This attitude is OK when it comes to inanimate, material things – but is dangerous when applied to people. Taurus needs to be careful and attentive to this possible trait within themselves.

Home and Domestic Life

Home and family are vitally important to Taurus. They like children. They also like a comfortable and perhaps glamorous home – something they can show off. They tend to buy heavy, ponderous furniture – usually of the best quality. This is because Taurus likes a feeling of substance in their environment. Their house is not only their home but their place of creativity and entertainment. The Taurus' home tends to be truly their castle. If they could choose, Taurus people would prefer living in the countryside to being city-dwellers. If they cannot do so during their working lives, many Taurus individuals like to holiday in or even retire to the country, away from the city and closer to the land.

At home a Taurus is like a country squire – lord (or lady) of the manor. They love to entertain lavishly, to make others feel secure in their home and to encourage others to derive the same sense of satisfaction as they do from it. If you are invited for dinner at the home of a Taurus you can expect the best food and best entertainment. Be prepared for a tour of the house and expect to see your Taurus friend exhibit a lot of pride and satisfaction in his or her possessions.

Taurus people like children but they are usually strict with them. The reason for this is they tend to treat their children – as they do most things in life – as their possessions. The positive side to this is that their children will be well cared for and well supervised. They will get every material thing they need to grow up properly. On the down side, Taurus can get too repressive with their children. If a child dares to upset the daily routine – which Taurus loves to follow – he or she will have a problem with a Taurus parent.

Horoscope for 2018

Major Trends

Sometimes the best way out of a rut is not climbing out of it, but simply blasting the rut away. When the blast is over, you'll find your path open. This is what is starting (and it is only the beginning) to happen this year, as Uranus enters your sign on May 16. This is a momentous transit that you will feel for the next seven years. Those of you born early in the sign of Taurus (April 20 to April 22) are going to feel this the most this year. But all of you will feel it in coming years.

The other major headline is the love life. The love life was good last year, but gets even better in the year ahead. Jupiter is firmly positioned in your 7th house of love almost all year – until November. For singles this brings romance and serious types of relationship. More on this later.

Jupiter will move into your 8th house on November 8. This will bring prosperity to the current love or spouse. He or she enters a peak prosperity period that will last well into 2019. It will also be a good time to pay off debt or attract outside investors. More on this later on.

Saturn moved into your 9th house late last year and will remain there for the next two years. This is basically a happy transit as Saturn makes harmonious aspects to you. You will be more disciplined and organized. For college students this is a difficult transit, however; it shows a need for more work, more effort, more discipline in the studies. You can't coast this year. It is also challenging for those of you involved in legal issues. You can expect many delays and setbacks.

Pluto has been in your 9th house for many years now, and will be there for many more. This indicates that a cosmic detox is going on in your religious and philosophical life. This is a long-term process. Old beliefs – those that don't belong in the mind – get flushed out so that a better, more realistic belief system can evolve.

Neptune has been in your 11th house for many years and, likewise, will be there for many more years to come. Neptune, like Pluto, is a very slow-moving planet. This transit is spiritualizing your friendships. You're attracting more spiritual friends, and perhaps are more involved in spiritual types of organizations too.

Your most important interests this year will be the body and image (from May 16 to November 6); love and romance (until November 8); sex, occult studies and personal reinvention (after November 8); religion, philosophy, higher education and foreign travel; friendships, groups and group activities; and spirituality (from January 1 to May 16 and from November 6 onwards).

Your paths of greatest fulfilment this year will be home and family (until November 17); love, romance and social activities (until November 8); sex, occult studies and personal transformation (from November 8 onwards); and communication and intellectual interests (after November 17).

Health

(Please note that this is an astrological perspective on health and not a medical one. In days of yore there was no difference, both these perspectives were identical. But now there could be quite a difference. For a medical perspective, please consult your doctor or health practitioner.)

Health and energy look excellent in the year ahead. There is only one long-term planet, Jupiter, in stressful alignment with you. All the others are mostly in harmonious aspect. So if you have any pre-existing conditions or health concerns you should hear good news about them this year. They are likely to be much milder, or even resolve themselves now.

Your empty 6th house of health is also a good sign: you don't need to focus on health as it is not a big issue. Why do drastic things when there's nothing wrong? You sort of take good health for granted this year. On November 8, even Jupiter will move away from his stressful aspect. So overall health will become even better.

Sure, there will be periods in the year when your health and energy are not as good as usual, but these are temporary things caused by the planetary transits. They are not trends for the year. When they pass, your normal good health and energy return.

Good though your health is, you can make it even better. Give special attention to the following – the vulnerable areas for Taurus (the reflex points are shown in the chart opposite):

Important foot reflexology points for the year ahead

*Try to massage all of the foot on a regular basis – the top of the foot as well as
the bottom – but pay extra attention to the points highlighted on the chart.
When you massage, be aware of 'sore spots' as these need special attention.
It's also a good idea to massage the ankles and below them.*

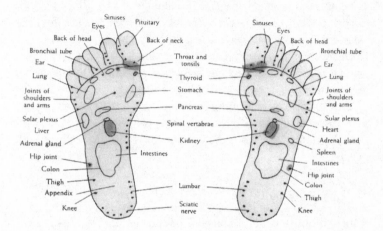

- The neck and throat. These are always important for Taurus and
  regular neck massage is always a good thing. Tension tends to
  collect there and needs to be released. Craniosacral therapy is said
  to be good for the neck.
- The kidneys and hips. These too are always important for Taurus.
  Hips (and the buttocks) should be regularly massaged. This will
  not only strengthen these areas but improve your overall posture.
  A herbal kidney cleanse might be a good idea if you feel under the
  weather.

Venus, your health planet, is a fast-moving planet and will move
through all the signs and houses of your Horoscope in any given
year. Thus there are many short-term health trends that depend on
where Venus is and the aspects she receives. Some months you
might respond better to one therapy and some months to another.
These short-term trends are best dealt with in the monthly reports
below.

Uranus, as we have mentioned, will move into your sign on May 16. From a health perspective it signals 'experimentation' with the body. There will be tendency to 'test the limits' of the body. This is a wonderful thing in that much of our physical limitations are self-imposed or have been inherited, and it is good to break these limits. On the other hand, this testing should be done in a mindful and conscious way, not recklessly. Thus disciplines like yoga, tai chi or other martial arts might be good. These are safe ways to test the body's limits.

This year Uranus is only making a foray into your sign. But next year – and for the next seven or so years – you will experience the full-blown transit and these tendencies will be a lot stronger.

Your health planet will move backwards this year. This is a relatively rare phenomenon that happens once every two years. So, from October 5 to November 16 avoid making major changes to the diet or health regime.

Home and Family

Your 4th house is not a house of power this year, Taurus. So the cosmos is not pushing you to make dramatic changes in your home life one way or another. It tends to the status quo and shows a sense of satisfaction with the way things are. You have more freedom in home and family affairs, but lack the interest to alter things. In spite of this, there will be changes and dramas in the family circle this year. Most likely you won't be initiating these things, but reacting to events that happen. This year we have three Solar Eclipses – usually there are only two. Since the Sun is your family planet the Horoscope is forecasting more than usual turbulence. Two eclipses – one Solar and one Lunar – will actually occur in your 4th house of home and family, reinforcing the sense of 'shakeup' and 'drama' that we see.

We will cover the eclipses in more detail in the monthly reports. In general it is wise to be more patient with family members (and with parents or parent figures) as they are apt to be more temperamental. The emotional life (and the dream life) will tend to be more volatile as well.

A parent or parent figure is likely to move, renovate the existing home, or buy an additional home. It seems happy and fortunate.

Another parent or parent figure seems very devoted to you and seems very focused on you. This is a double-edged sword: there is more support, but perhaps more control as well.

Siblings or sibling figures in your life could have moved in 2015 or 2016. Things are more stable for them this year. Children and children figures are likely to move after November 8, and perhaps next year too. This looks happy. Grandchildren of appropriate age have perhaps had multiple moves in recent years. This trend continues this year. Their wanderlust seems almost over with, however, and they will be more ready to settle down next year.

Though you are likely to need to make repairs to the home this year, major renovations aren't likely. (You have freedom to do them, but no pressing necessity.) However, if you're redecorating or updating the home in cosmetic kinds of way – or buying art objects for the home – June 13 to August 23 seems a good time.

One of the parents or parent figures in your life needs to watch his or her health more. A daily disciplined health regime is in order. He or she should pay more attention to the spine, knees, teeth, bones, colon, bladder and sexual organs. Surgery could be recommended to this person too.

Siblings or sibling figures have wonderful job opportunities this year. If there have been health problems there is good news on that front.

Finance and Career

Money and financial well-being are always important for Taurus, but this year less so than usual. I read this as a good thing. Finances are relatively stable – relatively satisfying – and you have no pressing need for major change. The money house is not a house of power this year. It is basically empty. Only short-term planets will briefly pass through there, so finances will be more or less like last year.

Your financial planet, Mercury, is, next to the Moon, the fastest and most erratic of the planets. Sometimes he moves very fast (passing through three signs and houses in a given month), sometimes he's slow and sometimes he goes backwards. The fact that he's your finan-cial planet shows that though you tend to be fixed in your ways, when it comes to finance, you're very flexible. You can change your opinions and attitudes at the drop of a hat.

This erratic nature of Mercury indicates that there are many short-term financial trends, all depending on where he is at any given time, how fast he's moving and the aspects he receives. These trends are best dealt with in the monthly reports.

We should mention that Mercury will go into retrograde motion three times this year (this is usual, although in the past two years he went retrograde four times each year). These are times to put the financial life (your goals and planning) under review. These are great periods for research and study, but not so good for making important purchases or financial moves. Mercury is retrograde from March 23 to April 15, July 26 to August 19 and November 17 to December 6.

The real action this year is in the career. Here we see many – and positive – changes. You tend to prefer status and prestige over mere money, Taurus. You sort of feel that 'if I'm successful, if I have status, money will follow eventually'.

There are two eclipse in your 10th career house this year – a Solar Eclipse on February 15 and a Lunar Eclipse on July 27. These indicate shakeups in your company or industry. Your career strategy and thinking will change. A lot of obstacles (or what you thought were obstacles) will be removed. But even more important than that is your career planet Uranus's entry into your sign on May 16. This signals you have the favour and support of the people with power in your life, the bosses and authority figures. This move is favourable for the career. It shows that career opportunities will start seeking you out rather than vice versa. The offers will come, you just have to go about your daily business.

With Uranus in your 1st house people will see you as successful. This will be your image and persona. You will dress and look the part. Personal appearance and overall demeanour will be a big factor in your career success.

Uranus in Aries for the past seven years has made the career highly unstable. There was always a feeling of insecurity. Uranus in Taurus is more stable – more solid – less volatile.

Love and Social Life

As we mentioned earlier, the year ahead is a banner love and social year. For some it will be the best ever, for others it will be up there among the best. Much depends on your age. Jupiter will spend the year in your 7th house of love. The stresses to your love planet, Pluto, are mostly over with. If you are single, this is a year for finding that special someone. Often this transit shows a literal marriage, but not always. Sometimes it shows a relationship that is 'like a marriage'.

All of you will be socializing more, making new and significant kinds of friendships. Often business partnerships happen under this transit too.

In spite of all this good, there are some complications (and this is especially so for those of you born early in the sign – from April 20 to April 23). Uranus in your sign is not the best aspect for serious relationships. There is a tendency to want absolute personal freedom and it is difficult having to compromise that. You want to do what you want to do when you want to do it. A committed relationship, by definition, implies a limitation of personal freedom. One needs to be able to sacrifice the latter in order to explore other kinds of freedom – the freedom of intimacy with another, the freedom to explore family life, etc. Too much self will might not stop romance, but it might stop committed relationships. Those of you involved romantically with a Taurus need to give them as much space – as much freedom – as possible, so long as it isn't destructive.

So romance is very likely this year – the opportunities are certainly there – but will it lead to marriage or commitment? That is the million dollar question.

Pluto, the generic planet of sex, is your love planet. Jupiter, the actual planet of sex, is in your house of love. This gives many messages. Sexual magnetism seems the most important thing for you (and for the people you're involved with). It seems the 'be all and end all'. While there is no question of its importance, we can't confuse that with real love, nor can one build a solid relationship only on that. More is needed.

Jupiter in your 7th house indicates an attraction to foreigners and to highly educated or religious kinds of people. You're attracted to mentor types. (Many of the people you meet seem eager to be mentor figures.) It shows an attraction to wealth too. In fact the people you're meeting seem well off; they seem like 'money people'.

There are romantic opportunities at your place of worship, at religious or educational functions or in foreign lands. Professors and the clergy in your life – as well as the people in your place of worship – like playing Cupid.

Self-Improvement

Uranus's brief venture into your 1st house this year is only a foretaste of things to come; an announcement. Much change is happening in your life, much of it sudden and unexpected. There is a cosmic lesson here. An important one. Taureans are conservative people. They like routine. They like predictability. And they don't do well with too much change. But now the cosmos is pushing change on you – and make no mistake, it is for your good. So the lesson here is to make change your friend. To embrace it. To roll and adapt with it. There is something very exciting about all this. Anything can happen at any time. Routines – comfortable though they may be – are not likely to last. It is important now to be flexible and ready to let things go. If you learn this, things will go easier for you down the road.

Uranus is your career planet. The worldly aspects of your career have been discussed above, but the 10th house has a deeper meaning than just the worldly career. Spiritually it represents your soul purpose, your spiritual mission for this life. This is going to become ever more important in the coming years. The message of the Horoscope is that your body and image is basically your mission. You're being called to create and personify the 'Divine Body' – the body as it was created to be – the Divine Idea of your body. This is perfection when we understand it correctly. But it is not just about the body, it's also about your outer personality. You are being called to perfect yourself, to make you as you are intended to be.

Uranus is going to initiate a long-term trend in 'self-redefinition'. You will be constantly redefining yourself, changing your image and your look – upgrading it the way you upgrade your computer and software. Every time you think you have it 'perfect' – a new idea comes to you and you change. You're not going to be the 'stodgy boring Taurus' any longer, but someone exciting, electrifying and fun to be around. You will have a magnetic, charismatic kind of presence.

For years now, Pluto has been detoxifying your belief systems – your philosophy of life. Everyone has a philosophy of life – consciously or unconsciously. This area of life is much more important (though less popular) than psychology. Your personal philosophy will shape your psychology. So, much change has happened in your belief systems over the years. Now Saturn's presence in your 9th house is going to test your new beliefs. They get a reality check. The changes you have made, are they real? Are they true? Can they hold up under the events of life? In the next two years, you will find out. Some will hold up, some will need to be changed, modified or thrown out completely.

Saturn in your 9th house favours what is called 'the old time religion'. Traditional religion. It has been fashionable to toss this out the window, to mock it in certain quarters. But the reason these religions have lasted so long is that underneath the human baggage lie deep spiritual truths. These should be understood and absorbed now. Once you have the essence you can throw away the outer trappings. But first one needs the essence.

Month-by-month Forecasts

January

Best Days Overall: 5, 6, 15, 16, 25, 26
Most Stressful Days Overall: 3, 4, 10, 11, 17, 18, 31
Best Days for Love: 5, 6, 10, 11, 15, 16, 25, 26, 27, 28
Best Days for Money: 1, 2, 3, 4, 10, 11, 15, 16, 20, 21, 25, 26, 27, 28, 29, 30
Best Days for Career: 4, 13, 14, 17, 18, 19, 23, 24, 31

You're in a very interesting situation these days. You begin your year with 90 per cent (and for half the month *all*) of the planets above the horizon. The upper half of your chart – the 'day side' – is chock-full of planets, while the lower half is empty. Only the Moon will move through the 'night side' of your chart this month, from the 3rd to the

9th and from the 25th to the 31st. This means that you are very much a 'day' person in the year ahead. A career person. A person focused on outer achievement. Home, family and emotional issues are taking a back seat. Also it means that the lower half of the Horoscope – even at its strongest point – will never dominate. You're in a strong career year – and the month ahead is a strong career month. If people accuse you of being 'career driven' – just humbly nod your head. It's in the stars.

A Lunar Eclipse on the 31st will force you – if only briefly – to pay more attention to the home and family. It occurs in your 4th house of home and family and brings dramas in the lives of family members – especially a parent or parent figure. Often repairs are needed in the home and you won't be able to avoid this. This is a powerful eclipse so reduce your schedule over that period. This eclipse will test cars and communication equipment, and in many cases they will need repair or replacement. Siblings and/or sibling figures in your life will have life-changing dramas. Since Venus is impacted by this eclipse (although not exactly, it's more like a glancing blow) the health regime will change in the coming months. Sometimes there is a health scare – but your health looks good and it probably won't be anything more than that. There can be upheavals in your neighbourhood and with neighbours too. If you employ others there is instability with employees.

It is interesting that this eclipse occurs right in the midst of a yearly career peak – one of your most successful (and demanding) times. It's a distraction to the career. Happily, the family (for the most part) is supportive of your career goals. They see it as a 'family project' and not just personal to you.

The love life is going well this month. Between the 8th and the 10th Venus travels with your love planet, Pluto. For singles this indicates a significant romantic meeting or opportunity. Jupiter is in your 7th house as well – serious love is in the air.

February

Best Days Overall: 2, 3, 11, 12, 21, 22
Most Stressful Days Overall: 6, 7, 14, 15, 27, 28
Best Days for Love: 2, 3, 4, 5, 6, 7, 11, 12, 16, 21, 22, 25, 26
Best Days for Money: 2, 3, 6, 7, 11, 12, 16, 17, 21, 22, 23, 24, 25, 26
Best Days for Career: 10, 14, 15, 19, 20, 28

Many of the trends discussed last month are still in effect now. You're still very much in a yearly career peak and seem very successful. Last month – on the 18th – Venus, the ruler of your Horoscope, crossed the Mid-heaven and entered your 10th house of career. This shows personal success and elevation. People look up to you. You're in charge (or aspire to be) and are at the top of your game. Venus will remain in your 10th house until the 11th. But another eclipse will distract you – and this one also looks to be powerful. It is a Solar Eclipse on the 15th, which occurs in your career house.

You need to be taking it more easy until the 18th anyway, but especially during the eclipse period. This Solar Eclipse affects the family, and especially the parents (both sets of parents or parent figures). There are dramas in their lives. The home might need more attention as hidden flaws there can be revealed. There are shakeups in your company and industry: perhaps the government changes the law and the rules of the game are changed. Bosses and authority figures have personal dramas. All these things are ultimately going to benefit your career, as obstructions to your progress are being blown away. But while it is happening there is usually a feeling of insecurity. A career course correction is very much in order now.

This eclipse is powerful in other ways too. Mercury, your financial planet, is affected. There is some financial disturbance, something that forces a course correction in your financial strategy and thinking. A love affair can be tested. Children and children figures need to redefine themselves. Jupiter, the ruler of your 8th house of regeneration, is also affected. Thus there can be near-death kinds of experiences, problems with the tax authorities or legal issues. Often people have dreams of death under these kinds of eclipses. But this is just to help you come to terms with it.

Health and energy will improve from the 18th onwards. Until then make sure to get enough rest. Enhance the health in the ways mentioned in the yearly report. Until the 11th pay attention to the ankles and calves. Massage them regularly. After the 11th give more attention to the feet – foot massage becomes very beneficial. Venus in Pisces, from the 11th onwards, favours spiritual kinds of therapies. If you feel under the weather, see a spiritual healer.

March

Best Days Overall: 1, 2, 10, 11, 12, 20, 21, 29, 30
Most Stressful Days Overall: 6, 7, 13, 14, 26, 27
Best Days for Love: 1, 2, 6, 7, 8, 10, 11, 12, 18, 19, 20, 21, 26, 27, 29, 30
Best Days for Money: 6, 7, 8, 15, 16, 17, 18, 19, 22, 23, 24, 25, 26, 27
Best Days for Career: 9, 13, 14, 18, 19, 27

Career is still very important, and this is how it will be all year. But the month ahead is more spiritual. There are many planets in the spiritual sign of Pisces this month: at least 40 per cent (and sometimes 50 per cent) of the planets are either there or moving through there. This shows involvement with spiritual-type groups and befriending spiritual people. The spiritual connection seems important in friendships these days. (Let's not forget that Neptune, the generic spiritual ruler, has been in your 11th house for many years now.)

Spirituality is further emphasized after the 20th as your 12th house becomes ultra-powerful. Your challenge this month will be to merge your spiritual values with the values of the world. This is not so easy to do. Your career approach will become more spiritual and your spiritual approach more worldly and practical.

Health and energy are superb this month. There is only one long-term planet in stressful alignment with you. All the short-term planets (except for the Moon on occasion) are either in harmony with you or leaving you alone. So long as you don't fritter away all this extra energy it should bring you success and prosperity. You can enhance your health further by giving more attention to the feet until the 6th, and to the head, face and scalp after that date. Scalp massage will not only strengthen the brain and head, but the entire body as well.

Mercury, your financial planet, spends most of the month in your spiritual 12th house – from the 6th onwards. This shows the importance of intuition, and a need – and an ability – to access the supernatural sources of supply. This is a time for miracle money, rather than natural money. Mercury will go into retrograde motion on the 23rd, so wrap up important purchases or investments before then. After the 23rd it's time to put your finances under review.

Love is good this year, as we've said, but after the 20th it does become more challenging. You have to work harder at your current relationship. There are some short-term personal disagreements with the beloved. Next month harmony is restored.

The planetary power is approaching its maximum Eastern position this month. Next month it will be even stronger. Now is the time to make the changes that need to be made. You have plenty of cosmic support. (If we have cosmic support we're not worried about what humans think.) Personal independence is unusually strong.

April

Best Days Overall: 7, 8, 16, 17, 25, 26
Most Stressful Days Overall: 2, 3, 9, 10, 11, 23, 24, 29
Best Days for Love: 2, 3, 7, 8, 16, 17, 25, 26, 27, 29
Best Days for Money: 2, 3, 4, 5, 6, 12, 13, 14, 15, 18, 19, 21, 22, 23, 24, 29, 30
Best Days for Career: 6, 9, 10, 15, 24

A happy and successful month Taurus, enjoy! Health and energy are terrific. And with more energy there is more happiness. (A good definition of depression, astrologically speaking, is 'lack of energy'.) With more energy your horizons expand. Things that were considered impossible – things you may have dismissed from your mind – are now eminently possible.

The planetary power is East – maximum East. This, as our regular readers know, is the sector of self. The planetary power is on your side, supporting you and your personal happiness. As we mentioned last month, this is the time to make any changes that need to be made in your life. Irksome conditions are easily alterable now, there's no need to suffer or compromise. Personal initiative matters. Personal skills matter. We are never disrespectful of others, but now you're not that dependent on them. It's time to have things your way – to have life on your terms. If you create wisely, the year ahead will be more comfortable. If you make mistakes you'll learn about them over the next six months, and when your next period of independence comes, you'll be able to make appropriate changes.

Spirituality is still important this month, until the 20th. Spiritual breakthroughs that happen will change both the financial and career situation for the better. Even the family situation will improve because of this. If parents or parent figures haven't been getting along, there is more togetherness from the 17th to the 19th. There is happy career success in that period too.

Venus spends most of the month in your sign, until the 24th. This brings beauty and glamour to the image. It is one of the best times to buy clothing or personal accessories as your taste will be excellent. Happy job opportunities are coming too: there is no need for any Taurus to be unemployed now.

The Sun moves into your sign on the 20th. This, too, improves the personal appearance. You have 'star quality' now. Charisma. A twinkle in your eye, a spring in your step. It is no surprise that the love life is vastly improved. The only complication is the retrograde of your love planet Pluto on the 22nd, which will go on for many months. This doesn't stop love, but it does slow things down a bit. And it should be slowed down – let love develop as it will.

May

Best Days Overall: 4, 5, 14, 15, 22, 23, 31
Most Stressful Days Overall: 7, 8, 20, 21, 26, 27, 28
Best Days for Love: 4, 5, 7, 8, 14, 15, 17, 22, 23, 26, 27, 28
Best Days for Money: 2, 3, 9, 10, 13, 14, 16, 17, 18, 19, 22, 23,
    26, 27, 31
Best Days for Career: 4, 7, 8, 14, 22, 31

Another happy and successful month, with just a few challenges to keep things interesting. (Too much happiness can get boring after a while.)

Last month, on the 20th, as the Sun entered your 1st house, you began one of your yearly personal pleasure peaks. This is a great time to pamper the body and to enjoy all the pleasures of the five senses. It's also good for getting your body and image in right shape. The cosmos supports these activities.

Mercury, now moving forward, crosses your Ascendant and enters your 1st house on the 13th, bringing financial windfalls to you. You start to dress more expensively and present an image of wealth. Financial opportunities seek you out. You have the financial favour of the money people in your life.

The big news – and we mentioned this in the yearly report – is Uranus's move into your sign on the 16th. Taureans have a tendency to get stuck in their ways. But those days are over (especially for those of you born early in the sign). Now change can happen at any time, in any place – sudden and dramatic change. During this period it seems to involve the career. Happy career opportunities come that can upend your whole status quo.

On the 21st the Sun enters your money house and you begin a yearly financial peak. Venus is in the money house until the 19th – also good for finances – and your money planet Mercury will enter on the 30th. So the month ahead is prosperous – Taurus heaven!

Mars crosses the Mid-heaven on the 16th and enters your 10th house of career. This indicates a lot of frenetic career activity. Perhaps there are some unpleasant revelations about your company or industry and much work has to be done. Perhaps you have to fend off competitors. It will keep you on your toes.

Money comes through your personal effort, your job, family and family connections and from good sales and marketing. A speedy Mercury (he moves through three signs and houses this month) shows financial confidence and fast, forward progress.

Family support is very good now. They seem devoted to you. Love is happy but Pluto is still retrograde, so no need to rush into anything. (Jupiter in your 7th house of love is also retrograde, just to reinforce what we're saying here.)

June

Best Days Overall: 1, 2, 10, 11, 18, 19, 28, 29
Most Stressful Days Overall: 3, 4, 16, 17, 23, 24, 30
Best Days for Love: 1, 2, 6, 7, 10, 11, 16, 18, 19, 23, 24, 28, 29
Best Days for Money: 3, 4, 5, 6, 7, 12, 13, 14, 15, 23, 24
Best Days for Career: 1, 3, 4, 10, 18, 28, 30

Planetary retrograde activity increases this month. By the 26th half the planets will be moving backwards – almost the maximum number for 2018. The pace of life slows down considerably. There are many delays and glitches in the world. On a psychological level it is useful to understand what's going on. Also, as an added bonus, we learn patience.

You're still very much into one of your yearly financial peaks. Things might be slower in the world, but your earnings are coming in as they should. By the 21st your short-term financial goals are more or less achieved and you can focus on other things – such as intellectual development. This is a great period to take courses in subjects that interest you. If you have expertise in a given field it's also a good time to teach others, to communicate what you know. Sales and marketing are always important on a financial level, but especially until the 29th.

Venus makes beautiful aspects to Neptune on the 1st and 2nd. This brings someone spiritual into your life. Your intuition is keen and the dream life is very active. From the 4th to the 6th, as Venus opposes Pluto, there are short-term conflicts with the beloved. These will pass. You're just seeing things from opposite perspectives.

Health and energy are basically good this month. Be careful of overworking though – Mars is still in your 10th house and career is frenetic.

You can enhance the health through right diet and emotional tranquillity until the 14th. After that date, give more attention to the heart. Heat-oriented therapies (and plain old sunshine) are healing from the 14th onwards.

Finances, as we mentioned, are basically good this month, but on the 15th and 16th there is some challenge or delay. On the 22nd or 23rd there can be a financial disagreement with the beloved.

Venus, the ruler of your Horoscope, is 'out of bounds' from the 1st to the 7th. So you're outside your normal sphere then. This might be because of your job.

Uranus is still in your 1st house this month and very near your Ascendant. So change and excitement is happening for many of you. Many of you are changing your image – experimenting with it. You keep upgrading your image the way some people update their software. It is an ongoing, continuous process.

July

Best Days Overall: 7, 8, 16, 17, 25, 26
Most Stressful Days Overall: 1, 14, 15, 20, 21, 27, 28, 29
Best Days for Love: 5, 6, 7, 8, 16, 17, 20, 21, 25, 26
Best Days for Money: 1, 5, 6, 10, 11, 12, 13, 14, 15, 20, 21, 22, 23, 24, 27, 28, 29
Best Days for Career: 1, 7, 16, 25, 27, 28, 29

Persistence – some might call it stubbornness – is one of the important virtues of Taureans. You have this innate ability to create success when others have long since given up. But this virtue is sometimes a vice. Sometimes you get too stuck in your ways and need a course correction. Uranus in your 1st house, and two very strong eclipses, are taking you out of your rut this month. Many of you saw the beginnings of this – the harbinger – last month.

Both eclipses – the Solar Eclipse of the 13th and the Lunar Eclipse of the 27th – affect you strongly, so take it nice and easy then. The Solar Eclipse not only impacts on your home and family planet, the Sun, but also occurs in the sign of Cancer, which generically rules family. So more family dramas are happening. Memories can arise about explosive past events. A parent or parent figure has to make a life-changing decision. Hidden flaws in the home can come to light so that you can deal with them. The family situation is not as it seemed to be, and the eclipse reveals this. The Solar Eclipse occurs in your 3rd house and so siblings and sibling figures in your life are affected here. They are experiencing personal and financial dramas. Cars and communication equipment will get tested, and will often need repair or replacement. Students below college level can change schools, or otherwise change their educational plans. There are disruptions in their school. Pluto, your love planet, is impacted too, so a current relationship gets tested. Repressed grievances tend to come up and need to be dealt with. Be more patient with the beloved at this time.

The Lunar Eclipse of the 27th also impacts on the home and family, as the Moon, the eclipsed planet, is the generic ruler of this area of the Horoscope. Siblings and sibling figures are once again affected, forcing important personal changes. Cars and communication equipment get tested once again. This eclipse occurs in your 10th house of career, so there are course corrections in your career. The rules of the game are changing. This eclipse impacts on the other parent figure in your life. Often there are dramas with bosses, elders and people involved in your career. This eclipse affects Mars, the ruler of your spiritual 12th house. Thus there are shakeups in a charitable or spiritual organization that you're involved with. There are dramas in the lives of guru figures. The dream life is likely to be hyperactive, but not very reliable. Don't put too much stock in your dreams for the moment.

August

Best Days Overall: 4, 5, 12, 13, 21, 22, 31
Most Stressful Days Overall: 10, 11, 16, 17, 24, 25
Best Days for Love: 4, 5, 12, 13, 14, 15, 16, 17, 21, 22, 24, 25, 31
Best Days for Money: 1, 2, 3, 6, 7, 8, 9, 10, 11, 16, 17, 19, 20, 26, 27, 29, 30
Best Days for Career: 4, 12, 21, 24, 25, 31

The turbulence of the past month is not yet over with. We have another Solar Eclipse – the third one of the year – on the 11th. This is more or less a replay of last month's eclipses (things never repeat in the same exact way, but the themes of the eclipses are similar). It occurs in your 4th house of home and family and the eclipsed planet, the Sun, is the ruler of your 4th house. So there are yet more family dramas, and perhaps more work needed on the physical home. (The hidden flaws there were more numerous than you thought.)

You should reduce your schedule this month, until the 22nd anyway – it's not your best health month – and especially around the eclipse period.

It is midnight in your year (allegorically speaking) and yet you seem wide awake. The outer world calls to you. You would like to sleep, but you need to focus on the activities of the day. It's a curious situation, and one that perhaps leaves you feeling sleep deprived.

Enhance the health by making sure you get enough rest. But also give more attention to the diet and the small intestine until the 7th, and to the kidneys and hips afterwards. Regular hip massage will not only strengthen the kidneys, but the lower back as well. Your health planet, Venus, spends most of the month in Libra – her own sign – which is a good health omen. She is strong in that sign. It also indicates a need for good social health, and good marital health. If there are problems there, resolve them as quickly as you can.

Your financial planet, Mercury, is retrograde until the 19th, so avoid major purchases and investments during this time. After the 19th there will be more clarity and it is safer to act. Mercury spends the month in your 4th house. So (no surprise), you're spending more on the home and family. Perhaps you're earning from there as well. Some of you will be earning money at home. Family and family connections are playing a huge role in the financial life this month.

Mars, your spiritual planet, is 'out of bounds' all month (an aspect that began last month). So in your spiritual life you're outside your normal sphere. This is the kind of aspect of someone who travels to some distant land on a spiritual pilgrimage. But it can also indicate exploring new and different types of spirituality from where you are.

September

Best Days Overall: 1, 9, 17, 18, 19, 27, 28
Most Stressful Days Overall: 7, 13, 14, 20, 21
Best Days for Love: 1, 2, 3, 9, 10, 13, 14, 18, 19, 22, 23, 27, 28
Best Days for Money: 2, 3, 4, 5, 9, 13, 14, 18, 19, 22, 23, 24, 29, 30
Best Days for Career: 1, 8, 9, 17, 20, 21, 27

Now that the excitement of the eclipses is over you can enjoy your life more. Your 5th house of creativity and fun is still very strong until the 22nd, so you're in another one of your personal pleasure peaks for the year. A good time to schedule more leisure and fun activities into your life.

Health and energy are much improved over last month. If there have been health problems you should hear good news about them this month. Continue to pay particular attention to the kidneys and hips until the 9th. After the 9th give more focus to the colon, bladder and sexual organs. Detox regimes are powerful after this date, and a herbal colon cleanse might be a good idea if you feel under the weather.

Finances are also good this month. Mercury is moving fast and financial progress happens quickly. You cover a lot of territory. The period between the 6th and the 22nd is particularly good. Mercury will be in your 5th house, showing that money is earned in happy ways. The act of making money is enjoyable (and we can't always say that). There is luck in speculations. Most importantly you're enjoying the wealth that you have. You're spending your money on fun activities. Children and children figures in your life seem important financially. Sometimes, especially if they are young, they motivate you to earn more. Sometimes they have ideas or insights that are profitable. If the children are older, they can be financially supportive in a more tangible way.

Your 6th house of health and work becomes strong from the 22nd onwards. This signals a good work ethic – something you need right now with Mars moving back into your 10th house of career. The demands of career are very strong, but you seem up to it. Those of you looking for work should have success during this period (and next month too).

On July 22 the planetary power started to shift from the East to the West, from the sector of the self to the sector of others. Now, it is approaching its maximum Western position. This means that the planetary power is more focused on others, flowing towards others, away from yourself. And, this is how you should be. Venus, the ruler of your Horoscope, moves into your 7th house on the 9th and stays there for the rest of the month ahead. You're taking a vacation from yourself (a much-needed one), and you're more concerned for others now. You put the interests of others ahead of your own. You feel good when you can do things for others. This tends to popularity, so love is going well too.

October

Best Days Overall: 6, 7, 15, 16, 25, 26
Most Stressful Days Overall: 4, 5, 10, 11, 17, 18, 19, 31
Best Days for Love: 2, 3, 6, 7, 10, 11, 15, 16, 20, 21, 25, 26, 29, 30
Best Days for Money: 1, 2, 3, 9, 10, 11, 20, 21, 27, 28, 29, 30
Best Days for Career: 6, 15, 17, 18, 24, 25

Love is the main headline in the coming month, but it is still a bit complicated. On the one hand, Pluto, your love planet, is finally moving forward again after many months of retrograde motion (this happens on the 20th). Jupiter in your 7th house is also moving forward, and on the 23rd the Sun will enter your 7th house, initiating a yearly love and social peak. So love is in the air for singles these days. There is only one problem. Venus, the planet of love and the ruler of your Horoscope, starts to go backwards on the 5th. So, love is happening, but you seem to be backing away from it. Perhaps you're taking a wait-and-see attitude. Perhaps you're being more cautious. But the love opportunities are there, and the social judgement is getting better.

Health is good this month and you're on the case – your 6th house of health is still very strong until the 23rd. After then, however, your health will need more attention being paid. We don't see any major disasters, just energy not up to its usual standards. So make sure, as always, to get enough rest. Enhance the health in the ways mentioned in the yearly report, and in the ways mentioned last month. Detox regimes are excellent. A herbal colon cleanse might be a good idea. Safe sex and sexual moderation are important.

The career has been important all year, but now, from the 23rd onwards, it becomes even more of a focus. After the 23rd 90 per cent of the planets will be above the horizon. Mars is still in your career house, however, and the career is frenetic. You need to be more aggressive here.

Finances looks good this month, but stronger after the 10th than before. The month will wind up being prosperous. Until the 10th money comes through your work – the old-fashioned way. On the 10th your money planet Mercury moves into Scorpio, your 7th house, and travels with the Sun. This signals good support from family and friends. Mercury will travel with Jupiter from the 28th to the 30th – indicating a nice payday. It also shows good financial cooperation with the spouse, partner or current love. Debts are easily paid. This is a good period to contact outside investors if you have good ideas for projects. A business partnership or joint venture could happen – the opportunity will come. Social connections are important all month.

November

Best Days Overall: 2, 3, 11, 12, 21, 22, 29, 30
Most Stressful Days Overall: 1, 6, 7, 8, 14, 15, 27, 28
Best Days for Love: 2, 3, 4, 5, 6, 7, 8, 11, 12, 14, 15, 21, 22, 23, 24, 29, 30
Best Days for Money: 1, 8, 9, 10, 19, 20, 23, 24, 27, 28
Best Days for Career: 2, 10, 14, 15, 20, 28

The spouse, partner or current love has had a good financial year, but this month it gets even better. On the 8th Jupiter will move into their money house, a classic signal of prosperity, and on the 22nd the Sun also moves into this house and they enter a yearly financial peak. You seem personally very involved with this.

Jupiter's move into your 8th house of regeneration shows the importance of tax efficiency. Good tax planning will play an important role in your bottom line. It is also excellent for paying debts, refinancing debt on more favourable terms, or for taking out loans – all depending on your need. Often this transit indicates inheritance, but hopefully no one has to die. You can profit from estates or be appointed to some administrative position in an estate.

You're still very much in the midst of a yearly love and social peak until the 22nd. However, Venus is still retrograde until the 16th, so while the love opportunities are still there you seem hesitant. This will start to change after the 16th. The New Moon of the 7th is going to clarify love issues as the month progresses. All the information you need will come to you effortlessly as the month progresses. You'll have all the information you need to make a correct decision.

Mercury, your financial planet, spends the month in Sagittarius, your 8th house. This shows involvement with the income of the spouse, partner or current love. It also shows the need for good tax and insurance planning. For those of you of appropriate age it is a good aspect for estate planning. Mercury is 'out of bounds' from the 4th to the 20th, showing that you're moving outside your normal sphere in pursuit of earnings. Sometimes it shows that there is a need to do this – that you can't attain your goals unless you think 'outside the box'. Mercury will go retrograde on the 17th, so try to wrap up important purchases and investment decisions before then. The Sun travels with Jupiter from the 24th to the 28th. This indicates a nice payday for you and for a parent or parent figure. He or she is likely to be more generous with you over that period.

Career is still important but it is a bit less frantic this month. Mars will leave your 10th house on the 16th.

Uranus's foray into your sign finishes on the 6th. He moves back into Aries for the next couple of months. But he did his job, he delivered his message; major changes will be happening from next year onwards.

December

Best Days Overall: 9, 10, 18, 19, 27, 28
Most Stressful Days Overall: 4, 5, 11, 12, 25, 26, 31
Best Days for Love: 2, 3, 4, 5, 9, 10, 14, 15, 18, 19, 23, 24, 27, 28, 31
Best Days for Money: 4, 5, 6, 13, 16, 21, 22, 23, 24, 26
Best Days for Career: 7, 11, 12, 17, 26

Though you're not in a yearly love and social peak, the love life seems active and positive this month. Venus is now moving forward and will spend almost all month in your 7th house of love. Pluto, your love planet, is going forward too. So the social confidence and judgement is good. Venus in your 7th house signals much social popularity. You're there for your friends and the beloved. You put their interests ahead of your own. You're very devoted to your existing relationship. This tends to popularity. Good social skills (and you have them now) are not only important in love but in finance as well. Mercury is also in your 7th house until the 13th.

Mercury resumes forward motion on the 6th, so your naturally sound financial judgement returns. This is a positive for finance. On the 13th Mercury moves into your 8th house again. This, as we have mentioned, is good for tax and estate planning (for those of you of appropriate age), for paying down or making debt (according to your need), and for focusing on the financial well-being of others. It is good for attracting outside money to your projects – in the form of either investors or credit.

Taureans tend to be hoarders. They take in, take in, take in. This a good month to detox your possessions – to get rid of the things that you don't need or use. Use should be the criterion. The things you use, keep. What you don't use, either sell or give to charity. Too many things clog up the internal system. You need to make room for the new and better things that want to come in.

On the 21st the Sun enters your 9th house and starts to travel with the ruler of that house. This signals foreign travel, foreign lands call to you. Spending the holidays with the family in some foreign spot seems a good idea. This is also a good aspect for college students. They seem more disciplined and more focused on their studies.

Mars, your spiritual planet, travels with Neptune from the 5th to the 7th. Pay attention to your dreams during this period as they seem significant. You could feel the effects of this aspect even before the 5th. It will bring spiritual breakthroughs. More spiritually minded friends will come into the picture.

Gemini

♊

THE TWINS

Birthdays from
21st May to
20th June

Personality Profile

GEMINI AT A GLANCE

Element – Air

Ruling Planet – Mercury
  Career Planet – Neptune
  Love Planet – Jupiter
  Money Planet – Moon
  Planet of Health and Work – Pluto
  Planet of Home and Family Life – Mercury

Colours – blue, yellow, yellow-orange

Colour that promotes love, romance and social harmony – sky blue

Colours that promote earning power – grey, silver

Gems – agate, aquamarine

Metal – quicksilver

Scents – lavender, lilac, lily of the valley, storax

Quality – mutable (= flexibility)

Quality most needed for balance – thought that is deep rather than superficial

Strongest virtues – great communication skills, quickness and agility of thought, ability to learn quickly

Deepest need – communication

Characteristics to avoid – gossiping, hurting others with harsh speech, superficiality, using words to mislead or misinform

Signs of greatest overall compatibility – Libra, Aquarius

Signs of greatest overall incompatibility – Virgo, Sagittarius, Pisces

Sign most helpful to career – Pisces

Sign most helpful for emotional support – Virgo

Sign most helpful financially – Cancer

Sign best for marriage and/or partnerships – Sagittarius

Sign most helpful for creative projects – Libra

Best Sign to have fun with – Libra

Signs most helpful in spiritual matters – Taurus, Aquarius

Best day of the week – Wednesday

Understanding a Gemini

Gemini is to society what the nervous system is to the body. It does not introduce any new information but is a vital transmitter of impulses from the senses to the brain and vice versa. The nervous system does not judge or weigh these impulses – it only conveys information. And it does so perfectly.

This analogy should give you an indication of a Gemini's role in society. Geminis are the communicators and conveyors of information. To Geminis the truth or falsehood of information is irrelevant, they only transmit what they see, hear or read about. Thus they are capable of spreading the most outrageous rumours as well as conveying truth and light. Geminis sometimes tend to be unscrupulous in their communications and can do both great good or great evil with their power. This is why the sign of Gemini is symbolized by twins: Geminis have a dual nature.

Their ability to convey a message – to communicate with such ease – makes Geminis ideal teachers, writers and media and marketing people. This is helped by the fact that Mercury, the ruling planet of Gemini, also rules these activities.

Geminis have the gift of the gab. And what a gift this is! They can make conversation about anything, anywhere, at any time. There is almost nothing that is more fun to Geminis than a good conversation – especially if they can learn something new as well. They love to learn and they love to teach. To deprive a Gemini of conversation, or of books and magazines, is cruel and unusual punishment.

Geminis are almost always excellent students and take well to education. Their minds are generally stocked with all kinds of information, trivia, anecdotes, stories, news items, rarities, facts and statistics. Thus they can support any intellectual position that they care to take. They are awesome debaters and, if involved in politics, make good orators. Geminis are so verbally smooth that even if they do not know what they are talking about, they can make you think that they do. They will always dazzle you with their brilliance.

Finance

Geminis tend to be more concerned with the wealth of learning and ideas than with actual material wealth. As mentioned, they excel in professions that involve writing, teaching, sales and journalism – and not all of these professions pay very well. But to sacrifice intellectual needs merely for money is unthinkable to a Gemini. Geminis strive to combine the two. Cancer is on Gemini's solar 2nd house of money cusp, which indicates that Geminis can earn extra income (in a harmonious and natural way) from investments in residential property, restaurants and hotels. Given their verbal skills, Geminis love to bargain and negotiate in any situation, and especially when it has to do with money.

The Moon rules Gemini's 2nd solar house. The Moon is not only the fastest-moving planet in the zodiac but actually moves through every sign and house every 28 days. No other heavenly body matches the Moon for swiftness or the ability to change quickly. An analysis of the Moon – and lunar phenomena in general – describes Gemini's financial attitudes very well. Geminis are financially versatile and flexible; they can earn money in many different ways. Their financial attitudes and needs seem to change daily. Their feelings about money change also: sometimes they are very enthusiastic about it, at other times they could not care less.

For a Gemini, financial goals and money are often seen only as means of supporting a family; these things have little meaning otherwise.

The Moon, as Gemini's money planet, has another important message for Gemini financially: in order for Geminis to realize their financial potential they need to develop more of an understanding of the emotional side of life. They need to combine their awesome powers of logic with an understanding of human psychology. Feelings have their own logic; Geminis need to learn this and apply it to financial matters.

Career and Public Image

Geminis know that they have been given the gift of communication for a reason, that it is a power that can achieve great good or cause unthinkable distress. They long to put this power at the service of the highest and most transcendental truths. This is their primary goal, to communicate the eternal verities and prove them logically. They look up to people who can transcend the intellect – to poets, artists, musicians and mystics. They may be awed by stories of religious saints and martyrs. A Gemini's highest achievement is to teach the truth, whether it is scientific, inspirational or historical. Those who can transcend the intellect are Gemini's natural superiors – and a Gemini realizes this.

The sign of Pisces is in Gemini's solar 10th house of career. Neptune, the planet of spirituality and altruism, is Gemini's career planet. If Geminis are to realize their highest career potential they need to develop their transcendental – their spiritual and altruistic – side. They need to understand the larger cosmic picture, the vast flow of human evolution – where it came from and where it is heading. Only then can a Gemini's intellectual powers take their true position and he or she can become the 'messenger of the gods'. Geminis need to cultivate a facility for 'inspiration', which is something that does not originate in the intellect but which comes through the intellect. This will further enrich and empower a Gemini's mind.

Love and Relationships

Geminis bring their natural garrulousness and brilliance into their love life and social life as well. A good talk or a verbal joust is an interesting prelude to romance. Their only problem in love is that their intellect is too cool and passionless to incite ardour in others. Emotions sometimes disturb them, and their partners tend to complain about this. If you are in love with a Gemini you must understand why this is so. Geminis avoid deep passions because these would interfere with their ability to think and communicate. If they are cool towards you, understand that this is their nature.

Nevertheless, Geminis must understand that it is one thing to talk about love and another actually to love – to feel it and radiate it. Talking about love glibly will get them nowhere. They need to feel it and act on it. Love is not of the intellect but of the heart. If you want to know how a Gemini feels about love you should not listen to what he or she says, but rather, observe what he or she does. Geminis can be quite generous to those they love.

Geminis like their partners to be refined, well educated and well travelled. If their partners are more wealthy than they, that is all the better. If you are in love with a Gemini you had better be a good listener as well.

The ideal relationship for the Gemini is a relationship of the mind. They enjoy the physical and emotional aspects, of course, but if the intellectual communion is not there they will suffer.

Home and Domestic Life

At home the Gemini can be uncharacteristically neat and meticulous. They tend to want their children and partner to live up to their idealistic standards. When these standards are not met they moan and criticize. However, Geminis are good family people and like to serve their families in practical and useful ways.

The Gemini home is comfortable and pleasant. They like to invite people over and they make great hosts. Geminis are also good at repairs and improvements around the house – all fuelled by their need to stay active and occupied with something they like to do. Geminis have many hobbies and interests that keep them busy when they are home alone.

Geminis understand and get along well with their children, mainly because they are very youthful people themselves. As great communicators, Geminis know how to explain things to children; in this way they gain their children's love and respect. Geminis also encourage children to be creative and talkative, just like they are.

Horoscope for 2018

Major Trends

Major, long-term planets are changing signs this year and this brings changes of direction in your own life. Nothing is settled right now. Everything is subject to change.

Jupiter spends most of the year in your 6th house of health and work. This is good news on the health front: if there have been problems in this area you should hear good news about them. It also shows very nice job opportunities coming your way. This can be with your present company or with another one. These job opportunities are happy. More on this later.

Jupiter, your love planet, will move into your 7th house of love on November 8. This shows happiness in love and a stellar kind of love life. Next year will also be good. There's more on this later.

Saturn moved into your 8th house of regeneration late last year, and most of you haven't felt the influence of this transit yet, but this year you will. It signals a need to rein in the sex drive and sexual activity – quality is to be preferred to quantity. The spouse, partner or current love is forced to reorganize the financial life. He or she is taking on new financial burdens.

Pluto has been in your 8th house for many years and will be there for many more to come. Since Pluto is your health planet, it indicates a tendency towards surgery. (This could have already happened.) But detox regimes should also be explored. More details later.

Uranus, the planet of change and experimentation, is making a foray into your 12th house of spirituality from May 16 to November 6, and next year he will move in for the long haul. Thus many of you will be changing your spiritual paths in the coming years, embracing a more scientific kind of approach. Many of you will change teachers and teachings – most likely multiple times – over the next seven years. Again, there are more details later.

Neptune, your career planet (and the most spiritual and idealistic of all the planets), has been in your 10th career house for some years now, and he will remain there for many more (he is a slow-moving planet). Thus idealism is important in the career. This aspect favours a spiritual type of career. More on this later.

Your most important interests in the year ahead will be health and work (until November 8); love and romance (from November 8 onwards); sex, occult studies and personal transformation; career; friends, groups and group activities (from January 1 to May 16 and from November 6 to December 31); and spirituality (from May 16 to November 6).

Your paths of greatest fulfilment this year are communication and intellectual interests (until November 17); finance (from November 17 onwards); health and work (until November 8); and love and romance (from November 8 onwards).

Health

(Please note that this is an astrological perspective on health and not a medical one. In days of yore there was no difference, both these perspectives were identical. But now there could be quite a difference. For a medical perspective, please consult your doctor or health practitioner.)

Health is good this year, as we mentioned. For most of the year until November, there is only one long-term planet in stressful alignment with you – Neptune. After November 8, however, Jupiter will move into Sagittarius and a stressful alignment. Most of the long-term planets are either in harmonious alignment or leaving you alone. So overall energy is good. Sure, there will be periods where your health and energy are less good than usual (and we will cover this in the monthly reports). But these are temporary periods caused by the short-term planets. They are not trends for the year. When the short-term planets move away, health and energy return to normal.

The other good health signal is Jupiter in your 6th house, as we mentioned. This shows 'good fortune' in matters of health. With this kind of transit cures are often found for things believed to be incurable. Medicines and therapies tend to be effective. The understanding of health and disease gets expanded.

Good though your health is, you can make it even better, as our regular readers know. Give attention to the following – the vulnerable areas of your Horoscope. (The reflex points are shown in the chart

Important foot reflexology points for the year ahead

Try to massage all of the foot on a regular basis – the top of the foot as well as the bottom – but pay extra attention to the points highlighted on the chart. When you massage, be aware of 'sore spots' as these need special attention. It's also a good idea to massage the ankles and, in particular, below them.

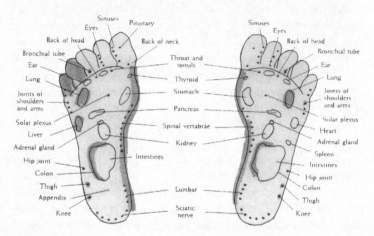

above.) Most of the time, problems can actually be prevented. But even in cases where they can't be totally prevented, they can be softened to a great extent. They need not be devastating.

- The lungs, arms, shoulders and respiratory system. These are always important for a Gemini. Regular arm and shoulder massage is always advisable as tension tends to collect in the shoulders and needs to be released.
- The liver and thighs. These became important in October of last year, when Jupiter moved into your 6th house, and remain so until November 8 when he moves on. The thighs should be regularly massaged. Thigh massage will not only strengthen the liver but the lower back as well – very important these days. If you feel under the weather a herbal liver cleanse might be just the ticket.
- The colon, bladder and sexual organs. Safe sex and sexual moderation are always important. If you have been neglectful of this, Saturn in your 8th house will probably enforce the issue. If

you feel under the weather, a herbal colon cleanse might be a good idea. Many natural healers affirm that all disease begins in the colon, so it is important to keep it clean.

- The spine, knees, teeth, skin and overall skeletal alignment. These have been important areas to you since December 2008, ever since Pluto moved into Capricorn, and they will remain so for many more years. Regular back (and knee) massage is recommended, as are regular visits to a chiropractor or osteopath: the vertebrae need to be kept in right alignment. Therapies such as The Alexander Technique, Rolfing or Feldenkrais are good. Yoga and Pilates are excellent for the spine. Give the knees more support when exercising. If you're out in the hot sun use a good sun-screen. Regular dental check-ups and cleaning are important too.

There is another issue to be considered in health. Jupiter, your love planet, is in your health house. So, good health for you (especially this year) means good social health – a healthy marriage or love life. If there are problems here it could impact on your physical health. So, if problems happen (God forbid), restore the harmony in the love and social life as quickly as possible and the health problem will weaken and disappear.

Home and Family

Your 4th house of home and family is not strong this year – it is not a house of power. Only short-term planets will move through there – and briefly. The planetary powers are not pushing you one way or another in this department. They give great freedom to shape this area as you will – but you lack the interest. Other things are more important these days. The tendency would be to the status quo. You seem basically content with things as they are.

Mercury, the ruler of your Horoscope, is also your family planet. This shows that family is important to you and perhaps part of your identity. In many cases, it takes time to forge your own identity as a separate individual within the family group.

As our regular readers know, Mercury, is a fast-moving and often erratic planet. (Doesn't this describe Gemini well?) Sometimes he is zipping along with great confidence. Sometimes he moves slowly and cautiously. And, sometimes, he goes backwards. He is the embodiment of 'flexibility' – a Gemini trait. In a given year he will move through every sign and house in your Horoscope. Thus there are many short-term home and family trends depending on where Mercury is and the kind of aspects he receives. These are best dealt with in the monthly reports.

This not an especially great year for doing major renovations to the home. However, if you're redecorating (repainting or re-arranging things), July 10 to August 7 and August 23 to September 22 are good times. These times are also good for buying furniture or objects of beauty for the home.

Siblings and sibling figures in your life are likely to move, renovate or buy an additional home this year. They have good fortune in the purchase or sale of a home. Their marriages are being tested. Children and children figures are prospering this year, but the home life seems stable. Parents or parent figures are likely to move or renovate their house after November 8 and into next year. Grandchildren (if you have them) are likely to move – and perhaps multiple times this year and in the coming years. They seem very unsettled.

The parent figures in your life – both sets – are making important changes to their health regimes. Perhaps there is some health scare that forces this. Their job situation seems unstable and, if they employ others, there is employee turnover.

Finance and Career

Your money house is not particularly active this year either. Again, only short-term planets will move through there, rather quickly. Finance is not a major concern. You seem more interested in the finances of others than in your own. This is generally a good thing. You seem satisfied with things as they are and have no need to make drastic changes. In spite of this I feel you will end the year richer than when you began. On November 17 the Moon's North Node will move into your money house and stay there for the rest of the year (and next year too). The North Node tends to show 'excess' – and in finance this is a good thing. Better too much than too little.

Should financial problems occur, it is most probably due to lack of attention. You have to force yourself to pay attention here.

Having said this, we do see some important financial shifts, changes and course corrections this year, more than usual. There will be two Lunar Eclipses (the usual number) and these always impact on finance. But in addition to this there is a Solar Eclipse on July 13 that occurs in your money house. This will create dramatic financial change. You probably won't be initiating these changes, but reacting to the events caused by the eclipse. We will deal with these more fully in the monthly reports.

The Moon, the fastest and most changeable of all the planets (even more so than Mercury) is your financial planet. Where Mercury will move through all the signs and houses of your Horoscope in one year, the Moon does so every month. Moreover, she is quite changeable, sometimes waxing, sometimes waning, sometime close to the earth and sometimes far away. Thus there are all kinds of short-term financial trends, depending on where the Moon is and the aspects she receives. These are best dealt with in the monthly reports.

You are more ambitious than usual these days. The long-term planets are mostly in the upper half of your chart this year, and by November 8, *all* the long-term planets will be there. The bottom half of your chart (the sector of home and family) will never match the power of the upper half. Your career 10th house is strong all year, whereas your family 4th house will only be strong for a couple of months. Jupiter is making beautiful aspects to your career planet Neptune almost all year. Thus you're successful – elevated in your status and profession. You have good career support from friends and social connections. Those of you who are attached are getting good support from the spouse, partner or current love interest. You're socializing with people who can help you careerwise. It is good for your career to attend or host the right kind of parties or gatherings this year.

Your professional skills are very important, but this year your social skills, your ability to get on with others – your likeability – seems very important. Of two people with equivalent professional skills, it is the more likeable one who will get the promotion.

It will also be good – and this has been the trend for many years – to be involved in charitable or altruistic causes. You're receiving perhaps more recognition for your spiritual activities than for your professional work now.

Jupiter in your 6th house of work shows that your good work ethic is noted by the people in authority in your life. It is an important factor in your success. 'Pray devoutly,' say the sages, 'but hammer stoutly.'

Love and Social Life

The year ahead, as we mentioned above, is a banner love and social year. And next year will be even better. You're in a very happy and active social cycle right now.

With Jupiter, your love planet, spending most of the year in your 6th house the workplace is not just your place of work but your social centre as well. Many of you are being offered happy job opportunities this year, and the social conditions of the job are playing a big role in your choices. The social atmosphere and opportunities could trump salary this year. For singles, this aspect signals romantic opportunities with co-workers or at company functions or events. It would also show an attraction to health professionals and for people involved in your health.

A good part of your socializing seems career- and job-related. And Jupiter in your 6th house making nice aspects to your career planet almost all year would also signal an attraction to people of power and prestige – people above you in the professional hierarchy. You find people who can help you careerwise alluring, and seem to get on with them.

Sometimes this aspect shows that parents, bosses and authority figures support your social goals and will often play Cupid. They seem to be playing an important – and positive – role in your love and social life.

The real romantic fun begins on November 8, however, as your love planet moves into your 7th house of love. This often signals marriage or relationships that are 'like marriage'. It signals 'committed' kinds of relationships. Often with this aspect you'll find that you're attending more weddings too. It's in the air. In general you will be attending more parties and gatherings. You will make new and significant friend-ships too.

You always have an attraction to foreigners, religious and highly educated kinds of people. As Jupiter moves into his own sign of Sagittarius in November, this becomes even stronger. The workplace will no longer be your social centre; instead now it will be the place of worship, the university or foreign countries.

For those of you in or working on the second marriage, the social life will also expand. If you're married or in an existing relationship, it will get tested in the year ahead – there are two eclipses in the house of the second marriage. Romantic opportunities will be found in spiritual settings – in prayer meetings, spiritual or meditation workshops, charity events. You seem to crave a more spiritual kind of relationship.

Those in or working on the third marriage have had much instability in love for the past seven years. Things are calming down this year. Marriage is not yet advisable, however; next year will be better than 2018.

Self-Improvement

Neptune, as we have mentioned, has been in your 10th house of career for many years now. So, many of the trends that we have written of in past years are still very much in effect. Long-term, slow-moving planets indicate long-term projects and developments. The transit of a long-term planet is not really an 'event' but a 'process'.

So you have been – and still are – in the process of spiritualizing your career. You're imbued with great idealism. Merely being successful in the worldly sense is not enough for you. Your work, your career has to be meaningful – something that uplifts all of humanity. It is an aspect that favours careers in charities, foundations and non-profit organizations. But there are other options too. Often we see people with this kind of aspect involved in worldly careers – mundane kinds of careers – but they are heavily involved in charitable activities. They are more known for these activities than for their worldly career.

There's another way to read this too – and it will fit in many cases. Your spiritual practice, your spiritual growth, becomes the career – the life work, the mission. This seems impractical and improbable as a career. Yet, it can be very powerful. One spiritual breakthrough –

perhaps as you are sitting in meditation by yourself – has the power to not only change your life, but your family, community, country and even the world – eventually. Many of the great world movements that we see right now began in this way.

Spirituality is becoming important in another way too. Uranus will move into your spiritual 12th house on May 16 and stay there until November 6. Next year he will move into your 12th house for the long haul – for the next seven years. This shows dramatic changes in your spiritual practice, teachings and teachers. Many of the old rulebooks – the 'thou shalt nots' – get thrown out, and you begin to learn through trial, error and experiment. The transit favours a more scientific, rational approach to spirituality, as opposed to the traditional, mystical ones. Thus it would favour paths such as Jnana yoga, hermetic science and kabbalah – all rational approaches. There is a deep science to spirituality (and some of this is being discovered by secular scientists and doctors). And this is a time to explore this.

Uranus rules astrology. So the esoteric – philosophical – side of astrology would be another viable path.

Month-by-month Forecasts

January

Best Days Overall: 8, 9, 17, 18, 19, 27, 28
Most Stressful Days Overall: 5, 6, 12, 13, 14, 20, 21
Best Days for Love: 1, 2, 5, 6, 10, 11, 12, 13, 14, 15, 16, 20, 21, 27, 28, 29, 30
Best Days for Money: 1, 2, 5, 6, 10, 11, 15, 16, 20, 21, 27, 28, 29, 30
Best Days for Career: 1, 2, 10, 11, 20, 21, 29, 30

You begin your year with most of the planets in your Western, social sector. Even the ruler of your Horoscope, Mercury, is in the West. This shows a need to 'go with the flow', to let others have their way (so long as it isn't destructive), to attain your ends through consensus and compromise rather than direct action. Right now you're having to live with the conditions that you created in the past. Try to make do as best you can. In a few months the planetary power will shift and it will be easier to make any necessary changes.

Your love and social peak occurred last month, but the month ahead is still very social. Mercury will be in your 7th house of love until the 11th, which shows that you're proactive in love. You are going after what you want and not waiting around for the phone to ring. It also indicates more personal popularity. You're there for your friends and for the current love. Their interests come before your own. You're devoted to them. This makes for popularity.

Health is better than last month and you can enhance it further in the ways mentioned in the yearly report. This is a good month to undertake detox or weight-loss regimes. A strong 8th house (until the 20th) is good for projects involving reinvention or personal transformation. There are things in our lives that might be in need of 'resurrection' – perhaps it is a relationship, a creative project, or a business venture. This is a good month to make it happen.

A Lunar Eclipse on the 31st seems to affect you strongly. It occurs in your 3rd house of communication, bringing dramas in the lives of siblings, sibling figures or neighbours. Students make important changes in their education plans; perhaps there are shakeups in their school. Every Lunar Eclipse impacts on your finances as the Moon is your financial planet. So course corrections are needed in the financial life. The events of the eclipse will show you what's necessary. Cars and communication equipment get tested and often repairs or replacements are necessary.

New Moons and Full Moons are always good financial days for you, Gemini. The Full Moon of the 1st and 2nd seems especially good as the Moon is at her closest distance to the Earth. In general, the waxing Moon is better financially than the waning moon – thus the 1st and the 2nd and the 17th to the 31st bring more enthusiasm and financial power.

February

Best Days Overall: 4, 5, 14, 15, 23, 24
Most Stressful Days Overall: 2, 3, 9, 10, 16, 17
Best Days for Love: 4, 5, 6, 7, 9, 10, 16, 17, 25, 26
Best Days for Money: 6, 7, 14, 15, 16, 17, 25, 26
Best Days for Career: 6, 7, 16, 17, 25, 26

A Solar Eclipse on the 15th creates excitement and change, but in spite of it, the month ahead looks prosperous and successful.

This eclipse happens in your 9th house of education, religion and thought, and impacts on legal matters. Pending issues take a dramatic turn, one way or another. Foreign lands call to you this month and you have the travel bug. But avoid foreign travel during the eclipse period. College-level students are forced to make changes to their educational plans. Sometimes they change schools or courses; sometimes the school they wanted rejects them but another one (perhaps even a better one) accepts them. The eclipse impacts on Mercury, the ruler of your Horoscope, and on Jupiter, your love planet. Thus there are personal and love dramas happening. Love is problematic anyway this month, as Mars spends the month in your 7th house, and the eclipse doesn't help matters. Perhaps you have got involved in power struggles with the beloved, and the eclipse brings this to a head. A good relationship will survive – but things are tense.

The eclipse's impact on Mercury is actually a healthy thing, in that you're forced to redefine yourself, to get clear in your own mind who you are and the kind of image you want to present. You will see changes here over the next six months or so. Every Solar Eclipse affects siblings, sibling figures and neighbours. There are dramas in their lives. Every Solar Eclipse also tests cars and communication equipment. You had this last month and now you have it again. The changes that weren't made last month happen now.

On the 18th both the Sun and Mercury – two very beneficent planets – cross your Mid-heaven and enter your 10th career house. You begin a yearly career peak and you seem very successful – you're in charge, on top, taking on responsibilities. There is more personal recognition for who you are and for your professional abilities. Your physical appearance and gift of the gab is playing a huge role in your career advancement.

Health is basically good this month, but it does need more attention after the 18th. At least half the planets are in stressful aspect with you then. Thus, if there are any vulnerabilities (genetic or otherwise) there is a greater likelihood that they will flare up. So, the first step is to make sure you get enough rest. Then enhance the health in the ways mentioned in the yearly report.

March

Best Days Overall: 3, 4, 13, 14, 22, 23, 31
Most Stressful Days Overall: 1, 2, 8, 9, 15, 16, 17, 29, 30
Best Days for Love: 6, 7, 8, 9, 15, 16, 17, 18, 19, 24, 25, 26, 27
Best Days for Money: 6, 7, 15, 16, 17, 24, 25, 26
Best Days for Career: 6, 7, 15, 16, 17, 24, 25

You're still in a yearly career peak until the 20th. The planets in your career house are friendly ones, helpful to you. This signals success. You have much cosmic support; the universe wills your success. By the 20th, as your short-term goals are achieved, your attention shifts to the social life – to friendships, groups and group activities. Though Mars is still in your 7th house until the 17th, creating some friction and perhaps power struggles, your love planet, Jupiter, is receiving good aspects and you seem in basic harmony with the beloved.

Jupiter starts to go backwards on the 9th, while Mercury goes into retrograde motion on the 23rd. This complicates love somewhat. Both you and the beloved seem indecisive and lacking in direction. You're not antagonistic or anything (Mars leaves your 7th house on the 17th), just kind of 'wishy washy'.

Health still needs attention until the 20th but is improving. Day by day you get stronger. On the 6th Mercury and Venus move into harmonious aspect with you; on the 17th Mars moves away from his stressful aspect (as we have seen); and on the 20th the Sun starts to make harmonious aspects. Early in the month continue to enhance the health in the ways mentioned in the yearly report. By the 20th you should be back to normal.

Finances don't seem a big issue these days. Your 2nd money house is empty of planets and this is basically a good sign. It shows a status quo kind of month. There is no need to make important changes or to pay undue attention here. The career is much more important than finance. Yet, prosperity seems greater than last month. First of all we have two Full Moons (the second is called the 'Blue Moon' – a rarity – and the origin of the expression 'once in a blue moon'). Full Moons are good financial days, and the 26th is an especially good financial day as the Moon is at 'perigee' – her closest distance to the Earth – and her impact is even stronger. In general the 17th to the 31st – the waxing Moon – is the best period for finances.

April

Best Days Overall: 1, 9, 10, 11, 18, 19, 27, 28

Most Stressful Days Overall: 4, 5, 6, 12, 13, 25, 26

Best Days for Love: 2, 3, 4, 5, 6, 7, 8, 12, 13, 16, 17, 21, 22, 27, 29, 30

Best Days for Money: 2, 3, 4, 5, 12, 13, 14, 15, 16, 21, 22, 25, 29, 30

Best Days for Career: 2, 3, 12, 13, 21, 22, 29, 30

On February 18 there was a decisive shift of planetary power, from the Western half (the social sector of your chart) to the independent Eastern sector (the sector of self). The shift is approaching its maximum point (this will happen in the next two months), and now it is time to develop your personal initiative and personal skills. These are what matter at present. It is wonderful to be popular socially, but one also needs a strong centre – strong core – a strong sense of who we are. This is the time to develop this. What do *you* like? What conditions make *you* happy? What is *your* opinion on politics or the world? Never mind what others think, or whether your opinions are popular or not – this is you and it is wonderful. It is time to be your authentic self. And since personal independence is so strong now, make the changes that need to be made in your conditions. Fashion your circumstances to your personal liking. You have the power and planetary support. Your happiness is very much up to you.

Health is miraculously good now. There is only one long-term planet in stressful alignment; all the others are either in harmony or leaving you alone. Perhaps the easing of the career demands have something to do with this.

Venus moves into your sign on the 24th. For women of childbearing age this signals heightened fertility. In general it brings more fun into life. You're more playful. Venus in your sign enhances the personal appearance. There is more grace and charm in your demeanour. You are more involved with children and are perhaps a bit of a child yourself. This is a very good period for buying clothing or accessories, as your taste will be spot on. For single men, this aspect brings young women into the personal sphere. For a woman it shows more beauty and grace in the appearance.

Your love planet Jupiter is still retrograde, and this will go on for some more months. So there is no need to rush love or make important decisions one way or another. Let love develop as it will.

Your spiritual 12th house becomes powerful from the 20th onwards, so it is a good time for spiritual-type pursuits – meditation, spiritual studies, the study of sacred scripture and charitable activities. It is a period for internal growth.

May

Best Days Overall: 7, 8, 16, 17, 24, 25
Most Stressful Days Overall: 2, 3, 9, 10, 22, 23, 29, 30
Best Days for Love: 2, 3, 7, 8, 9, 10, 17, 18, 19, 26, 27, 29, 30
Best Days for Money: 4, 5, 9, 10, 14, 15, 18, 19, 24, 26, 27
Best Days for Career: 9, 10, 18, 19, 26, 27

A happy, prosperous month ahead, Gemini – enjoy!

Health was good last month and is even better in the month ahead (Mars moves into harmonious alignment with you from the 16th onwards). With more energy there are more possibilities open to you. Things that seemed beyond your reach even a few months ago are now eminently do-able. If you like, you can enhance your health even further in the ways mentioned in the yearly report.

Job opportunities have been good all year, and especially so now. The only issue here is a need to do more research on these things. Ask more questions. Resolve all doubts. Things are not what they seem.

You're still very much in a strong spiritual period until the 21st. So it is good to focus on your inner life and your inner growth. When we are right spiritually, the other areas of life tend to fall into place.

Uranus's major move into your spiritual 12th house on the 16th signals impending spiritual changes. You're going to be changing teachers, teachings and your spiritual practice over the coming years, perhaps multiple times. You will be taking a more scientific approach to it. You're going to be more experimental, learning through trial and error.

Venus remains in your 1st house until the 19th and you can refer to our discussion of this last month. On the 19th she moves into your money house and brings added prosperity. She will bring luck in speculations – especially on the 31st – and prosperity for the children or children figures in your life. They should be more supportive of you as well (there are many ways they can do this, depending on their age and stage in life). Money is earned in happy ways. The Moon is at her perigee on the 17th and it should be a good financial day. The New Moon of the 15th and the Full Moon of the 29th are powerful financial days. In general, earnings will be stronger from the 15th to the 29th – as the Moon waxes – than before the 15th. The waxing Moon gives more enthusiasm and power to your earning ability.

The Sun enters your sign on the 21st and you begin one of your yearly personal pleasure peaks. You look and feel great!

June

Best Days Overall: 3, 4, 12, 13, 20, 21, 22, 30
Most Stressful Days Overall: 5, 6, 7, 18, 19, 25, 26
Best Days for Love: 5, 6, 7, 14, 15, 16, 23, 24, 25, 26
Best Days for Money: 3, 4, 5, 6, 7, 12, 13, 14, 15, 23, 24
Best Days for Career: 5, 6, 7, 14, 15, 23, 24

During last month and this month the planetary power is at its maximum Eastern position for the year. Thus you're in your most independent period. If you haven't yet made the changes that need to be made – changes that enhance your happiness – now is the time to act. Later on, as the planets move towards the West, it will be more difficult to do. At times like these we realize that the cosmos cares about our happiness and takes a personal interest. It cares even about the seeming 'little things' – that you have the right clothes, accessories and image. And, later, as the Sun enters your money house on the 22nd, you will see that it cares about your finances and wants you to be rich. (The only caveat is that you have to allow it to do things its way and not your way. You sort of have to stand aside and allow 'affluence' to be affluence.)

Career is still important these days – you still have a lot of planets in the upper half of your chart – but since last month the lower half of your Horoscope has become much stronger. It is time to pay more attention to your self, your family and your emotional well-being. Time also to have some fun and to pamper yourself a bit, and to get your body and image to where you want it to be.

The Sun in your own sign enhances the mind and communication skills (which are always good). There is star quality to the image. You shine and the opposite sex takes notice. As the expression goes 'you are the message that you want to send', and because you dazzle more, your message gets across.

Finances have not been a major issue this year, but this month they are. Venus has been in your money house since the 19th of last month and she will be there until the 14th of this month. On the 1st and 2nd she makes beautiful aspects to both Jupiter and Neptune. This brings luck in speculations, perhaps a pay rise (either official or unofficial) and great financial intuition. On the 12th Mercury also moves into the money house, indicating strong personal interest in finances (which is 90 per cent of the battle – we get what we focus on). And on the 22nd the Sun, too, moves into the 2nd house. You're in a yearly financial peak. Prosperity is happening. Family support also looks good. From the 19th to the 21st Mercury will make nice aspects to Jupiter and to Neptune, signalling a nice payday. This aspect is excellent for the career as well – you have the favour of the authority figures in your life. It is also a happy romantic period.

July

Best Days Overall: 1, 10, 11, 18, 19, 27, 28, 29
Most Stressful Days Overall: 3, 4, 16, 17, 22, 23, 24, 30, 31
Best Days for Love: 1, 5, 6, 12, 13, 16, 20, 21, 22, 23, 24, 25, 26, 27, 28, 29
Best Days for Money: 1, 3, 4, 12, 13, 20, 21, 22, 27, 28, 29
Best Days for Career: 3, 4, 12, 13, 20, 21, 30, 31

The month ahead is basically happy and prosperous, but two eclipses will ensure that things never get boring. They will keep you on your toes.

The Solar Eclipse of the 13th occurs in your money house and indicates a need for financial course corrections. Your financial thinking and strategy hasn't been realistic, as the events of the eclipse will show. Sometimes, this kind of eclipse brings some unplanned expense and this forces change. The changes you have to make will be good in the long run, but usually the process isn't pleasant. Every Solar Eclipse impacts on the siblings, sibling figures and neighbours in your life. Siblings will have to redefine themselves. Cars and communication equipment get tested too, and often need repair or replacement. Drive more carefully at this time. Pluto, your health planet, is affected by this eclipse, and thus there will be important changes in your health regime. Often people change doctors or therapists under an eclipse like this; sometimes there is a health scare. However, your health is good these days and this is most likely no more than a scare – get a second opinion. Job changes are likely, but don't worry; you have awesome job prospects this year. Sometimes the conditions of work are changed. If you employ others, there is instability with them.

The Lunar Eclipse of the 27th occurs in your 9th house, so avoid foreign travel during this period. If you must travel, schedule it around the eclipse. College students (or college-bound students) make important changes to their educational plans. Sometimes they change schools or courses. Finances are affected by this eclipse too, as the eclipsed planet, the Moon, is your financial planet. There's no doubt that your financial thinking hasn't been realistic and needs a good course correction, and the changes you make now will set the course for future prosperity. This eclipse affects both Mars and Uranus, so there are dramas in the lives of friends – life-changing events – and your high-tech equipment and gadgetry gets tested. Make sure important files are backed up and that your anti-virus, anti-hacking software is up to date. I have found, in my personal experience, that the movements of the universe definitely affect sensitive mechanical equipment. The only question is how, and that is not yet clear.

August

Best Days Overall: 6, 7, 14, 15, 24, 25
Most Stressful Days Overall: 12, 13, 19, 20, 26, 27
Best Days for Love: 5, 8, 9, 14, 15, 16, 17, 19, 20, 24, 25, 26, 27
Best Days for Money: 2, 3, 8, 9, 10, 11, 16, 17, 20, 26, 27, 31
Best Days for Career: 8, 9, 16, 17, 26, 27

You thought you were finished with eclipses last month, but not yet. There is one more, the third Solar Eclipse of the year, on the 11th. It mirrors, in many ways, the previous one of July 13, but more so. It occurs in your 3rd house of communication and impacts on the planetary ruler of that house. So you should drive more carefully and defensively this period. If you don't need to drive, it would be better not to. If you must do so, be more careful. Cars and communication equipment will get tested once again. The universe wants only the best for you; anything less will go by the board. Once again there are dramas in the lives of siblings, sibling figures and neighbours. Sometimes there are upheavals in your neighbourhood – new construction, etc. Students are also affected. They may change schools or educational plans, and sometimes there are shakeups and disturbances in the smooth running of their institutions.

The month ahead, in spite of the eclipse, looks happy, however. Your 3rd house of communication and intellectual interests – your favourite house – is very strong. The mental faculties (always good) are even stronger right now. Students learn faster. Information is retained.

Health is basically good this month, but you need to pay a bit more attention after the 22nd. It is nothing serious here, only a reduction of your normal energy. (Often this is not felt as this is very subtle, but it can make one more susceptible to opportunistic infections.) Enhance the health in the ways mentioned in the yearly report.

The planetary power (the short-term planets) is now energizing the bottom half of your chart. Thus it is time to shift some energy and attention to the home, family and emotional concerns. Time to get more into 'emotional wellness'. Career is still very important – the upper half of the Horoscope is still very strong – so you're not going to ignore it completely. But now you should work on creating a stable home life as well. This is the main challenge at present – to be success-ful in the career and at home.

Finance is not a big issue this month. The Full Moon of the 26th will be a strong financial day, and so will the Moon's perigee (the point when it is closest to the Earth) on the 10th. The 11th to the 26th – the Moon's waxing period – will tend to be better than when the Moon is waning (from the 1st to the 9th and the 26th to the 31st).

September

Best Days Overall: 2, 3, 11, 12, 20, 21, 29, 30
Most Stressful Days Overall: 9, 15, 16, 22, 23, 24
Best Days for Love: 2, 3, 4, 5, 13, 14, 15, 16, 22, 23, 24
Best Days for Money: 1, 4, 5, 9, 13, 14, 18, 19, 22, 23, 24, 29
Best Days for Career: 4, 5, 13, 14, 22, 23, 24

With Neptune, your career planet, in retrograde motion since June 18, and with your 4th house of home and family very strong right now, career issues need time to resolve themselves and you may as well focus on domestic matters. However, though career issues seem cloudy, the demands on you are still strong.

The power in the 4th house, as our regular readers know, means more than just home and family. It involves cosmic therapy. Many, many problems have their origin in the memory body. Old traumas, unresolved, can be retriggered or restimulated. When challenging events happened in childhood, powerful (and usually negative) state-ments were made and then forgotten about. Yet, these statements (commands, if you will) are still operating and are often impeding progress. So, when the 4th house is strong, nature will bring up old memories so that they can be viewed from your current level of under-standing. What is terrifying to a three-year-old brings only smiles to an adult. It's not so much about rewriting history – the events happened – but it's about reinterpreting history, giving the events a different (and, hopefully, healthier) 'spin'. This makes all the difference in the world to our emotional wellness. Apparently random memories will come up, but they're not random. They have significance for your life in the 'here and now'. Look at them and the feelings they arouse in you. Examine them. They will lose any power they once had over you.

This is also a good month for those of you involved in formal kinds of psychological therapy. There is more progress happening. The New Moon of the 9th is going to clarify both emotional issues and the family situation as the month progresses. The information you need to make a good decision will come to you naturally and normally, with little stress on your part.

Health still needs watching until the 22nd, but there will be a big improvement after then. In the meantime, as always, make sure to get enough rest. Enhance the health in the ways mentioned in the yearly report.

This is an excellent month for job seekers – especially until the 22nd. The Sun in Virgo favours work, and Pluto, your planet of work, receives good aspects until that date. (The 10th, 11th, 15th and 16th are especially good days for job seekers.)

October

Best Days Overall: 1, 8, 9, 17, 18, 19, 27, 28
Most Stressful Days Overall: 6, 7, 12, 13, 14, 20, 21
Best Days for Love: 2, 3, 10, 11, 12, 13, 14, 20, 21, 29, 30
Best Days for Money: 1, 2, 3, 8, 9, 10, 11, 18, 19, 20, 21, 29, 30
Best Days for Career: 2, 3, 10, 11, 20, 21, 29, 30

Last month, on the 22nd, you entered another one of your yearly personal pleasure peaks. This is not just about having fun – which will happen – but about recharging the batteries so that future work will go better. If you take advantage of this period, you'll find new ideas and a new zest for work after the 23rd of this month. This is a good period (until the 23rd) to explore your personal creativity – especially your writing.

Last month, the planetary power began to shift from the independent Eastern sector (the sector of the self) to the social Western sector (the sector of others). At least 70 per cent (and sometimes 80 per cent) of the planets are now in the West and this will be the situation for a few months. Personal independence is therefore weaker, but the cosmos compensates you in other ways. You're forced to develop (and rely on) your social skills – your ability to gain the cooperation of others. The planetary power flows towards others now, rather than towards you, and your way is probably not the best way right now. Let others have their way, so long as it isn't destructive. Adapt to unpleasant conditions as best you can. Make a note of what needs to be changed: when the planetary power moves towards your sector (the Eastern half of your chart) again, you'll be able to make these changes and they will happen easier.

Uranus has been in your 12th house of spirituality since May and is causing much ferment in your spiritual life. You've been making all kinds of changes to your practice and teachings (especially those of you born early in the sign of Gemini). But now, with your spiritual planet (Venus) going retrograde on the 5th, it will be better to study things further before making any important changes. (In fact, all the planets involved in your spirituality are retrograde this month – along with Venus, Neptune, the generic spiritual planet and Uranus, the occupant of your 12th house are both moving backwards.) Dreams and your intuition need more verification these days. They are accurate, but the meaning might not be what you think.

The retrograde of Venus (which is rare – it only happens every two years) affects children and children figures in your life. While they are prospering this year (and especially this month) they seem to lack personal direction. They are not sure what they really want or what their personal goals should be.

November

Best Days Overall: 4, 5, 14, 15, 23, 24
Most Stressful Days Overall: 2, 3, 9, 10, 16, 17, 29, 30
Best Days for Love: 4, 5, 8, 9, 10, 14, 15, 19, 23, 24, 27
Best Days for Money: 6, 7, 8, 16, 17, 19, 25, 26, 27
Best Days for Career: 6, 7, 8, 16, 17, 25, 26

Love and romance is the major headline of the month ahead. For those of you already in a relationship there is more (and happy) social activity, while those of you who are unattached are sure to meet interesting prospects. Jupiter, your love planet, moves into your 7th house of love on the 8th. Thus he is in his own sign and house and is both celestially and terrestrially strong. He is ultra-powerful on your behalf and your social grace – your social magnetism – is unusually strong. It is as if you've taken a 'love pill' or love potion. People are attracted to you.

Many a Gemini will marry in the next twelve months. Many will be involved in relationships that are 'like' marriage but without the formalities. Business-type partnership could also happen. On the 22nd the Sun will join Jupiter in your 7th house and you enter a yearly love and social peak. For some of you (much depends on your age) it will be a life-time peak.

Mercury, the ruler of your Horoscope, spends the month in your 7th house too. This adds to your popularity. You are there for others – and especially for the beloved. You're in the mood for romance. You reach out to others and take a proactive approach to love. All month is good for love, but the 24th to the 28th (when the Sun travels with Jupiter) and the 29th and 30th (when Mercury travels with Jupiter) seem best.

The social life is active, but so is the career and it will be a challenge to juggle both. Mars crosses your Mid-heaven on the 16th and enters your 10th house of career, signalling a need to be more aggressive in the career. Friends are succeeding and helping out, and your technological expertise is playing a huge role from the 16th onwards. The planetary shift from the bottom half to the top half of your Horoscope also indicates a focus on career. You're working hard, but the work seems to pay off. There is success.

The New Moon of the 7th and the Full Moon of the 23rd are powerful financial days – especially the latter as it occurs in your own sign. The 26th, when the Moon is closest to the Earth, is also an especially good financial day. (She is at her perigee in your money house.)

December

Best Days Overall: 2, 3, 11, 12, 21, 22, 29, 30
Most Stressful Days Overall: 6, 7, 14, 15, 27, 28
Best Days for Love: 2, 3, 6, 7, 14, 15, 16, 23, 24, 26
Best Days for Money: 6, 7, 16, 17, 23, 24, 26, 27
Best Days for Career: 4, 5, 14, 15, 23, 24, 31

Many of the trends we wrote of last month are still in effect in December. Career and love are the main focuses.

Mars is still in your 10th house career. However, your career planet, Neptune, started moving forward on November 25. There is mental clarity in your career and career path now; it is starting to move forward again. Mars is travelling with Neptune this month and from the 5th to the 7th they will be conjunct. This shows, as we mentioned last month, much activity in the career. Success comes from boldness and being more aggressive. Neptune by himself can be too passive, but Mars will rouse him into activity.

This aspect also shows the success and help of friends. Online activities and technological expertise boost the career too. Bosses and parents (or parent figures) are having an excellent financial month, and your industry is doing well this month. Venus will give a boost to your career on the 20th and 21st as she makes beautiful aspects to Neptune. Children and children figures in your life are succeeding themselves, and also supporting your career. An appeal to the youth market is helpful careerwise.

Health got more delicate from November 22 onwards, and it will need more attention being paid to it until the 21st of this month. Make sure you get enough sleep. Don't allow yourself to get over tired and enhance your health in the ways mentioned in the yearly report. The good news is that your 6th house of health is stronger than usual this month. Mercury is there until the 13th, and Venus will be there from the 2nd onwards. This shows that you are paying attention here.

The love life still shines this month. You're still in a yearly love and social peak until the 21st. Mercury enters your 7th house of love again (this time in forward motion) on the 13th: someone you may have met last month and perhaps backed away from is being given another chance. This aspect makes for social popularity and good fortune in love.

The holiday season tends to be a more social period in the world, but for you it is more so than usual – more so than past holiday seasons.

Cancer

THE CRAB

Birthdays from
21st June to
20th July

Personality Profile

CANCER AT A GLANCE

Element – Water

Ruling Planet – Moon
  Career Planet – Mars
  Love Planet – Saturn
  Money Planet – Sun
  Planet of Fun and Games – Pluto
  Planet of Good Fortune – Neptune
  Planet of Health and Work – Jupiter
  Planet of Home and Family Life – Venus
  Planet of Spirituality – Mercury

Colours – blue, puce, silver

Colours that promote love, romance and social harmony – black, indigo

Colours that promote earning power – gold, orange

Gems – moonstone, pearl

Metal – silver

Scents – jasmine, sandalwood

Quality – cardinal (= activity)

Quality most needed for balance – mood control

Strongest virtues – emotional sensitivity, tenacity, the urge to nurture

Deepest need – a harmonious home and family life

Characteristics to avoid – over-sensitivity, negative moods

Signs of greatest overall compatibility – Scorpio, Pisces

Signs of greatest overall incompatibility – Aries, Libra, Capricorn

Sign most helpful to career – Aries

Sign most helpful for emotional support – Libra

Sign most helpful financially – Leo

Sign best for marriage and/or partnerships – Capricorn

Sign most helpful for creative projects – Scorpio

Best Sign to have fun with – Scorpio

Signs most helpful in spiritual matters – Gemini, Pisces

Best day of the week – Monday

Understanding a Cancer

In the sign of Cancer the heavens are developing the feeling side of things. This is what a true Cancerian is all about – feelings. Where Aries will tend to err on the side of action, Taurus on the side of inaction and Gemini on the side of thought, Cancer will tend to err on the side of feeling.

Cancerians tend to mistrust logic. Perhaps rightfully so. For them it is not enough for an argument or a project to be logical – it must feel right as well. If it does not feel right a Cancerian will reject it or chafe against it. The phrase 'follow your heart' could have been coined by a Cancerian, because it describes exactly the Cancerian attitude to life.

The power to feel is a more direct – more immediate – method of knowing than thinking is. Thinking is indirect. Thinking about a thing never touches the thing itself. Feeling is a faculty that touches directly the thing or issue in question. We actually experience it. Emotional feeling is almost like another sense which humans possess – a psychic sense. Since the realities that we come in contact with during our lifetime are often painful and even destructive, it is not surprising that the Cancerian chooses to erect barriers – a shell – to protect his or her vulnerable, sensitive nature. To a Cancerian this is only common sense.

If Cancerians are in the presence of people they do not know, or find themselves in a hostile environment, up goes the shell and they feel protected. Other people often complain about this, but one must question these people's motives. Why does this shell disturb them? Is it perhaps because they would like to sting, and feel frustrated that they cannot? If your intentions are honourable and you are patient, have no fear. The shell will open up and you will be accepted as part of the Cancerian's circle of family and friends.

Thought-processes are generally analytic and dissociating. In order to think clearly we must make distinctions, comparisons and the like. But feeling is unifying and integrative.

To think clearly about something you have to distance yourself from it. To feel something you must get close to it. Once a Cancerian has accepted you as a friend he or she will hang on to you. You have to be really bad to lose the friendship of a Cancerian. If you are related to Cancerians they will never let you go no matter what you do. They will always try to maintain some kind of connection even in the most extreme circumstances.

Finance

The Cancer-born has a deep sense of what other people feel about things and why they feel as they do. This faculty is a great asset in the workplace and in the business world. Of course it is also indispensable in raising a family and building a home, but it has its uses in business. Cancerians often attain great wealth in a family business. Even if the business is not a family operation, they will treat it as one. If the Cancerian works for somebody else, then the boss is the parental figure and the co-workers are brothers and sisters. If a Cancerian is the boss, then all the workers are his or her children. Cancerians like the feeling of being providers for others. They enjoy knowing that others derive their sustenance because of what they do. It is another form of nurturing.

With Leo on their solar 2nd money house cusp, Cancerians are often lucky speculators, especially with residential property or hotels and restaurants. Resort hotels and nightclubs are also profitable for the Cancerian. Waterside properties attract them. Though they are basically conventional people, they sometimes like to earn their livelihood in glamorous ways.

The Sun, Cancer's money planet, represents an important financial message: in financial matters Cancerians need to be less moody, more stable and fixed. They cannot allow their moods – which are here today and gone tomorrow – to get in the way of their business lives. They need to develop their self-esteem and feelings of self-worth if they are to realize their greatest financial potential.

Career and Public Image

Aries rules the 10th solar career house cusp of Cancer, which indicates that Cancerians long to start their own business, to be more active publicly and politically and to be more independent. Family responsibilities and a fear of hurting other people's feelings – or getting hurt themselves – often inhibit them from attaining these goals. However, this is what they want and long to do.

Cancerians like their bosses and leaders to act freely and to be a bit self-willed. They can deal with that in a superior. They expect their leaders to be fierce on their behalf. When the Cancerian is in the position of boss or superior he or she behaves very much like a 'warlord'. Of course the wars they wage are not egocentric but in defence of those under their care. If they lack some of this fighting instinct – independence and pioneering spirit – Cancerians will have extreme difficulty in attaining their highest career goals. They will be hampered in their attempts to lead others.

Since they are so parental, Cancerians like to work with children and make great educators and teachers.

Love and Relationships

Like Taurus, Cancer likes committed relationships. Cancerians function best when the relationship is clearly defined and everyone knows his or her role. When they marry it is usually for life. They are extremely loyal to their beloved. But there is a deep little secret that most Cancerians will never admit to: commitment or partnership is really a chore and a duty to them. They enter into it because they know of no other way to create the family that they desire. Union is just a way – a means to an end – rather than an end in itself. The family is the ultimate end for them.

If you are in love with a Cancerian you must tread lightly on his or her feelings. It will take you a good deal of time to realize how deep and sensitive Cancerians can be. The smallest negativity upsets them. Your tone of voice, your irritation, a look in your eye or an expression on your face can cause great distress for the Cancerian. Your slightest gesture is registered by them and reacted to. This can be hard to get used to, but stick by your love – Cancerians make great partners once you learn how to deal with them. Your Cancerian lover will react not so much to what you say but to the way you are actually feeling at the moment.

Home and Domestic Life

This is where Cancerians really excel. The home environment and the family are their personal works of art. They strive to make things of beauty that will outlast them. Very often they succeed.

Cancerians feel very close to their family, their relatives and especially their mothers. These bonds last throughout their lives and mature as they grow older. They are very fond of those members of their family who become successful, and they are also quite attached to family heirlooms and mementos. Cancerians also love children and like to provide them with all the things they need and want. With their nurturing, feeling nature, Cancerians make very good parents – especially the Cancerian woman, who is the mother *par excellence* of the zodiac.

As a parent the Cancerian's attitude is 'my children right or wrong'. Unconditional devotion is the order of the day. No matter what a family member does, the Cancerian will eventually forgive him or her, because 'you are, after all, family'. The preservation of the institution – the tradition – of the family is one of the Cancerian's main reasons for living. They have many lessons to teach others about this.

Being so family-orientated, the Cancerian's home is always clean, orderly and comfortable. They like old-fashioned furnishings but they also like to have all the modern comforts. Cancerians love to have family and friends over, to organize parties and to entertain at home – they make great hosts.

Horoscope for 2018

Major Trends

The year ahead is best described as a 'bittersweet' kind of year. Jupiter in the sign of Scorpio brings many happy events – more money, more fun in life, optimism and personal creativity. But Saturn's move into Capricorn late last year says 'hold on a minute, you've got real responsibilities, you can't just be having a good time'. Your challenge will be to enjoy your life while handling all your responsibilities – and there may be a few extra ones this year.

Pluto has been in your 7th house of love since January 2008. This has caused great changes in your love and social life. There have been many a divorce and separations during these past ten years. Spiritually speaking, you're giving birth to the social life of your dreams: your ideal love and social life. This always involves purging the old and effete. Usually these are inner attitudes and beliefs but often it manifests in outer ways as well, such as the death of old relationships and the beginning of new ones. Now that Saturn has moved into your 7th house these new relationships will get 'stress tested'. Only the good ones will survive. More on this later.

Uranus has been in your 10th house of career for the past seven years, which has brought multiple career changes to many of you. In some cases the career changes involved your industry or company. In others it involved your approach to the career. And sometimes it brought actual career changes – lawyers became talk-show hosts; doctors started writing blogs or entering online businesses – things of this nature. Uranus will still be in your 10th house for some of this year, but he leaves it between May and November and next year he will move out for good. So there is more stability happening in the career. A greater sense of security. Again, there is more on this later.

Uranus's move into your 11th house from May 16 to November 6 will test many of your friendships. Over the next seven years your whole social circle will be changed and radically different.

Neptune has been in your 9th house of religion, education and ideas for some years now and he will be there for many more to come. This indicates a spiritualizing of your religious and philosophical beliefs. Many of you will be exploring the mystical side of the religion you were brought up in.

On November 8, Jupiter will move into your 6th house, his own sign and house. Thus he is very powerful. This brings happy job opportunities – very nice ones. It will bring good news on the health front as well. More on this later.

Your most important interests this year are fun, children and creativity (until November 8); health and work (from November 8 onwards); love and romance; foreign travel, higher education and religion; and career (from January 1 to May 16 and from November 6 to December 31).

Your paths of greatest fulfilment this year are fun, creativity and children (until November 8); health and work (from November 8 onwards); finance (until November 17); and the body, image and personal pleasure (from November 17 onwards).

Health

(Please note that this is an astrological perspective on health and not a medical one. In days of yore there was no difference, both of these perspectives were identical. But now there could be quite a difference. For a medical perspective, please consult your doctor or health practitioner.)

Health needs some attention this year. You have three powerful long-term planets in stressful alignment with you, so overall energy is not what it should be. And this tends to make a person more vulnerable to things. Add to this that there will be times in the year when the short-term planets increase this stress and the vulnerabilities become greater. This doesn't mean illness *per se* – it only means that more work, more attention, needs to be given to your health. It's not just something to take for granted.

Until November 8, your 6th house will generally be empty, with only short-term planets passing through it. So there is a tendency toward 'lack of attention'. You will have to force yourself to concentrate on health.

The good news, as our regular readers know, is that much can be done to enhance the health and prevent problems from developing. Give more attention to the following – the vulnerable areas in your Horoscope this year (the reflex points are shown overleaf):

- The heart. This area became important in 2008 and will be important for many more years to come. Since many spiritual healers affirm that worry (i.e. lack of faith) is a prime root cause of heart problems, it is good to cultivate faith.
- The stomach (for women, the breasts). These are always important for the Cancerian. Eating right is always an important issue for you. What you eat is important, and should be checked with a professional, but *how* you eat can be just as important. The act of eating needs to be elevated from mere animal appetite to an act of

Important foot reflexology points for the year ahead

Try to massage all of the foot on a regular basis – the top of the foot as well as the bottom – but pay extra attention to the points highlighted on the chart. When you massage, be aware of 'sore spots' as these need special attention. It's also a good idea to massage the ankles – and below them especially.

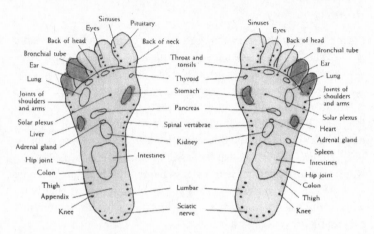

worship. Bless your food. Give thanks for it. Say grace (in your own words) before and after meals. Have soothing music playing when you eat. This will change the energy vibrations of both the food and your digestive system; the food will be digested better and you'll get only the highest and best qualities from what you eat.

- The liver and thighs. These too are very important for the Cancerian, as Jupiter, the ruler of these areas, is your health planet. Thighs should be regularly massaged, and a herbal liver cleanse every now and then – especially if you feel under the weather – is a good idea.

- The colon, bladder and sexual organs. These have only become important recently – since last October – although they continue to be important until November 8. Safe sex and sexual moderation are crucial these days. There should be neither too much nor too little. Listen to the body and not the mind. The body will tell you when enough is enough. A herbal colon cleanse every now and then is a good idea.

Your health planet Jupiter's position in the sign of Scorpio shows a tendency to surgery. You sort of see it as the 'quick' solution to a health problem. But keep in mind that Scorpio also rules detoxification and often this will do the same job (though it does take somewhat longer). You respond well to detoxes this year.

Jupiter in your 5th house of fun and creativity indicates a need to 'stay happy'. Watch the moods (Cancerians are very moody). Avoid depression like the plague. Keep the creative juices flowing. A creative hobby would be fun and therapeutic these days.

Home and Family

Home and family are always important to you, but the intensity of this feeling is less than usual this year. Your house of home and family is basically empty: only short-term planets will move through there this year.

Many of you have moved or refurbished the home in the past two years. Your family circle has expanded as well. This year you seem well content here and have no need to make major changes. It is a year that favours the status quo.

Cancerians of childbearing age were unusually fertile last year, and this trend continues in the year ahead. A pregnancy wouldn't be a surprise.

This year, your focus is more on your children (or the children figures in your life) rather than other family members. You get on well with them. They seem to bring great happiness and joy. They also seem very prosperous – living on a higher than usual standard – and inclined to travel as well. They seem like 'happy campers'.

Major renovations or repairs to the home don't seem likely this year (though the short-term planets and your personal Horoscope, cast for you, could modify this). But if you are repainting or re-arranging the furniture – beautifying the home in a cosmetic kind of way, the periods of August 7 to September 9 and November 16 to December 2 would be good times. These would also be good times to buy decorative objects for the home.

Your home and family planet is Venus. She is a fast-moving planet and in any given year she will move through every sector of your

Horoscope. Thus there are many short-term trends with home and family, depending on where Venus is and the aspects she receives. These are best dealt with in the monthly reports.

Venus will make one of her rare once-every-two-years retrograde moves this year, between October 5 and November 16. This will not be a time for major family decisions or major expenditure on the home. This is a time for reviewing things and for seeing where improvements can be made. You can put your plans into action when Venus moves forward again on November 16.

A parent or parent figure has gone through many personal changes over the last seven years, but now things are starting to settle down a bit. The other parent or parent figure is having a very prosperous year and seems generous with you. He or she can have job changes this year. Moves are not likely for them – these seem fraught with delays and difficulties. As we mentioned, children and children figures in your life are prospering, but a move is not likely. Siblings or sibling figures can move or renovate property, especially after November 8. (It could happen next year too.) Grandchildren (if you have them) are having a stable family year.

Finance and Career

The year ahead looks very prosperous. Jupiter is making beautiful aspects to you, so there is financial expansion. Happy opportunities. What the world calls 'good luck' (which is only the application of spiritual laws). There is luck in speculations and it probably wouldn't hurt to invest modest sums in some form of speculation (although not your rent or food money please, and not automatically – only under intuition). Speculations are favourable but the cosmos has many ways to prosper you.

There are going to be many dramatic financial shifts and course corrections this year – more than usual. We have three Solar Eclipses this year, rather than the more usual two. And since the Sun is your financial planet, these bring changes and dramas. Also, two eclipses – one Solar and one Lunar – will occur in your money house. So, four out of the five eclipses this year impact finance. My feeling is that you might be underestimating your earnings and need to change strategy.

If there is a financial weakness this year it is the lack of power in your money house. Only short-term planets will move through there. Generally this indicates satisfaction with earnings as they are. You sort of take prosperity for granted and have no need to overly focus here. However, if financial problems arise, lack of attention could be the cause.

Jupiter's beautiful aspects to your Natal Sun suggests earning through work. Your work will create the good fortune. It also shows earning from the health field.

Jupiter in your 5th house shows that children or children figures are important financially. Often they are the motivating force for financial success, but they can also come up with ideas or inspirations. If they are of appropriate age they can be physically and materially supportive too. Jupiter's position here also indicates earnings from industries that cater to the youth market – music, entertainment, sports or companies that supply these industries.

Uranus has been in your 10th house of career for many years, as we have said, and he is still here for part of the year ahead. There have been many career changes over the time, but now this career uncertainty is starting to settle down now. It's not quite over yet, but by next year it will be and there will be more stability and security here.

Uranus in your career house favours a freelance kind of career – a career that offers a lot of freedom and change. The electronic media and the online world are favoured. The only problem with a freelance career is the insecurity and uncertainty. Learning to live with this has been one of your main lessons over the past seven years.

There are a lot of short-term career trends, depending on where Mars, your career planet, is and the aspects he receives. These are best dealt with in the monthly reports.

Love and Social Life

The love and social life is challenging this year. But, the challenges can bring many rewards if you handle them properly.

Saturn, as we have mentioned, will be in your 7th house of love for the next two years. This is a transit not conducive to marriage or to committed, contractual love. Even if you meet a 'special someone' it is not advisable to marry. Enjoy the relationship for what it is. Next year might be a better time for that.

As we mentioned, if you're already in a marriage or serious relationship, it will get tested this year. This is not usually pleasant, but it has some good points. We never know if love is real during the good times, when everything is idyllic. We only find out during the tough times. If your marriage or relationship can handle the stress of the next two years it can probably survive anything.

Saturn is your love planet. So, in general, you tend to be traditional and conservative in marriage and relationships. But now, with Saturn in his own sign and house, you are apt to be more conservative than usual. And this goes for the spouse, partner or the people you get involved with.

Those of you who are single will tend to favour older, more settled kinds of people. Corporate types. Business types. There is a feeling of practicality in love (you always have this tendency, but more so now). You gravitate to the good provider, the ambitious person, the person who can help you in your career. The problem here is that 'relationships of convenience' rather than of real love are likely.

The spouse, partner or current love seems very 'business-like' these days: cool, aloof, standoffish. The element of passion seems missing. This will need to be ignited artificially. Both of you will have to work on this. Both of you will have to practise – make it a project – sending love and warmth to others.

For singles there is less dating and party-going this year. The cosmos is calling you to be more selective about these things. There is a need to focus on quality rather than quantity. You will date less, but the dates will be of higher quality.

Often this aspect brings social disappointments. Perhaps your expectations were too high. Perhaps you were too naive. You should look at this not as disappointment, but as 'revelation from the Divine'. Truth sometimes hurts, but it is better than living a lie.

Those of you in or working toward the second marriage have a much easier time in the marriage. If you are unattached there is romance in store, but no need to rush into a marriage. Those in or working toward the third marriage will also have the relationship tested. If you are unattached, it would be better not to marry. You have the aspects for serial relationships rather than marriage.

Self-Improvement

Saturn in your 7th house, as we mentioned, brings challenges to the love and social life, which is being reorganized and made more stable. But this is a process, not one event. Saturn is going to reorganize – and test – your current love attitudes, your notions of what love is all about. Saturn, involved in love, often makes one a 'non-believer' in love – at least in the romantic love that is idealized in our culture. One sort of feels, 'love is an illusion anyway, so I might as well be practical about it'. This was the concept in many cultures for thousands of years – and is still prevalent in many parts of the world. Marriages were arranged by the parents, who, presumably, were more clear-headed than their children. The chemistry between the two people was rarely an issue. Marriage was practical; it created bonds – either financial or diplomatic – between families. It was often an instrument of state policy. It was never about 'personal fulfilment'. The thinking was that one can learn to love anybody, so one might as well learn to love someone who is useful to the state or to the family fortunes. Almost all marriages were marriages of convenience.

This concept has been largely abandoned in the Western world, yet, upon analysis, there *is* something very spiritual in this attitude. One *can* learn to love anyone – with practice and patience. Spiritually speaking, it is merely a choice that one makes, a moment-by-moment choice. Perhaps the chemistry is not what it should be. Perhaps the habits and mannerisms are off-putting. Yet, as any meditator knows, these are not obstructions to love. Spiritual love is above any and all human conditions. It is not dependent on 'objects'. It is a spiritual force that anyone can tap into. It will flow, without distinction, to every part of life – the good, the bad or the ugly. This love might not approve of certain actions – it doesn't whitewash reality – but it loves in spite of these things.

Learning this kind of love will be a great help over the next two years. Meditation will help you.

There is another lesson that Saturn teaches about love – not popular to be sure, but valid. Duty and Love are generally seen as opposites, as antagonistic attitudes. Duty is seen as involving discipline, the stiff upper lip, effort and exertion. Love, on the other hand, is seen as effortless. Yet, duty performed in a loving way is perhaps the highest form of love. Someone who truly loves another will always do their duty to that person.

As we have said earlier on, Saturn in your 7th house is apt to bring disappointment, not only in love but with friends as well. Perhaps your expectations are too high. Perhaps the spouse or friend is undergoing a personal drama. Perhaps these people were never who you thought them to be. No matter. This is a year to practise the art of forgiveness. It isn't wise (or healthy) to hold on to grievances. You need all the help you can get in your relationships, and forgiveness will be a huge help.

Real forgiveness is never about 'whitewashing' history. We don't paper things over. The people did what they did. It was wrong. Yet, we forgive. Real forgiveness happens when we can put ourselves in their shoes and understand why they did what they did. The realization often comes that had I been in that situation, I too might have acted that way.

Finally, some relationships will not survive the coming stresses. In the dissolution there are lessons too. In this situation you have a choice. You can maximize or minimize the negativity. Dissolution always brings negativity; the issue is, do you want to maximize or minimize it? It is best to minimize, wherever possible. Sadly, most choose the former course.

Month-by-month Forecasts

January

Best Days Overall: 1, 2, 10, 11, 20, 21, 29, 30
Most Stressful Days Overall: 8, 9, 15, 16, 22, 23
Best Days for Love: 5, 6, 15, 16, 25, 27, 28
Best Days for Money: 1, 2, 3, 4, 5, 6, 10, 11, 15, 16, 20, 21, 27, 28, 29, 30, 31
Best Days for Career: 1, 2, 10, 11, 20, 21, 22, 23

Saturn in your 7th house shows a year of reduced social activity. But this month, there is an increase. You're in the midst of a yearly love and social peak. A lot of this socializing seems business related though, rather than romance related: business partnerships or joint ventures could happen – the opportunities are there.

Last month, on December 21, the upper half of your Horoscope began to become dominant, and this continues this month, after the 11th, as Mercury moves from the lower to the upper half of the chart. You're entering the period to focus on your career. You're not yet at the peak – this will come in a few months – but there is more focus. Home and family issues become less important. You serve your family best by being successful in the world.

Health needs watching this month, especially until the 20th. Sixty per cent of the planets (and sometimes 70 per cent) are in stressful alignment with you. So make sure you get enough rest. Aches and pains might not be as serious as they feel but just the natural consequence of low energy. When your energy is low pre-existing conditions can start to flare up. Enhance your health in the ways mentioned in the yearly report. Spiritual healing seems powerful until the 11th. After the 27th pay more attention to the head, face and scalp. Craniosacral therapy might be a good idea. The most important thing is to maintain high energy levels. You will see big improvement after the 20th, but you still need to pay attention.

A Lunar Eclipse on the 31st occurs in your money house, signalling a need to rethink and change your financial strategy and planning. The events of the eclipse will show you where you are off the mark. Every Lunar Eclipse is especially powerful on Cancerians as the Moon is the ruler of your Horoscope. So, take it easy that period. Spend more quiet time at home. You will be redefining yourself, changing your image and self-concept over the next few months. This is a healthy thing to do, but with an eclipse involved, it is forced on you.

On the 20th the Sun, your financial planet, moves into Aquarius, your 8th house of regeneration. This is good for paying off debt (or for taking on loans), tax and estate planning and for buying insurance (or collecting on it). If you have good investment ideas it is a good time to attract outside backers to your projects.

February

Best Days Overall: 6, 7, 16, 17, 25, 26
Most Stressful Days Overall: 4, 5, 11, 12, 19
Best Days for Love: 2, 4, 5, 11, 12, 16, 21, 25, 26
Best Days for Money: 4, 5, 6, 7, 14, 15, 16, 17, 25, 26, 27, 28
Best Days for Career: 9, 10, 19, 20, 27, 28

Finance has not been a big issue in your life so far this year (and nor was it last year). Perhaps you haven't paid enough attention here – the Lunar Eclipse last month and the upcoming Solar Eclipse on the 15th of this month are forcing you to pay more attention and make the changes that need to be made. It is tempting to have the financial life on 'automatic pilot' – but sometimes human intervention is necessary.

The Solar Eclipse this month occurs in your 8th house and affects not only your personal finances but the finances of the spouse, partner or current love. If you're involved in business partnerships it applies to your partner here as well. You both need to make course corrections in the financial life. Your thinking hasn't been realistic, as the events of the eclipse will show. The 8th house connection often shows 'near death' experiences (or fears of death). Here it involves financial 'near death' rather than physical. This eclipse also impacts on Mercury and Jupiter. Thus job changes can be in the works. The conditions of the workplace change. Your health is good this month, but the impact on Jupiter can bring some kind of health scare. It will bring – over the coming months – dramatic changes in your health regime. If you employ others there is instability in the workplace and dramas in the lives of employees. The impact on Mercury will test cars and communication equipment – you should drive more careful this period, more defensively. Indeed, if you don't need to drive, don't. Since Mercury rules your 12th house of spirituality, there can be upheavals and shakeups in a charitable or spiritual organization you belong to. There are dramas in the lives of gurus or guru figures in your life.

Avoid speculations on the 9th and 10th and be careful of overspending. Marriage is not advisable this year, but the love life improves from the 18th onwards. You still need to go slowly in love, and to be more choosey about who you date and what parties you attend.

Health is good this month and will get even better after the 18th. There is a lot of water in the Horoscope from the 18th onwards – at least half of the planets are in water signs. This is comfortable for you, but watch your mood. Water-based therapies are beneficial all year, but especially this month.

March

Best Days Overall: 6, 7, 15, 16, 17, 24, 25
Most Stressful Days Overall: 3, 4, 10, 11, 12, 18, 19, 31
Best Days for Love: 1, 8, 10, 11, 12, 18, 19, 20, 26, 27, 29
Best Days for Money: 6, 7, 15, 16, 17, 24, 25, 26, 27
Best Days for Career: 8, 9, 18, 19, 20, 29, 30

A happy, prosperous and successful month ahead, Cancer, enjoy

Last month on the 18th, your 9th house – considered one of the happiest – became very strong, and this is the situation until the 20th of this month. The financial planet, the Sun, in the 9th house shows prosperity, the enlargement of wealth. Foreign companies, foreign investments and foreigners in general are playing a huge role in earnings. The Sun in spiritual Pisces at the start of the month shows 'miracle money' rather than 'natural money'. It shows an ability to access the supernatural sources of supply. It shows a good financial intuition too.

Power in the 9th house indicates good fortune for college students. If you're involved in legal issues there is good fortune here too. Foreign lands are calling to you – travel is in the air. The planets favour sea travel rather than air or land travel: a cruise looks interesting.

With the north node of the Moon in your 2nd money house, your problem might be too much money rather than too little. (The north node tends to excess.) But this is a nice problem to have.

On the 20th the Sun crosses the Mid-heaven and enters your career house. Forty per cent of the planets will be here – a strong percentage. The career is going well. You're succeeding. There can be pay rises (official or unofficial) too. You have the financial favour of the authority figures in your life. Your good professional reputation is important financially – guard it. Your career planet, Mars, will move into your 7th house of love on the 17th, so you advance your career by social means. Attend the right parties and gatherings – perhaps you can host them as well.

Health needs more attention being paid to it from the 20th onwards, as many, many planets are in stressful alignment with you. Make sure to get enough rest. Try not to overwork in your career. Take breaks. Enhance your health in the ways mentioned in the yearly report. Until the 17th (with Mars in your 6th house), scalp and face massage will be good. Good muscle tone seems important too.

April

Best Days Overall: 2, 3, 12, 13, 21, 22, 29
Most Stressful Days Overall: 1, 7, 8, 14, 15, 27, 28
Best Days for Love: 7, 8, 16, 17, 25, 27
Best Days for Money: 2, 3, 4, 5, 12, 13, 14, 15, 16, 21, 22, 23, 24, 25, 29, 30
Best Days for Career: 7, 8, 14, 15, 16, 17, 25, 26

Many of the trends we wrote about in March are still very much in effect for most of the month ahead. The career is still the main head-line this month. You still have the financial favour of those in authority in your life. Your good professional reputation is still playing a role in earning.

Although home and family are always important to you, they are less pressing right now. Your success in the world is the best way to serve your family these days.

The Sun, your financial planet, travels with Uranus from the 17th to the 19th (although you could feel the effects of this even earlier). This transit indicates a sudden financial disturbance – perhaps an unex-pected expense or some change that requires action. The good news is that it is a short-term change. Sometimes (very often) the sudden expense is balanced with a sudden, unexpected inflow of money. On the 20th, as the Sun moves into your 11th house, the high-tech and online world become important. This is a good financial transit as the Sun will be in conservative Taurus – your financial judgement will be sound. It will be a very good time to get involved with groups and organizations after the 20th. It will be fun and will help the bottom line. Most likely you will be spending more on computers and high-tech gadgetry.

Love has been stressful since March 17. Mars entered your 7th house and spends the month here. This can produce power struggles in love, which are never healthy. Also it can lead to relationships of convenience rather than of real love. (With Saturn in your 7th house all year, you have this tendency anyway. Now it becomes stronger.) The good news is that you advance your career in social ways – as we mentioned last month. You have a knack for meeting just the right people who can help your career. Like last month, a lot of your social-izing is career related (or with people involved in your career).

Health still needs watching this month, especially until the 20th. The good news is that health is improved over last month. You can enhance the health in the ways mentioned in the yearly report. Most importantly, do your best to maintain high levels of energy. Health will further improve after the 20th, but still needs some attention (plane-tary heavy hitters in Capricorn, Mars, Pluto and Saturn are not powers to be trifled with).

May

Best Days Overall: 9, 10, 18, 19, 26, 27, 28
Most Stressful Days Overall: 4, 5, 11, 12, 13, 24, 25, 31
Best Days for Love: 4, 5, 7, 8, 14, 17, 22, 26, 31
Best Days for Money: 4, 5, 9, 10, 14, 15, 18, 19, 20, 21, 24, 26, 27
Best Days for Career: 4, 5, 11, 12, 13, 15, 16, 24

On March 20 the planetary power started to shift from the Western, social sector of your chart, to the independent Eastern sector. This represents a psychological shift in you. The planetary power moves in your direction. It supports you. Because of this you are more independ-ent than usual. There's more of a 'can do' spirit. The Western social sector is still very strong – at least half of the planets are still there – so others and their favour are still important, but a bit less so now. This is a time to have things your way. Your personal initiative and skills matter. You are less in need of the approval of others than usual. So, this is a time to make those changes that need to be made. This is a time to take responsibility for your own happiness. You have a few more months of heightened independence. If you wait too long – when the planets start moving away from you again – changes can be made but with greater difficulty.

Finances look good this month. If there is a weakness here it is your empty money house, which indicates you might not be paying enough attention here. If financial challenges arise, start paying more attention. We get what we focus on. On the 1st your financial planet makes nice aspects to Saturn. This shows good financial cooperation with your spouse, partner or current love. Friends in general seem helpful. On the 11th and 12th the Sun makes very nice aspects to Pluto. This gives us a few messages. There is more luck in speculations. Children and children figures in your life are more financially supportive – young people in general are more supportive. You probably spend more on children too, but they can also inspire earnings. On the 21st the Sun enters your spiritual 12th house. This shows good financial intuition. This is a good period to delve deeper into the spiritual dimensions of wealth. The Horoscope is saying that if you're right spiritually, finance and family will take care of themselves.

Venus, your family planet, moves into your own sign on the 19th. This is a happy kind of aspect. Your looks improve; there is more grace and glamour to the image. Family members seem very devoted to you. Love is still problematic, but your looks are not the problem!

Venus spends most of the month 'out of bounds' – from the 6th to the 31st. Thus family members are outside their normal spheres. They are looking for solutions in far away or unfamiliar places.

June

Best Days Overall: 5, 6, 7, 14, 15, 23, 24
Most Stressful Days Overall: 1, 2, 8, 9, 20, 21, 22, 28, 29
Best Days for Love: 1, 2, 6, 7, 10, 16, 18, 23, 24, 28, 29
Best Days for Money: 3, 4, 5, 6, 7, 12, 13, 14, 15, 16, 17, 23, 24
Best Days for Career: 3, 4, 8, 9, 12, 13, 20, 21, 22, 30

A happy month ahead. Not perfect, but basically happy. The planetary power is now (especially after the 21st) in its maximum Eastern position and you are in a period of maximum independence for the year ahead. There have been periods in your life where you were more independent, but this year the Western sector (the social sector) of your chart is still strong. It's the kind of month where you need to balance your personal interests with those of others. Your personal desires are strong, but so are the social demands. Still, if conditions need changing this is the time to make those changes.

This is a prosperous month ahead. On the 1st and 2nd Venus makes beautiful aspects to Jupiter and Neptune (there is an exact Grand Trine at that time – a very positive aspect). The family as a whole prospers, especially a parent or parent figure. He or she will be more generous with you. Family support is good all month. Your financial planet remains in your 12th house until the 21st, which again emphasizes the financial intuition. Intuition is eminently logical, only we generally don't see it right away. We see it in hindsight. On the 21st the Sun crosses your Ascendant and enters your 1st house – a very happy financial aspect. Financial windfalls come to you. Financial opportunities seek you out. You have the 'look' of a money person during this period and others see you this way. 'You're flush' as the saying goes. Aside from his position in your own sign, your financial planet will be part of a Grand Trine in Water – a rare and fortunate aspect. Finances flow smoothly to you.

Like last month, the love life could be better, but personal appearance is not the issue here. You and the beloved see things from opposite perspectives. The tendency is to separate (you live your life; he or she lives theirs). Even if there is no actual physical separation, emotionally there is. The challenge of both of you is to bridge your differences. Respect them, and bridge them. Sometimes one way is best, sometimes another. Both perspectives are valid. In astrology, opposites are always the best marriage partners (if they don't kill each other first).

July

Best Days Overall: 3, 4, 12, 13, 20, 21, 30, 31
Most Stressful Days Overall: 5, 6, 18, 19, 25, 26
Best Days for Love: 5, 6, 7, 8, 16, 25, 26
Best Days for Money: 1, 3, 4, 12, 13, 14, 15, 20, 21, 22, 27, 28, 29
Best Days for Career: 1, 5, 6, 10, 11, 18, 19, 27, 28, 29

Finance has not been a big deal this year. For most of the year, your money house has been basically empty and you have seemed satisfied with the status quo. But last month the money house started to get powerful. Venus moved in on June 19 and Mercury on the 29th. This month your 2nd house will get even stronger as the Sun moves into it on the 22nd. Last month was prosperous – this month even more so. There is a strong focus on finance, and this makes all the difference in the world.

Venus's presence in the money house since June 14 indicates spending on the home and family – not a surprise. It also shows good family support and that family connections play an important role in earnings. Venus leaves the money house on the 10th. Mercury will spend the entire month in the 2nd house, signalling a good financial intuition. This aspect favours buying, selling and trading. Good sales, marketing and PR are important in whatever you do. The Sun's move into the money house is also wonderful. He is in his own sign and house – and is more powerful than usual. This favours speculations, and industries that appeal to youth – entertainment, music, etc. For those of you who are more conservative, it also favours electric utilities and gold.

Mars, your career planet, spends most of the month 'out of bounds' – from the 9th onwards. This shows that career activities are pulling you into unknown territory, outside your normal sphere.

Two eclipses shake things up this month and keep things interesting. The Solar Eclipse of the 13th occurs in your own sign. Take it easy over this period. As with every Solar Eclipse there's a need for a course correction in finance. The events of the eclipse will show you what's needed. The eclipse in your sign indicates a need to redefine yourself – your image and self-concept.

The Lunar Eclipse of the 27th occurs in your 8th house and also impacts on your image and self-concept. This month is definitely a time to take stock of yourself and to decide on what image you want to project to the world. This eclipse affects Mars, so career changes and shakeups are happening. It could bring a happy career opportunity too. Perhaps surgery is recommended to you or to bosses or parent figures in your life.

August

Best Days Overall: 8, 9, 16, 17, 26, 27
Most Stressful Days Overall: 1, 2, 3, 14, 15, 21, 22, 29, 30
Best Days for Love: 4, 5, 12, 14, 15, 21, 22, 24, 25, 31
Best Days for Money: 2, 3, 8, 9, 10, 11, 16, 17, 20, 26, 27, 31
Best Days for Career: 1, 2, 3, 6, 13, 22, 29, 30

Your career planet, Mars, is both retrograde and 'out of bounds' this month. This suggests that you're in unknown, unfamiliar territory and lack confidence and direction. Very understandable. Now is the time to gain as much mental clarity as you can. Career issues need time to resolve themselves. In the meantime you can focus more on the home and family and your emotional wellness. Back in June the planetary power began to shift to the lower half of your Horoscope. Now it is approaching its nadir. Career is important all year, but you can shift some attention to the home and family.

You're still in the midst of yearly financial peak this month. The focus is on finance – as it should be. It is a prosperous month ahead. Mercury spends the month in your money house, showing, like last month, that good sales, marketing, advertising and PR are important in whatever you're doing. The word has to get out about your product or service. We see this all month (and even next month too). On the 22nd your financial planet moves into your 3rd house, reinforcing this message. Buying, selling, trading and retailing are also paths to profits. It is probable that you're spending more on books and magazines – on education – this month.

A Solar Eclipse on the 11th occurs in your money house, showing a need for more course corrections in the financial life. Financial thinking and planning hasn't been realistic lately, as the events of the eclipse will show. The good news is that you'll be able to make the necessary changes. This eclipse also affects the money people in your life and they have dramas – often life-changing kinds of dramas. Sometimes this kind of eclipse brings shakeups at your bank or brokerage.

Health and energy are reasonable this month. You must keep in mind, though, that after the 13th (as Mars moves back into your 7th house) there are three powerful planets in stressful alignment with you. So stay in your body. Be aware of it. If you're tired, rest. Enhance the health in the ways mentioned in the yearly report.

Love is still very stressful.

September

Best Days Overall: 4, 5, 13, 14, 22, 23, 24
Most Stressful Days Overall: 11, 12, 17, 18, 19, 25, 26
Best Days for Love: 1, 2, 3, 8, 9, 13, 17, 18, 19, 22, 23, 27
Best Days for Money: 1, 4, 5, 7, 9, 13, 14, 18, 19, 22, 23, 24, 29
Best Days for Career: 1, 10, 11, 20, 21, 25, 26, 29, 30

Finance is becoming less important this month. On the 6th Mercury leaves the money house and it is basically empty this month. (Only the Moon visits there on the 7th.) So, short-term financial goals have been more or less achieved and you don't need to pay too much attention here now. Your financial planet will be in your 3rd house until the 22nd. Thus, as we have seen for the past two months, sales, marketing and advertising – getting the word out about your product or service – is vital. It also favours buying, selling, trading and retailing. On the 22nd the Sun moves into your 4th house of home and family. So you're spending more here. You can also earn from the home and family too. Sometimes people work more from home. Sometimes, the family or family connections provide financial support or opportunity. Sometimes the family inspires earnings through ideas and advice. Sometimes people earn through industries that cater to the home.

Health needs some attention after the 22nd. As always – and this is the number one priority – make sure you get enough rest (quality rest).

Focus more on what is really essential in your life and let go of trivialities. Enhance the health in the ways mentioned in the yearly report.

Your career planet, Mars, remains 'out of bounds' until the 24th, but you seem to be acclimatized to your strange environment. Mars is moving forward now, however, and there is more career confidence, more direction.

This month you face one of the classic conflicts that many people face – only with you, Cancer, it is more dramatic. Your 4th house of home and family is strong, but the demands of the career are also powerful. Somehow, you have to give each their due. Your job is to be successful at home *and* in the career.

The family as a whole have prospered this year – children and children figures as well. Very soon their financial goals (the short-term ones at least) will have been attained and they will branch out to other interests.

Mars leaves your 7th house on the 11th and love should go a little bit better. But even so, it still needs much work.

October

Best Days Overall: 2, 3, 10, 11, 20, 21, 29, 30
Most Stressful Days Overall: 8, 9, 15, 16, 22, 23
Best Days for Love: 2, 3, 6, 10, 11, 15, 16, 20, 21, 24, 25, 29, 30
Best Days for Money: 1, 2, 3, 4, 5, 8, 9, 10, 11, 18, 19, 20, 21, 29, 30, 31
Best Days for Career: 1, 8, 9, 17, 18, 19, 22, 23, 27, 28

A happy and prosperous month ahead. Enjoy!

Until the 22nd your 4th house of home and family – your favourite house – is still powerful. The cosmos impels you to focus on what you most love. Like last month, though, you have to divide your time with the demands of career, which are still very strong. Your career planet Mars has been in your 8th house of regeneration since September 11 and will be there for the rest of this month. Often this brings 'near death' experiences in the career. Transformations. On the other hand, it indicates a very intense focus, which generally leads to success.

With Jupiter in your 5th house all year, you're had a fun kind of year. But this coming month – especially after the 23rd – even more so. The Sun's entry into your 5th house on the 23rd initiates a yearly personal pleasure peak. Personal creativity has been strong all year, but now even more so. There is much involvement with children and children figures in your life. And, those of appropriate age are perhaps creating children these days.

Prosperity will be much stronger after the 23rd than before. Until then you need to work harder for earnings – work harder to achieve your financial goals. But after the 23rd it happens easier and in happier ways.

The financial planet in your 5th house favours speculation and risk taking. Money comes to you easily and is spent easily. You spend more on the children (or children figures) in your life, but they can also be financial inspirations. If they are of appropriate age, they are likely to be supportive or provide opportunity. The good thing about this position is that one enjoys the money one has. One spends on fun kinds of activities. The Sun in the 5th house is all about 'happy money'. Financial opportunities come as you are at the theatre, on holiday or at a party – while you're having fun. Avoid speculations on the 11th and 12th. And from the 23rd to the 25th there is a short-term financial disturbance. You may have to make some changes.

Health and energy are dramatically better after the 22nd. In the meantime enhance the health in the ways mentioned in the yearly report.

November

Best Days Overall: 6, 7, 8, 16, 17, 25, 26
Most Stressful Days Overall: 4, 5, 11, 12, 19, 20
Best Days for Love: 2, 4, 5, 10, 11, 12, 14, 15, 21, 23, 24
Best Days for Money: 1, 6, 7, 8, 16, 17, 19, 27, 28
Best Days for Career: 4, 5, 15, 16, 19, 20, 25, 26

This is a very eventful kind of month. Uranus moves back into your 10th house of career on the 6th, creating more changes in the career. But by now – after seven years of this – you know how to handle it.

More importantly, Jupiter, your health planet, moves into Sagittarius your 6th house on the 8th. This shows job changes. Work might be less fun than it has been. On the positive side, you will have wonderful new job opportunities in the next twelve or so months. Your job prospects are bright indeed.

You're still in the midst of a yearly personal pleasure peak until the 22nd. By then, your urge for leisure is sated and you're in the mood for work. This will be a good period (from the 22nd onwards) for doing all those mundane, boring, detail-oriented jobs that you've been putting off. You'll have the energy and the drive to do them. Jupiter's move into your 6th house brings changes to the health regime too. The liver and thighs – always important for you – become even more so, but it will not be necessary to focus on the colon, bladder and sexual organs now. Some of you might benefit from foreign doctors or foreign treatments. Some of you will want to travel abroad for treatment.

Jupiter in your 6th house (in his own sign and house) is a positive for health. Here he is much stronger on your behalf than last year.

The planetary power is now mostly in the Western, social sector of your chart. This has been the case since late September and is now approaching its maximum. It is time to develop your social skills. Time to get things done by consensus, not by direct action. Let others have their way, so long as it isn't destructive. Likeability is more important financially and in your career than personal skills. If you're OK with others, the finances and career will fall into place.

Your financial planet is still in your 5th house of 'happy money' until the 22nd. So keep in mind our discussion of this last month. On the 22nd it enters your 6th house, indicating money from work and productive service. Probably you will spend more on your health and on health issues during this period, but you will have opportunities to earn from these things too. Children and children figures have prospered over the past year, and this month is especially strong for them.

December

Best Days Overall: 4, 5, 14, 15, 23, 24, 31
Most Stressful Days Overall: 2, 3, 9, 10, 16, 17, 29, 30
Best Days for Love: 2, 3, 8, 9, 10, 14, 15, 18, 23, 24, 27
Best Days for Money: 6, 7, 16, 17, 25, 26, 27
Best Days for Career: 4, 5, 14, 15, 16, 17, 23, 24, 31

Mars, your career planet, has been making nice aspects to you since November 16, and this trend continues in the month ahead. You're getting on with bosses, elders, parents and parent figures. The authority figures in your life seem kindly disposed to you. Happy career developments are happening. A foreign trip might be necessary (looks like from the 5th to the 7th) for business. Career is furthered by your willingness to travel.

Your 5th house of fun is strong this month, but so is your 6th house of work. So, you're working hard and playing hard.

Money comes, like last month, through work. (In many cases there are extra jobs or overtime pay available.) A very nice job opportunity comes on the 21st or 22nd. This is also an excellent financial time. Health is basically good this month, but don't let the normal ups and downs of finances get you down. Health is health and money is money. Keep them separate in your mind. Health will need watching after the 21st. Give more attention to the liver and thighs. Regular thighs massage will not only strengthen the liver, but the lower back as well. A herbal liver cleanse might be a good idea if you feel under the weather.

On the 21st the Sun enters your 7th house, signalling the importance of social connections in finance. Who you know is more important than how much you actually have. Often this shows a business-type partnership or joint venture. You seem very involved, financially, with the spouse, partner or current love.

With the planetary power now in its maximum Western position, likeability becomes more important for success than personal abilities. Likeability becomes an issue in finance as well. Perhaps you don't have the best product or service, but if your customers like you, that's enough.

On the 21st you begin a yearly love and social peak. It probably won't compare to past years' peaks, but it is the most active time for the current year. Singles will probably be dating more, but serious romance, isn't likely. Enjoy things for what they are.

Leo

♌

THE LION

Birthdays from
21st July to
21st August

Personality Profile

LEO AT A GLANCE

Element – Fire

Ruling Planet – Sun
  Career Planet – Venus
  Love Planet – Uranus
  Money Planet – Mercury
  Planet of Health and Work – Saturn
  Planet of Home and Family Life – Pluto

Colours – gold, orange, red

Colours that promote love, romance and social harmony – black, indigo, ultramarine blue

Colours that promote earning power – yellow, yellow-orange

Gems – amber, chrysolite, yellow diamond

Metal – gold

Scents – bergamot, frankincense, musk, neroli

Quality – fixed (= stability)

Quality most needed for balance – humility

Strongest virtues – leadership ability, self-esteem and confidence, generosity, creativity, love of joy

Deepest needs – fun, elation, the need to shine

Characteristics to avoid – arrogance, vanity, bossiness

Signs of greatest overall compatibility – Aries, Sagittarius

Signs of greatest overall incompatibility – Taurus, Scorpio, Aquarius

Sign most helpful to career – Taurus

Sign most helpful for emotional support – Scorpio

Sign most helpful financially – Virgo

Sign best for marriage and/or partnerships – Aquarius

Sign most helpful for creative projects – Sagittarius

Best Sign to have fun with – Sagittarius

Signs most helpful in spiritual matters – Aries, Cancer

Best day of the week – Sunday

Understanding a Leo

When you think of Leo, think of royalty – then you'll get the idea of what the Leo character is all about and why Leos are the way they are. It is true that, for various reasons, some Leo-born do not always express this quality – but even if not they should like to do so.

A monarch rules not by example (as does Aries) nor by consensus (as do Capricorn and Aquarius) but by personal will. Will is law. Personal taste becomes the style that is imitated by all subjects. A monarch is somehow larger than life. This is how a Leo desires to be.

When you dispute the personal will of a Leo it is serious business. He or she takes it as a personal affront, an insult. Leos will let you know that their will carries authority and that to disobey is demeaning and disrespectful.

A Leo is king (or queen) of his or her personal domain. Subordinates, friends and family are the loyal and trusted subjects. Leos rule with benevolent grace and in the best interests of others. They have a powerful presence; indeed, they are powerful people. They seem to attract attention in any social gathering. They stand out because they are stars in their domain. Leos feel that, like the Sun, they are made to shine and rule. Leos feel that they were born to special privilege and royal prerogatives – and most of them attain this status, at least to some degree.

The Sun is the ruler of this sign, and when you think of sunshine it is very difficult to feel unhealthy or depressed. Somehow the light of the Sun is the very antithesis of illness and apathy. Leos love life. They also love to have fun; they love drama, music, the theatre and amusements of all sorts. These are the things that give joy to life. If – even in their best interests – you try to deprive Leos of their pleasures, good food, drink and entertainment, you run the serious risk of depriving them of the will to live. To them life without joy is no life at all.

Leos epitomize humanity's will to power. But power in and of itself – regardless of what some people say – is neither good nor evil. Only when power is abused does it become evil. Without power even good things cannot come to pass. Leos realize this and are uniquely qualified to wield power. Of all the signs, they do it most naturally. Capricorn, the other power sign of the zodiac, is a better manager and administrator than Leo – much better. But Leo outshines Capricorn in personal grace and presence. Leo loves power, whereas Capricorn assumes power out of a sense of duty.

Finance

Leos are great leaders but not necessarily good managers. They are better at handling the overall picture than the nitty-gritty details of business. If they have good managers working for them they can become exceptional executives. They have vision and a lot of creativity.

Leos love wealth for the pleasures it can bring. They love an opulent lifestyle, pomp and glamour. Even when they are not wealthy they live as if they are. This is why many fall into debt, from which it is sometimes difficult to emerge.

Leos, like Pisceans, are generous to a fault. Very often they want to acquire wealth solely so that they can help others economically. Wealth to Leo buys services and managerial ability. It creates jobs for others and improves the general well-being of those around them. Therefore – to a Leo – wealth is good. Wealth is to be enjoyed to the fullest. Money is not to be left to gather dust in a mouldy bank vault but to be enjoyed, spread around, used. So Leos can be quite reckless in their spending.

With the sign of Virgo on Leo's 2nd money house cusp, Leo needs to develop some of Virgo's traits of analysis, discrimination and purity when it comes to money matters. They must learn to be more careful with the details of finance (or to hire people to do this for them). They have to be more cost-conscious in their spending habits. Generally, they need to manage their money better. Leos tend to chafe under financial constraints, yet these constraints can help Leos to reach their highest financial potential.

Leos like it when their friends and family know that they can depend on them for financial support. They do not mind – and even enjoy – lending money, but they are careful that they are not taken advantage of. From their 'regal throne' Leos like to bestow gifts upon their family and friends and then enjoy the good feelings these gifts bring to everybody. Leos love financial speculations and – when the celestial influences are right – are often lucky.

Career and Public Image

Leos like to be perceived as wealthy, for in today's world wealth often equals power. When they attain wealth they love having a large house with lots of land and animals.

At their jobs Leos excel in positions of authority and power. They are good at making decisions – on a grand level – but they prefer to leave the details to others. Leos are well respected by their colleagues and subordinates, mainly because they have a knack for understanding and relating to those around them. Leos usually strive for the top positions even if they have to start at the bottom and work hard to get there. As might be expected of such a charismatic sign, Leos are always trying to improve their work situation. They do so in order to have a better chance of advancing to the top.

On the other hand, Leos do not like to be bossed around or told what to do. Perhaps this is why they aspire so for the top – where they can be the decision-makers and need not take orders from others.

Leos never doubt their success and focus all their attention and efforts on achieving it. Another great Leo characteristic is that – just like good monarchs – they do not attempt to abuse the power or success they achieve. If they do so this is not wilful or intentional. Usually they like to share their wealth and try to make everyone around them join in their success.

Leos are – and like to be perceived as – hard-working, well-established individuals. It is definitely true that they are capable of hard work and often manage great things. But do not forget that, deep down inside, Leos really are fun-lovers.

Love and Relationships

Generally, Leos are not the marrying kind. To them relationships are good while they are pleasurable. When the relationship ceases to be pleasurable a true Leo will want out. They always want to have the freedom to leave. That is why Leos excel at love affairs rather than commitment. Once married, however, Leo is faithful – even if some Leos have a tendency to marry more than once in their lifetime. If you are in love with a Leo, just show him or her a good time – travel, go to casinos and clubs, the theatre and discos. Wine and dine your Leo love – it is expensive but worth it and you will have fun.

Leos generally have an active love life and are demonstrative in their affections. They love to be with other optimistic and fun-loving types like themselves, but wind up settling with someone more serious, intellectual and unconventional. The partner of a Leo tends to be more political and socially conscious than he or she is, and more libertarian. When you marry a Leo, mastering the freedom-loving tendencies of your partner will definitely become a life-long challenge – and be careful that Leo does not master you.

Aquarius sits on Leo's 7th house of love cusp. Thus if Leos want to realize their highest love and social potential they need to develop a more egalitarian, Aquarian perspective on others. This is not easy for Leo, for 'the king' finds his equals only among other 'kings'. But perhaps this is the solution to Leo's social challenge – to be 'a king among kings'. It is all right to be regal, but recognize the nobility in others.

Home and Domestic Life

Although Leos are great entertainers and love having people over, sometimes this is all show. Only very few close friends will get to see the real side of a Leo's day-to-day life. To a Leo the home is a place of comfort, recreation and transformation; a secret, private retreat – a castle. Leos like to spend money, show off a bit, entertain and have fun. They enjoy the latest furnishings, clothes and gadgets – all things fit for kings.

Leos are fiercely loyal to their family and, of course, expect the same from them. They love their children almost to a fault; they have to be careful not to spoil them too much. They also must try to avoid attempting to make individual family members over in their own image. Leos should keep in mind that others also have the need to be their own people. That is why Leos have to be extra careful about being over-bossy or over-domineering in the home.

Horoscope for 2018

Major Trends

Three Solar Eclipses this year will bring dramatic (more so than usual) personal change. Usually there are only two such eclipses, but this year we have three. With the Sun as your ruling planet, you're very affected by them. Two eclipses – one Solar and one Lunar – will occur in your own sign, and this further reinforces the changes we see. You will be redefining yourself, reinventing yourself, more than usual. Generally the events of the eclipse force the issue. (More on this in the monthly reports).

The main headline this year is Uranus's move from Aries into Taurus. This is major. This year his move is a brief foray – from May 16 to November 6. But next year he will move into Taurus for the long term, for the next seven years. This will affect two important areas of your life – the love life (Uranus is your love planet) and the career (as Taurus is your 10th solar house of career). Health is also affected here as Uranus will be making stressful aspects to you. More on this later.

Jupiter will spend most of the year in your 4th house of home and family. This often shows a move, renovation or the buying of an additional home (sometimes one doesn't buy the home, but has access to it). It also shows happiness from the family. More on this later.

Pluto has been in your 6th house of health and work for ten years now, and this year, Saturn joins him there. This will bring changes to the health regime and a stronger work ethic. You will probably need to work harder this year, and you might feel the job situation could be better. You'll have to grin and bear it. More details later.

Jupiter will move into Sagittarius on November 8 and Uranus will move away from his stressful aspect on November 6. These powerful planets will then be making harmonious aspects to you. So the latter part of the year – the last two months – will be much happier and easier than the previous months. Jupiter in Sagittarius signals more fun in life, more creativity and more involvement with children (in happy ways).

Neptune has been in your 8th house of regeneration for many years (and will be there for many more, too). We have discussed this in previous years and the trends are still in effect. Neptune is spiritualizing your sexuality and sexual attitudes. Sexual activity will be more elevated, more refined. It will become less an act of lust and more an act of worship.

Your most important areas of interest this year are home and family (until November 8); fun, children and personal creativity (from November 8 onwards); health and work; sex, occult studies, personal reinvention; foreign travel, religion, higher education (until May 16 and from November 6 onwards); and career (from May 16 to November 6).

Your paths of greatest fulfilment this year are home and family (until November 8); fun, children and personal creativity (from November 8 onwards); the body, image and personal pleasure (until November 17); and spirituality (from November 17 onwards).

Health

(Please note that this is an astrological perspective on health and not a medical one. In days of yore there was no difference, both of these perspectives were identical. But now there could be quite a difference. For a medical perspective, please consult your doctor or health practitioner.)

Health is basically good this year. Until May 16 only one long-term planet is in stressful alignment with you – Jupiter – and his stresses are not usually serious. On May 16 Uranus will move into a stressful alignment as well, and these two will be the maximum planetary stress (of the long-term planets), through to the beginning of November. And after November 8 both Jupiter and Uranus will move into harmonious alignment with you.

The other good news is that your 6th house of health is very strong this year. You're paying attention here. You're not letting little things develop into big things. With Saturn in your 6th house you seem more open to daily, disciplined health regimes. You seem more disciplined in your health attitudes.

Uranus's move into Taurus will be felt most strongly by those of you born between July 23 and July 26, early in the sign of Leo. Most of you won't feel this too strongly this year (but you will in future years).

Your health is good, but you can make it even better by giving more attention to the following areas – the vulnerable areas of your

Horoscope (the reflex points are shown in the below above). This will tend to prevent problems before they develop.

- The heart. This is always an important area for you, Leo as Leo rules the heart. The important thing here is to avoid worry and anxiety, the two emotions that stress the heart.
- The spine, knees, teeth, skin and overall skeletal alignment. These are also always important for you, as Saturn, the ruler of these areas, is your health planet. This year (and next) they become even more important as Saturn is now in your house of health. So, regular back and knee massage is important. Spinal health is vital, so regular visits to a chiropractor or osteopath would be a good idea. Therapies such as Alexander Technique, Feldenkrais or Rolfing would be good. Yoga and Pilates are also very beneficial for the spine and posture. Make sure you have regular dental check-ups, and if you're out in the sun use a good sun screen. Give the knees more support when you exercise.

Important foot reflexology points for the year ahead

Try to massage all of the foot on a regular basis – the top of the foot as well as the bottom – but pay extra attention to the points highlighted on the chart. When you massage, be aware of 'sore spots' as these need special attention. It's also a good idea to massage the ankles, and especially below them.

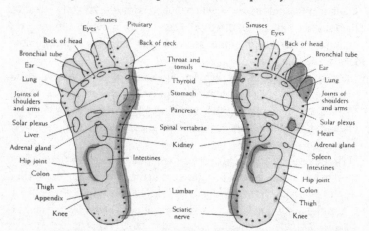

- The colon, bladder and sexual organs. These areas became important when Pluto entered your 6th house in 2008, and they will remain so for many more years. Safe sex and sexual moderation (a big issue for Leo) continues to be important. The tendency of Leo is to overdo this. If you listen to your body and not your mind, you will know when enough is enough. A herbal colon cleanse every now and then – especially when you feel under the weather – might be a good idea.

With Saturn as your health planet you tend to be conservative in health matters and to gravitate to orthodox medicine. This year, with Saturn in his own sign and house, this tendency is even stronger and you tend to shun any new or experimental treatments. You might want to be a bit more flexible in your approach this year.

Pluto is your home and family planet. His position in your 6th house shows that for you good health means a healthy home and family life – domestic harmony. So, if problems (God forbid) arise, bring this area into harmony as quickly as you can. Also work to maintain emotional harmony. Moods should be kept positive and constructive.

Home and Family

Home and family interests have become both happy and important since October 2017, when Jupiter moved into your 4th house. He spends most of the year ahead here. For Leos of childbearing age, this aspect indicates heightened fertility. (This will be true next year as well.)

Often, as we have mentioned, Jupiter in the 4th house will signal a move, home renovations or the acquisition of an additional home. There are many scenarios as to how this happens, but the end result is a larger, more comfortable home. People often buy expensive items for the home too. It is 'as if' one had moved or enlarged the living space.

This aspect shows the prosperity of a parent or parent figure and his or her generosity towards you, too. The family as a whole becomes more prosperous. Your present home increases in value, as does many of the furnishings in the home. It generally shows the fortunate purchase or sale of a home.

The family circle expands this year. Generally this happens through birth or marriage. But often it shows meeting people who are 'like' family to you. You have this feeling towards them and vice versa.

Pluto, your family planet, has been in your 6th house for ten years now. So, there is much focus on the health of the family and family members, and on making the home 'healthier'. Sometimes one spends on getting rid of mould or harmful substances (and they're always finding new threats). Sometimes one buys health equipment or health gadgets for the home. We have written of this in previous years and the trend is still very much in effect. Your home is as much a 'health spa' as a home.

This position also indicates working from home – perhaps setting up a home office or home-based business.

Renovations will go well all year, but January 1 to January 26 seems the best time for this. If you're redecorating or rearranging things in a cosmetic way, or beautifying the home, September 9 to October 5, October 23 to November 22 and December 2 to December 31 seem best. These are also good periods for buying objects of beauty for the home – paintings or sculptures and things of this nature.

The marriage of a parent or parent figure seems stressful this year and will be severely tested. There can be repairs in the home (there are two eclipses in his or her 4th house) but not necessarily a move. Children and children figures in your life are likely to move this year. They become more prosperous from November 8 onwards. Siblings and sibling figures are prospering, but they're better off not moving. Grandchildren (if you have them) have a stable kind of family year.

Finance and Career

With your money house basically empty this year (only short-term planets will move through there) finance is a not a big deal for you. Other things are much more important. Usually this shows a stable situation. You seem basically satisfied with things as they are and have no need to make major changes. You have a lot of financial freedom this year, a lot of free will in this area. But, you lack the interest. The financial passion is not there. If financial problems do occur (God forbid) this is probably the reason. You will need to pay more attention here.

Jupiter in your 4th house for most of the year signals good fortune in real estate or in industries that cater to the home – furniture makers, landscapers, interior designers. It shows a good feeling for the hotel and food industries too, and good family support. Family connections also bring good fortune.

Mercury, your financial planet, is a fast-moving and often erratic planet, and, this would be a good description of your financial life. Sometimes it moves fast, and you make great progress. Sometimes, it moves slowly. And sometimes you feel like you're going backwards. It reflects the movements of Mercury in the heavens. As our regular readers know by now, in any given year Mercury will move through all the sectors of your Horoscope. He will make aspects – good or bad – with every planet in your chart. So, there are many short-term financial trends depending on where Mercury is and the aspects he is receiving. These are best covered in the monthly reports.

The good thing about having Mercury as your financial planet is that money and earnings opportunities can happen in many ways and through many kinds of people and activities.

Mercury will go retrograde three times this year (an improvement over the past two years, where he went retrograde four times in each year). These are times to put the financial life under review and to refrain from making important purchases or investments. Your financial judgement is not up to par during those periods. This year these periods are from March 23 to April 15, July 26 to August 19, and November 17 to December 6.

Finances might not be a big deal this year, but the career will be important with Uranus's move into your career house. Those of you born early in the sign of Leo (from July 23 to July 26) are going to feel this the most in 2018, but in the coming years all of you will feel it. Major career changes will be happening – and they happen suddenly and unexpectedly. It favours a more 'free' kind of career – the freelance life. Many Leos are involved with electronic media. (I would wager that if we did a poll of media figures – especially in the entertainment world – we would find a disproportionate number of Leos, or people strong in the sign.) There will be a lot of changes in your company and industry as well. Over the next few years I wouldn't be surprised if you actually changed your career and career path.

Uranus, is your love planet. His position near your Mid-heaven from May 16 to November 6 shows that your social grace is maybe more important (or at least just as important) as your professional skills. Likeability becomes a factor, so you should cultivate this. It will be important to attend (or perhaps host) the right kind of parties and gatherings. You'll make more career progress in social settings than in the normal, conventional ways.

The spouse, partner or current love seems very successful this year and is perhaps opening doors for you. The same is true of friends and social connections.

Love and Social Life

Though your 7th house is empty this year we do see many changes and upheavals in love. First off, there will be two eclipses in this house – one a Solar Eclipse on February 15 and the second, a Lunar Eclipse on July 27. This will test existing relationships. The good ones – the ones that are basically healthy – tend to survive these things and get even better. But the inherently flawed ones tend to dissolve. But more important than the eclipses is the shift of your love planet from Aries into Taurus, from your 9th to your 10th house. This is not just the shift of a major long-term planet; it signals a shift – a sea change – in your love attitudes and needs. This is more difficult to handle.

Uranus has been Aries for the past seven years and you have been a 'love at first sight' kind of person. You tended to jump into relationships rather quickly and often paid the price for it. You were attracted to the 'excitement' of love – to the adventure, to the conquest. You could fall in and out of love rather quickly. But now (and this is only the beginning) your love planet moves into conservative Taurus. You begin to want more stability in love. You want something that will last. You want 'reliability' and 'steadiness' in a lover. There is a whole shift in psychology. (As we mentioned earlier, those of you born early in the sign of Leo – from July 23 to July 26 – will feel this most strongly this year.)

And since Uranus is hovering around your Mid-heaven – the cusp of your 10th house of career – you are attracted to 'high and mighty' people. People who are already successful. People of status and prestige. Wealth will also be an allurement (much more so than over the past seven years). Wealth and power are exciting these days (especially from May 16 to November 6).

You will find love and romantic opportunities as you pursue your career goals and with people involved in your career. Often this aspect indicates the 'office romance' – a relationship with a boss or someone higher up either in your company or your industry or profession.

You want someone who supports and who can help your career and life work. And you will find this, either this year or in the coming years. Though there are many love and social changes happening, I feel you will be successful in love. Uranus will be the most 'elevated' planet in the chart. Love will be high on your priorities. There will be great focus here – and this is 90 per cent of success. By the spiritual law, we always get what we focus on – good, bad or indifferent.

This position can also be read as love actually being the career. Your mission is really your love life – your marriage and friends – to be there for them.

Uranus in your 10th house shows that you will be mixing socially with powerful people – the 'elites' as they are called. Much of your social life will be career and business related.

Self-Improvement

Jupiter in your 4th house has many more meanings than just home and family, which we have discussed. In esoteric science, your subconscious mind, often called the 'deeper mind', is considered a person's true home. We live in it and the conditions it has created for us (through our conscious or unconscious commands). It is the repository of everything that has ever happened to us – not only in this life, but in past lives. This mind is a slumbering, silent giant, capable of all kinds of supernatural feats, but always under the control of the conscious mind. If there are challenges in life, or undesirable conditions, this mind needs to be understood.

This is a year for getting this deeper understanding. So, those of you in conventional kinds of therapy should make good progress this year. But even if you're not in any formal kind of therapy, you will experience 'nature's therapeutics' this year.

Most people are not suffering from physical, financial or social maladies. These are only the side-effects of deeper issues. Generally they suffer from 'undigested or partially digested experiences'. Things happened in the past that were evaluated by a young, immature mind. Conclusions were reached. Judgements were made. Often passionate statements – negative and destructive affirmations – were made. These, if left unattended, continue to operate in the psyche (and in our affairs) long after they have been consciously forgotten. (Even statements made when we were little children will continue to act in our adult lives on an unconscious level.)

Jupiter in the 4th house is often interpreted as 'nostalgia' – a love for the past. This is true, but this too is only a side-effect. Nature, through the planetary powers, is bringing up old, long-forgotten memories. This will happen out of the blue (seemingly). Often a person has dreams of past events. Or, they might meet a person who reminds them of some past event. And though it might seem 'random' to the conscious mind, these memories are significant. Nature is helping you to confront old experiences that are still active in the mind, and to look at them from your current state of consciousness. What, to the child, is a terrifying trauma is viewed very differently by the adult. When this is realized, the past trauma loses its power and you're free to create new conditions and circumstances. The emotional content is no longer active.

This is not about 'rewriting history'. The facts are still the facts. The events are still the events. But history is being reinterpreted. The meaning of past events will change. And this will make all the difference in the world. In many cases, from your present perspective, you will see some past trauma as a great blessing in your life and actually give thanks for it. It was never what you thought it to be, only the tough love of the cosmos acting in your highest and best interest. Then healing happens.

Month-by-month Forecasts

January

> Best Days Overall: 3, 4, 12, 13, 14, 22, 23, 31
> Most Stressful Days Overall: 10, 11, 17, 18, 25, 26
> Best Days for Love: 4, 5, 6, 13, 14, 15, 16, 17, 18, 19, 23, 24, 27, 28, 31
> Best Days for Money: 1, 2, 3, 4, 5, 6, 10, 11, 15, 16, 20, 21, 25, 26, 29, 30
> Best Days for Career: 5, 6, 15, 16, 25, 26, 27, 28

You begin your year with *all* the planets in the social, Western sector of your Horoscope. This is highly unusual. Only the Moon (and for only half the month) will visit the Eastern sector. Thus this is not a time for personal power struggles or for self-assertion. The planetary power is for others this month. You're a naturally strong and independent kind of person, but right now less so than usual. Adapt to situations as best you can. Seek consensus in all that you do. Let others have their way, so long as it isn't destructive. Let go of your wishes and be for others. If you do this, the month ahead looks happy. On the 20th the Sun enters your 7th house of love and you enter a yearly love and social peak. Your policy of putting others first will make you very popular this period. If you're in a relationship you seem very devoted to the beloved. Those not yet in a relationship will have more romantic opportunity from the 20th onward.

(Putting others first might seem saintly, but it's not really the case from the perspective of Astrology. It's just the cycle you're in at the moment.)

A Lunar Eclipse on the 31st occurs in your own sign, revealing a need to redefine yourself and your image. A need to be clear on who you are and how you want others to perceive you. The eclipsed planet, the Moon, rules your 12th house of spirituality, and thus there are spiritual changes happening. You change your practice, teachers or teachings. Often this comes about through interior revelation – a good thing. Often an eclipse in this house signals shakeups in spiritual or charitable organizations that you're involved with. There are dramas with guru figures in your life. Friends have financial crises and are forced to make changes. The spouse, partner or current love could have a health scare, and there are probably job changes ahead.

Your health needs watching from the 20th onwards, and especially during the eclipse period. Make sure to get enough rest – this is always the most important thing. Then enhance your health in the ways mentioned in the yearly report.

February

Best Days Overall: 9, 10, 19, 27, 28
Most Stressful Days Overall: 6, 7, 14, 15, 21, 22
Best Days for Love: 4, 5, 10, 14, 15, 16, 19, 20, 25, 26, 28
Best Days for Money: 2, 3, 4, 5, 6, 7, 14, 15, 16, 17, 25, 26
Best Days for Career: 4, 5, 16, 21, 22, 25, 26

Health still needs attention until the 18th. A Solar Eclipse on the 15th will not help matters and will have a strong effect on you. Take it easy over that period. Spend more quiet time at home and avoid stressful situations.

This eclipse occurs in your 7th house of love and will test your current relationship (and friendships too). Long-repressed grievances are forced to the surface so that they can be dealt with. Often there are dramatic events in the life of the beloved that complicate things. Be more patient with the beloved and with friends this period. Good relationships survive these things, but flawed ones are in danger.

Every Solar Eclipse affects you on a very personal level, because the Sun rules your Horoscope. This one is no different. It forces a need to redefine yourself, your image and self-concept. (In this sense it is a repeat of last month's Lunar Eclipse.) New events – that come from this month's eclipse – force this new re-evaluation. Over the coming months you will change your wardrobe, hair style and overall presentation (a six-month process that goes on until the next set of eclipses).

A Solar Eclipse in the 7th house often shows an impending change in the marital status. Singles will often decide to marry with this kind of aspect. Married couples (in flawed relationships) will often separate or divorce.

This eclipse affects two other planets, Mercury and Jupiter. Its impact on Mercury shows a need for financial changes – this usually comes because of some financial disturbance or crisis. The events of the eclipse will show you why your financial thinking and strategy have been unrealistic. The impact on Jupiter affects children or children figures in your life. They should stay out of harm's way at this time. They too are forced to redefine themselves. This is not a good period for speculations or for travelling. Avoid these things if you can.

Health and energy improve after the 18th. In the meantime, enhance your health in the ways mentioned in the yearly report.

March

Best Days Overall: 8, 9, 18, 19, 26, 27
Most Stressful Days Overall: 6, 7, 13, 14, 20, 21
Best Days for Love: 8, 9, 13, 14, 18, 19, 26, 27
Best Days for Money: 1, 2, 6, 7, 8, 15, 16, 17, 18, 19, 24, 25, 26, 27, 29, 30
Best Days for Career: 8, 18, 19, 20, 21, 26, 27

Your devotion to others extends to the financial life as well this month. Your financial gift lies in making other people rich. Sometimes this implies material support; sometimes advice or other kinds of help. With your 8th house very strong until the 20th, this is a good period for tax planning. If you are of the appropriate age, it is good for estate planning too.

This is also a good month for detox regimes of all kinds, and for weight loss if you need it. This is a very good month to go through your possessions and get rid of the things you don't need or use. There is something very magical about this. One feels 'lighter', less burdened, less clogged up. The excess baggage is cluttering the mind as well as the physical space. It is a month for prospering by 'pruning' – by getting rid of waste and redundancy. A pruned tree grows better afterwards.

On the 20th your 9th house becomes very strong. This is a whole different psychological approach to life. Under this aspect you are more happy-go-lucky, more like your normal Leo self. There is optimism, travel and the expansion of one's horizons. Students at the university level should have a good month.

Your financial planet, Mercury, will be in your 9th house from the 6th onwards. This shows increased earnings. Foreigners, foreign companies and foreign investments seems good. These kinds of people can be important in your financial life as well.

Pluto has been in your 6th house of health for many years. On the 17th Mars moves into this house as well. You've had a tendency towards surgery for many years and now the tendency is even stronger. If surgery is recommended it would not be a surprise. Sometimes these things are called for, but sometimes not. Keep in mind that cleansing and detoxing are especially powerful this month and will often have the same result as surgery, but will take a little longer.

The upper half of your Horoscope is now dominant. So it is time to focus more on your career and outer objectives. Venus, your career planet, will be in your 9th house from the 6th onwards, which is a good career aspect. The career horizons are enlarged. You are optimistic about the career. Business travel is likely.

April

Best Days Overall: 4, 5, 6, 14, 15, 23, 24
Most Stressful Days Overall: 2, 3, 9, 10, 11, 16, 17, 29
Best Days for Love: 6, 7, 8, 9, 10, 11, 15, 16, 17, 24, 27
Best Days for Money: 2, 3, 4, 5, 6, 12, 13, 14, 15, 21, 22, 23, 24, 25, 26, 29, 30
Best Days for Career: 7, 8, 16, 17, 27

A happy and successful month ahead, Leo. Enjoy!

Your 9th house remains very powerful until the 20th, which is good for those of you involved in legal matters – you have much cosmic help. College level students are succeeding in their studies, and college-bound students should hear good news this month. The urge to travel is also very strong, but Mars conjunct to Saturn from the 1st to the 3rd indicates delays. It will probably be better to schedule these journeys (and they seem business related) for after the 3rd.

The love life will shine this month. Uranus, your love planet, receives positive stimulation. The 17th to the 19th brings happy romantic opportunities for singles. For those already in a relationship it signals more romance within the relationship. It shows a 'closeness' – a togetherness – with the beloved. You're on the same page, physically and philosophically. Foreign travel can bring romance this month. There are romantic opportunities at college or religious functions too.

The financial life is good, but your financial planet is in retrograde motion until the 15th. This won't stop earnings, but it does slow things down a bit. Your financial judgement is not up to its usual standard, so you should avoid rash expenditures – especially of big ticket items – until after the 15th. You tend to be rash in financial matters normally. You like things in a hurry. But this month, with Mercury in Aries you are even more so. Avoid the lure of the 'quick buck'. Financial clarity will be much improved after the 15th. You can also expect increased earnings too.

As we mentioned, the month ahead is successful. Venus spends the entire month in your 10th house, showing that your social grace – your likeability – is ultra-important to your career. Your gift of the gab and good ideas are recognized. On the 20th the Sun crosses the Mid-heaven and enters your career house. You're on top of your game, where you belong. People look up to you. Honours and recognition can come – both for professional achievements and for who you are. Personal appearance and overall demeanour seem important in the career, and you are dressing accordingly.

May

Best Days Overall: 2, 3, 11, 12, 13, 20, 21, 29, 30
Most Stressful Days Overall: 7, 8, 14, 15, 26, 27, 28
Best Days for Love: 3, 7, 8, 13, 17, 22, 26, 31
Best Days for Money: 2, 3, 9, 10, 13, 14, 18, 19, 22, 23, 26, 27, 31
Best Days for Career: 7, 8, 14, 15, 17, 26

This is an eventful kind of month. Many changes, but basically successful. In order for your goals to be achieved changes have to happen, and we see the beginning of this process this month.

Mars makes dynamic aspects with Uranus from the 14th to the 18th. Avoid confrontations and watch the temper at this time. People tend to overreact under this kind of aspect. It is probably not such a good idea to travel over this period either. If you must, try and schedule your trip around these days. The beloved should also take it easy.

You're still in the midst of a yearly career peak and this is where the focus should be. Home and family issues will take care of themselves – your family seems supportive of the career. Uranus makes a major move into your 10th house on the 16th and this brings much change to the career – to your company and industry. Some of you (especially those of you born early in Leo) could change your career path.

Uranus's move into your house of career is good for the love life. It now becomes prominent – important – a major focus in your life. Your social skills are always important careerwise, but now even more so than usual. Make sure to attend or host the right kinds of gatherings. The spouse, partner or current love is also successful this month and is helping your career. He or she is in a position to do so. Now love opportunities happen as you pursue your career path and with people involved in your career. You're attracted to people of power and prestige (and you're meeting and mingling with these kinds of people too).

Health needs watching until the 21st. As always, make sure to get enough rest. Enhance the health in the ways mentioned in the yearly report.

Earnings will be strong this month. Your financial planet Mercury is now moving forward again. Until the 13th he is in your 9th house – the house of expansion. On the 13th he crosses your Mid-heaven and enters your 10th house of career, an aspect that often shows pay rises (official or unofficial). The authority figures in your life are supporting your financial goals. Your increased status leads naturally to more money.

June

Best Days Overall: 8, 9, 16, 17, 25, 26
Most Stressful Days Overall: 3, 4, 10, 11, 23, 24, 30
Best Days for Love: 1, 3, 4, 6, 7, 10, 16, 18, 23, 24, 28, 30
Best Days for Money: 3, 4, 5, 6, 7, 14, 15, 18, 19, 23, 24
Best Days for Career: 6, 7, 10, 11, 16, 23, 24

The planetary power is now moving into the Eastern sector of the self. The Western sector is still strong (this is a trend for the entire year) but you're in a period of more independence these days and changes that you want to make will be easier to accomplish. You are less dependent on others' goodwill (but not completely free to do your own thing). Your challenge these days is to balance your personal interests with those of others. You can't go too far either way. Sometimes your way is best, sometimes the other person's.

Mars entered your 7th house of love on May 16 and is there all of the month ahead. This is a mixed blessing. On the one hand, you might be overly aggressive in love – too pushy. On the other hand it shows an enlargement of the social circle – Mars rules your 9th house of expansion. If you can avoid power struggles with the beloved or prospective romantic partners, things should go well.

Uranus is still in your 10th house this month, still creating sudden changes. In the career anything can happen at any time. The old expression 'expect nothing but be ready for anything' is apposite now. Venus makes beautiful aspects with Jupiter between the 1st and 2nd – and this brings career success. Your career planet is 'out of bounds' from the 1st to the 7th, so you're exploring career paths outside your normal sphere. Perhaps the career demands are pulling you away from your normal horizons.

Earnings look good this month – although there are some bumps in the road. Mercury, your financial planet, moves very quickly through three signs and houses of your Horoscope this month. You're covering much territory and making quick progress. There is also financial confidence. Until the 12th Mercury is in Gemini, your 11th house. This is his own house. He is at 'home' and very powerful on your behalf. It signals the importance of social connections, online activities and the technological world in earnings. On the 12th Mercury enters your spiritual 12th house. Thus the intuition, rather than practical logic, should be your guiding force. There are some financial dramas – perhaps delays – on the 15th and 16th and the 22nd and 23rd. But these are merely short-term hiccups. The 19th and 20th brings a nice payday as Mercury trines Jupiter. Speculations are more favourable in that period, but good luck can come in other forms too. On the 29th Mercury crosses your Ascendant and enters your 1st house, bringing financial windfalls and opportunity. It is a prosperous month.

July

Best Days Overall: 5, 6, 14, 15, 22, 23, 24
Most Stressful Days Overall: 1, 7, 8, 20, 21, 27, 28, 29
Best Days for Love: 1, 5, 6, 7, 16, 25, 26, 27, 28, 29
Best Days for Money: 1, 5, 6, 12, 13, 14, 15, 16, 17, 20, 21, 22, 23, 24, 27, 28, 29
Best Days for Career: 5, 6, 7, 8, 16, 25, 26

A basically happy month, Leo, but two eclipses this month shake things up and bring about needed changes. These changes are not always pleasant in the short term, but in the long term they are good. Both eclipses affect you strongly, so reduce your schedule over these periods.

The Solar Eclipse of the 13th occurs in your 12th house of spirituality. This can bring shakeups – turmoil – in a spiritual or charitable organization you're involved with. It often brings dramatic events in the lives of guru figures in your life. There are changes in your spiritual regime – in your teachings and practice. The dream life will be more active this period, but not very significant. Much of it is just psychic flotsam and jetsam caused by the eclipse. More importantly, this eclipse (and there will be another one next month too) forces a personal review - a personal re-evaluation - a redefinition of who you are, your self-concept and the image you project to others. It is important now for you to define yourself for yourself, otherwise others will define you and this is usually not pleasant. Over the next six months, your image - the face you present to the public - your personal 'look' will be changed. This is in accord with spiritual law. Change the way you think and your appearance will follow suit. This eclipse impacts on Pluto, your family planet, so there can be dramas in the family over the next six months or so, and a need for repairs in the home. A parent or parent figure experiences personal, life-changing dramas.

The Lunar Eclipse of the 27th also has a strong effect. It occurs in your 7th house of love and will test a current relationship or business partnership. Often there are dramas in the lives of these people that cause the testing. Often old dirty laundry is dug up for cleaning. Good relationships survive these things - and get even better. It is the flawed ones that are in danger. Since this eclipse impacts on Uranus, your love planet, everything we've just said is magnified. Mars is affected by this eclipse too. Thus it is not wise to be travelling during the period of the eclipse. (In addition, Mars is also retrograde all month.) College-level students can make important changes in their educational plans. A legal matter (if you're involved in something like this) starts to take a dramatic turn, one way or another. There are shakeups in your place of worship.

August

Best Days Overall: 1, 2, 3, 10, 11, 19, 20, 29, 30
Most Stressful Days Overall: 4, 5, 16, 17, 24, 25, 31
Best Days for Love: 4, 5, 12, 14, 15, 21, 24, 25, 31
Best Days for Money: 1, 2, 3, 8, 9, 10, 11, 12, 13, 16, 17, 19, 20, 26, 27, 29, 30
Best Days for Career: 4, 5, 14, 15, 24, 25, 31

Another eclipse, a rare third Solar Eclipse of the year, occurs on the 11th. All Solar Eclipses affect you strongly, but this one more so than normal. It occurs in your own sign of Leo. Once again you're forced to redefine yourself, to re-evaluate who you are and how you want others to think of you. It brings a change of the personality and image. Changes that weren't made last month are made now. If you haven't been careful in dietary matters, this kind of eclipse can produce a detox of the body. This is not disease, though it can feel this way. It is cleansing. Cooperate with it. Partners and friends can have crises in their love relationships now. Bosses and elders are having family dramas. Health is good this month, but take it easy over the period of the eclipse, for a few days before the 11th and a few days after.

Since July 22 you have been in the best period of the year for changing irksome conditions. Take advantage of this, as later on it will be more difficult. The Sun in your sign brings energy and star quality to the image. You look great. You have energy and charisma. Finances are also good – although earnings are slower than usual. There are glitches and delays. Mercury, your financial planet, is retrograde until the 19th. In spite of this, the month should be prosperous (as long as you handle the delays). Mercury is in your own sign. You look wealthy and feel wealthy and others see you this way. The eclipse might shake your confidence and self-esteem, but once the period is over your natural self-confidence will returns, perhaps even stronger than before.

There are still many changes going on in your career, in your company and in your industry, but now it's time to be more involved with the family and home. Your emotional wellness is important now. Venus has her 'solstice' from the 5th to the 9th. She pauses in the heavens (in her latitudinal motion) and then changes direction. This is what is happening in the career too.

Mercury goes forward again on the 19th, and the Sun enters your money house on the 23rd. So you can expect greater prosperity from the 19th onwards. From the 23rd onward you will be in a yearly financial peak.

September

Best Days Overall: 7, 15, 16, 25, 26
Most Stressful Days Overall: 1, 13, 14, 20, 21, 27, 28
Best Days for Love: 1, 2, 3, 8, 9, 13, 17, 20, 21, 22, 23, 27
Best Days for Money: 4, 5, 9, 13, 14, 18, 19, 22, 23, 24, 29
Best Days for Career: 1, 2, 3, 13, 22, 23, 27, 28

Mars has been 'out of bounds' since July 9 and this continues for most of the month ahead – until the 24th. Thus college students are moving 'outside the box' in their studies – experimenting with new ways and new educational subjects. Same old, same old seems boring. This is also happening in your religious life. You're exploring other religions and philosophies and looking for answers that are not in your own native tradition. This is basically healthy. Many of you are also travelling to exotic places – or, rather, to places you would normally never visit.

Finance is the main headline this month. You're still in the midst of a yearly financial peak (this continues until the 22nd). Earnings are strong. You're focused here. The ruler of your Horoscope in your money house is always a positive financial indicator. He is always friendly to you – always helpful. You spend on yourself, you adopt the image of wealth and you 'feel' wealthier than usual. Probably you're flaunting it more to the world. (Leos love to flaunt!) Mercury, your financial planet, is moving forward all month and very quickly. This shows fast financial progress; fast (and generally accurate) financial decision making. Until the 6th, Mercury is in your sign – a positive financial signal. He brings windfalls and financial opportunity and you don't need to go looking for it. The money people in your life are favourably disposed to you. On the 6th he enters your money house (his own sign and house), where he is extra powerful on your behalf. You will probably spend more on health and health products but you can earn from this as well. Financial judgement is sound too and the details of finance are easily handled. By the 22nd, as both Mercury and the Sun leave your money house, your short-term financial goals should have been achieved and you can focus on other things – education, reading, intellectual interests and pastimes.

Venus, your career planet, moves into your 4th house of home and family on the 9th. This, couple with most of the planets being below the horizon as well, indicate that now your mission, your career, is the home and family. Sometimes this shows pursuing the career from home.

Health is good this month. Those of you born early in the sign of Leo (July 22–25) need to be more careful healthwise, but for the rest of you, health is basically good. You can enhance it further in the ways mentioned in the yearly report.

October

Best Days Overall: 4, 5, 12, 13, 14, 22, 23, 31
Most Stressful Days Overall: 10, 11, 17, 18, 19, 25, 26
Best Days for Love: 2, 3, 6, 10, 11, 15, 17, 18, 19, 20, 21, 24, 25, 29, 30
Best Days for Money: 1, 2, 3, 6, 7, 9, 10, 11, 20, 21, 29, 30
Best Days for Career: 2, 3, 10, 11, 20, 21, 25, 26, 29, 30

The ruler of your Horoscope is in Libra until the 23rd, so you have more social grace these days, however it doesn't seem to be helping the love life. Mars, the planet of war and conflict, will be in your 7th house of love all month. And, later in the month, the Sun will oppose your love planet Uranus. Love can work out, but it is going to take a lot more effort on your part (and the beloved's). Try not to make matters worse by getting involved in power struggles with the beloved. Respect your differences. You and the beloved see things from opposite perspectives these days. If you can bridge these differences, things can work out and be stronger than before.

Your 4th house of home and family is easily the strongest house in the chart this month. Half of the planets are either there or moving through there. This is a lot of energy. Moreover, your career planet Venus spends the month in the 4th house, which just emphasizes its importance. Your real career at the moment is the home and family – to be there for the family. Venus is going retrograde on the 5th while your family planet, Pluto, is moving forward on the 2nd – another indication to pay more attention to the family. Career matters will resolve in a month or two – they need time. So, you might as well focus on the family.

With both your financial planet (from the 10th) and your career planet (all month) in the 4th house, the message of the Horoscope is stay in emotional harmony, get the family situation right, and finance and career will fall into place naturally.

Finances look strong this month. Until the 10th Mercury is in Libra, your 3rd house. This favours sales, marketing and communication activities. Financial opportunities happen in your neighbourhood. This aspect favours retailing and trading too. Neighbours can play an important role in the financial life. When Mercury moves into your 4th house after the 10th, it shows family support and family connections. It favours residential real estate, the food business, hotels and industries that cater to the home. It favours earning money from home – from a home office or home-based business.

This is a good month to move or buy an additional home. It is also good for beautifying the home or redecorating it.

Perhaps the most important function of the 4th house is to restore emotional harmony – to digest and come to terms with the past. Those of you involved in formal types of therapy will make good progress.

November

Best Days Overall: 1, 9, 10, 19, 20, 27, 28
Most Stressful Days Overall: 6, 7, 8, 14, 15, 21, 22
Best Days for Love: 2, 4, 5, 10, 14, 15, 20, 23, 24, 28
Best Days for Money: 1, 2, 3, 8, 9, 10, 19, 20, 27, 28, 29, 30
Best Days for Career: 4, 5, 14, 15, 21, 22, 23, 24

Love is getting much easier this month. The beloved is backing away from a previous position to a position that is more harmonious to you. Mars will move out of your 7th house on the 16th. Love will be even better next month.

Your 4th house is still strong until the 22nd. So continue to focus on the home, family and your emotional wellness. This will lay the groundwork for your future career push, which will start next year. Your career planet is still retrograde – until the 16th – so career matters need more research and study. Important decisions shouldn't be made just yet. When Venus starts moving forward on the 16th you can further the career through good marketing and good communication. The career planet in the 3rd house is a good aspect for students below college level. It shows focus on their studies and success. Good grades, learning what needs to be learned, is seen as their mission in life these days.

Jupiter makes a major move into your 5th house on the 8th – a very happy transit. Not only will it bring prosperity for the next twelve months, but fun, happiness and enhanced creativity. Leo is one of the most creative signs in the zodiac and these days even more so. This is a party time of the year in general, but for you especially. More so than in past years.

Leos love speculation. But now this love is even greater than usual. On the 22nd, the Sun moves into your 5th house and starts to travel with Jupiter. The casinos and night spots are calling to you.

Mercury, your financial planet, spends the month in your 5th house. This is generally a good financial signal. It shows happy money, money that is earned while you're having fun. Generally it favours speculation, but after the 17th Mercury starts to move backwards, which complicates things. If you're going to speculate (and it is difficult to see how you won't), do so with half (or even a quarter) of what you originally intended. There is a very nice payday on the 29th or 30th as Mercury travels with Jupiter, but there could be delays involved.

Health is good this month, but will get even better after the 22nd. Until then, enhance the health in the ways mentioned in the yearly report.

December

Best Days Overall: 6, 7, 16, 17, 25, 26
Most Stressful Days Overall: 4, 5, 11, 12, 18, 19, 31
Best Days for Love: 2, 3, 7, 11, 12, 14, 15, 17, 23, 24, 26
Best Days for Money: 4, 5, 6, 13, 16, 23, 24, 26, 27, 28
Best Days for Career: 2, 3, 14, 15, 18, 19, 23, 24

There's no need to lecture Leo on the importance of enjoying life. You are our teachers in that department. You're still very much in a yearly personal pleasure peak until the 21st, and so let the good times roll! For singles the month ahead is more about love affairs than serious romance. However, there is a serious love opportunity around the 20th and 21st. Your love planet is still retrograde however, so there's no need to rush into anything.

Mercury starts moving forward on the 6th and the financial judgement is much clearer after then. Until the 13th he is in your 4th house, signalling good family support and someone who also spends on the home and family. Family connections are important in the financial life. On the 13th Mercury will move into your 5th house and we have a repeat of last month, only better. Last month Mercury was retrograde. Now he is direct. This aspect shows, like last month, happy money – money that is earned in happy ways and that is spent on joyful things. Speculations are favourable from the 13th onwards, and especially from the 20th to the 22nd. That period is an especially good financial period and you will gain one way or another (the cosmos has many ways to prosper you). The main danger with your financial planet in your 5th house is over-spending. One can be unrealistically over-confident. So try to keep this in check.

Health and energy are super these days. When Jupiter moved out of Scorpio last month, the last stressful planet moved away from you. Only Venus (and she is mild) is making a stressful aspect. So you have energy to spare. If there have been pre-existing conditions they are in abeyance. On the 21st, the Sun moves into your 6th house and will be there until January 18 next year. You are focused on health – perhaps overly so. But it is a good aspect for setting up long-term health regimes.

Your powerful 6th house from the 21st onwards is also wonderful for doing those boring, detailed jobs that need to be done – but which you usually put off. Now you will have the energy and patience for them.

Children and children figures in your life are going to have a fabulous year ahead. Jupiter is giving them a grand lifestyle – travel, good food, nice clothing, etc. If these children are of childbearing age, they are very fertile now. This month – after the 21st – they enter a yearly financial peak. For them, the challenge is good financial management.

Virgo

♍

THE VIRGIN

Birthdays from
22nd August to
22nd September

Personality Profile

VIRGO AT A GLANCE

Element – Earth

Ruling Planet – Mercury
  Career Planet – Mercury
  Love Planet – Neptune
  Money Planet – Venus
  Planet of Home and Family Life – Jupiter
  Planet of Health and Work – Uranus
  Planet of Pleasure – Saturn
  Planet of Sexuality – Mars

Colours – earth tones, ochre, orange, yellow

Colour that promotes love, romance and social harmony – aqua blue

Colour that promotes earning power – jade green

Gems – agate, hyacinth

Metal – quicksilver

Scents – lavender, lilac, lily of the valley, storax

Quality – mutable (= flexibility)

Quality most needed for balance – a broader perspective

Strongest virtues – mental agility, analytical skills, ability to pay attention to detail, healing powers

Deepest needs – to be useful and productive

Characteristic to avoid – destructive criticism

Signs of greatest overall compatibility – Taurus, Capricorn

Signs of greatest overall incompatibility – Gemini, Sagittarius, Pisces

Sign most helpful to career – Gemini

Sign most helpful for emotional support – Sagittarius

Sign most helpful financially – Libra

Sign best for marriage and/or partnerships – Pisces

Sign most helpful for creative projects – Capricorn

Best Sign to have fun with – Capricorn

Signs most helpful in spiritual matters – Taurus, Leo

Best day of the week – Wednesday

Understanding a Virgo

The virgin is a particularly fitting symbol for those born under the sign of Virgo. If you meditate on the image of the virgin you will get a good understanding of the essence of the Virgo type. The virgin is, of course, a symbol of purity and innocence – not naïve, but pure. A virginal object has not been touched. A virgin field is land that is true to itself, the way it has always been. The same is true of virgin forest: it is pristine, unaltered.

Apply the idea of purity to the thought processes, emotional life, physical body and activities and projects of the everyday world, and you can see how Virgos approach life. Virgos desire the pure expression of the ideal in their mind, body and affairs. If they find impurities they will attempt to clear them away.

Impurities are the beginning of disorder, unhappiness and uneasiness. The job of the Virgo is to eject all impurities and keep only that which the body and mind can use and assimilate.

The secrets of good health are here revealed: 90 per cent of the art of staying well is maintaining a pure mind, a pure body and pure emotions. When you introduce more impurities than your mind and body can deal with, you will have what is known as 'dis-ease'. It is no wonder that Virgos make great doctors, nurses, healers and dieticians. They have an innate understanding of good health and they realize that good health is more than just physical. In all aspects of life, if you want a project to be successful it must be kept as pure as possible. It must be protected against the adverse elements that will try to undermine it. This is the secret behind Virgo's awesome technical proficiency.

One could talk about Virgo's analytical powers – which are formidable. One could talk about their perfectionism and their almost superhuman attention to detail. But this would be to miss the point. All of these virtues are manifestations of a Virgo's desire for purity and perfection – a world without Virgos would have ruined itself long ago.

A vice is nothing more than a virtue turned inside out, misapplied or used in the wrong context. Virgos' apparent vices come from their inherent virtue. Their analytical powers, which should be used for healing, helping or perfecting a project in the world, sometimes get misapplied and turned against people. Their critical faculties, which should be used constructively to perfect a strategy or proposal, can sometimes be used destructively to harm or wound. Their urge to perfection can turn into worry and lack of confidence; their natural humility can become self-denial and self-abasement. When Virgos turn negative they are apt to turn their devastating criticism on themselves, sowing the seeds of self-destruction.

Finance

Virgos have all the attitudes that create wealth. They are hard-working, industrious, efficient, organized, thrifty, productive and eager to serve. A developed Virgo is every employer's dream. But until Virgos master some of the social graces of Libra they will not even come close to fulfilling their financial potential. Purity and perfectionism, if not handled correctly or gracefully, can be very trying to others. Friction in human relationships can be devastating not only to your pet projects but – indirectly – to your wallet as well.

Virgos are quite interested in their financial security. Being hard-working, they know the true value of money. They do not like to take risks with their money, preferring to save for their retirement or for a rainy day. Virgos usually make prudent, calculated investments that involve a minimum of risk. These investments and savings usually work out well, helping Virgos to achieve the financial security they seek. The rich or even not-so-rich Virgo also likes to help his or her friends in need.

Career and Public Image

Virgos reach their full potential when they can communicate their knowledge in such a way that others can understand it. In order to get their ideas across better, Virgos need to develop greater verbal skills and fewer judgemental ways of expressing themselves. Virgos look up to teachers and communicators; they like their bosses to be good communicators. Virgos will probably not respect a superior who is not their intellectual equal – no matter how much money or power that superior has. Virgos themselves like to be perceived by others as being educated and intellectual.

The natural humility of Virgos often inhibits them from fulfilling their great ambitions, from acquiring name and fame. Virgos should indulge in a little more self-promotion if they are going to reach their career goals. They need to push themselves with the same ardour that they would use to foster others.

At work Virgos like to stay active. They are willing to learn any type of job as long as it serves their ultimate goal of financial security. Virgos may change occupations several times during their professional lives, until they find the one they really enjoy. Virgos work well with other people, are not afraid to work hard and always fulfil their responsibilities.

Love and Relationships

If you are an analyst or a critic you must, out of necessity, narrow your scope. You have to focus on a part and not the whole; this can create a temporary narrow-mindedness. Virgos do not like this kind of person. They like their partners to be broad-minded, with depth and vision. Virgos seek to get this broad-minded quality from their partners, since they sometimes lack it themselves.

Virgos are perfectionists in love just as they are in other areas of life. They need partners who are tolerant, open-minded and easy-going. If you are in love with a Virgo do not waste time on impractical romantic gestures. Do practical and useful things for him or her – this is what will be appreciated and what will be done for you.

Virgos express their love through pragmatic and useful gestures, so do not be put off because your Virgo partner does not say 'I love you' day-in and day-out. Virgos are not that type. If they love you, they will demonstrate it in practical ways. They will always be there for you; they will show an interest in your health and finances; they will fix your sink or repair your video recorder. Virgos deem these actions to be superior to sending flowers, chocolates or Valentine cards.

In love affairs Virgos are not particularly passionate or spontaneous. If you are in love with a Virgo, do not take this personally. It does not mean that you are not alluring enough or that your Virgo partner does not love or like you. It is just the way Virgos are. What they lack in passion they make up for in dedication and loyalty.

Home and Domestic Life

It goes without saying that the home of a Virgo will be spotless, sanitized and orderly. Everything will be in its proper place – and don't you dare move anything about! For Virgos to find domestic bliss they need to ease up a bit in the home, to allow their partner and children more freedom and to be more generous and open-minded. Family members are not to be analysed under a microscope, they are individuals with their own virtues to express.

With these small difficulties resolved, Virgos like to stay in and entertain at home. They make good hosts and they like to keep their friends and families happy and entertained at family and social gatherings. Virgos love children, but they are strict with them – at times – since they want to make sure their children are brought up with the correct sense of family and values.

Horoscope for 2018

Major Trends

Saturn's move out of Sagittarius late last year is a great thing for you. You feel as if a major burden has been taken off your shoulders. You have more energy and optimism, and health will definitely improve. More on this later.

Jupiter spends most of the year in your 3rd house of communication and intellectual interests. So this is a great year for expanding your knowledge, for taking courses in subjects that interest you and for doing more reading. Students below college level will be successful in school. The mind is sharp and absorbs information quickly. It is also a wonderful aspect for writers, teachers, journalists and bloggers. You communicate well and easily. Sales, marketing, PR and advertising people should also do well. Their skills are enhanced.

On November 8 Jupiter will move into his own sign and house – where he can operate in a much stronger fashion. This shows moves (fortunate ones) or renovations of the existing home. The family circle gets enlarged. More details later.

Late last year – very late – Saturn made a major move from your 4th to your 5th house, where he'll remain for the year ahead (and next year too). You will need to be more selective in your leisure pursuits. Perhaps you will cut back on these things. Those of you in the creative arts will have to be more disciplined in your creativity. Children and children figures seem more difficult to handle.

Pluto has been in your 5th house for many years now – since 2008. So the above areas have been undergoing radical change anyway. Children or children figures could have had surgery or near-death kinds of experiences. On the other hand, they seem focused on their school work and are probably doing well in school.

The most notable headline this year is Uranus's major, major move from Aries into Taurus, your 9th house. Since Uranus is your health and work planet, this is signalling job changes and changes in your health regime and health needs. More on this later.

Neptune has been in your 7th house of love for many years now. We have discussed this in previous years and the trend is still very much in effect (not trying to be repetitious here). There is still great idealism in love, with all the good and bad points that this brings. The whole love life – the love attitudes – are becoming more spiritualized. Again, there are more details later.

Your most important areas of interest this year are communication and intellectual interests (until November 8); home and family (from November 8 onwards); children, fun and personal creativity; love and romance; sex, occult studies, personal transformation (from January 1 to May 6 and from November 6 onwards); and foreign travel, religion and higher education (from May 16 to November 6).

Your paths of greatest fulfilment this year will be communication and intellectual interests (until November 8); home and family (from November 8 onwards); spirituality (until November 17); and friends, groups and group activities (from November 17 onwards).

Health

(Please note that this is an astrological perspective on health and not a medical one. In days of yore there was no difference, both of these perspectives were identical. But now there could be quite a difference. For a medical perspective, please consult your doctor or health practitioner.)

Health is always important to a Virgo and this year we see many, many changes here. This is in spite of the fact that health is unusually good. There is only one long-term planet in stressful alignment with you; the others are either making harmonious aspects or leaving you alone. Saturn's move into Capricorn late last year, and Uranus's move into Taurus this year are also enhancing the health. It is only later in the year – after November 8 – that another long-term planet begins to put stress on you. This will be Jupiter, and his effects are usually mild.

Health may be good this year, but you're still making important changes. There will be two eclipses in your 6th house this year – a Solar Eclipse on February 15 and a Lunar Eclipse on July 27. This always produces change, and sometimes it produces a health scare. But since your energy is so good, it is not likely to be anything more than that.

Uranus, your health planet, will be making a brief excursion into your 9th house this year. This will also bring much change. During his stay in Taurus the head, face and scalp – which have been important for the past seven years – become less important. Physical exercise – though a good thing – can be down-played as well. You will feel all these changes more strongly next year, as Uranus moves into Taurus for the long haul.

Good though your health is, you can make it even better. And what Virgo doesn't want better health? Give more attention to the following areas – the most vulnerable areas of your chart (the reflex points are shown overleaf). This attention is likely to prevent problems from developing, and even if they do (because of strong karmic momentum) they will be much less severe – more like annoyances than disease.

- The small intestine, which is always important to Virgo.
- The ankles and calves are also always important to Virgo. Uranus, the planet that rules these areas, is your health planet, so regular massage of the ankles and calves (and the shin bone as well)

Important foot reflexology points for the year ahead

Try to massage all of the foot on a regular basis – the top of the foot as well as the bottom – but pay extra attention to the points highlighted on the chart. When you massage, be aware of 'sore spots' as these need special attention. It will also be good to massage the ankles.

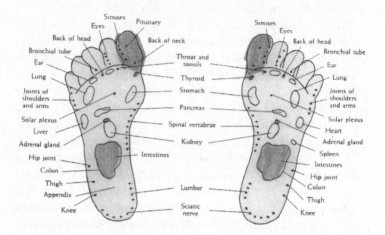

should be part of your normal health regime. Give the ankles more support when you exercise.

- The head, face and scalp. These have become important since Uranus has been in Aries for the past few years. So continue to massage these areas regularly (especially until May 16 and from November 6 onwards). Craniosacral therapy is also good for the head.

- The musculature has been important for the past seven years and is still important for a while this year (until May 16 and from November 6 onwards). So it is still important to maintain good muscle tone. Weak or flabby muscles will knock the spine and skeleton out of alignment and this will create all kinds of other problems. So, vigorous exercise – according to your age and stage in life – is important.

- The adrenals have also been important for the past seven years. It is important to avoid anger and fear as these two emotions stress the adrenals.

- The neck and throat start to become important from May 16 to November 6. Neck massage will be good. Tension tends to collect here and needs to be released. Craniosacral therapy is good for the neck as well.

With Uranus as your health planet, you tend to be experimental in health matters. You like to follow the 'latest', most trendy therapies or diets. This coming year (and in future years) you become a bit more conservative in health matters, and less likely to embrace the 'new' merely because it is new. You will be slower to make changes.

Home and Family

Your 4th house is not a house of power for most of the year. But this will change, as we mentioned, after November 8 as Jupiter moves into this house. Until then you're more or less treading water here.

However, Jupiter in your 3rd house can be read as in the spiritual 12th house of the family. (Make the 4th house the 1st house – since we're dealing with family – and count forward.) Thus the family – and especially one of the parents or parent figures in your life – are in a highly spiritual kind of period for much of this year. There is much internal growth happening – behind the scenes growth – which will become visible after November 8 and well into next year.

This parent or parent figure seems financially stressed. He or she is reorganizing the finances. It's not more income that they need, just better financial management – better use of their existing resources. Usually the problem is caused by taking on some additional financial responsibility. They can feel a sense of lack even if they are prospering on the objective level. The feeling is still there. Their financial picture changes for the better after November 8.

Jupiter in the 4th house brings happiness in the home and with the family. If there have been problems, there is much relief. Even good fortune. The family as a whole becomes more prosperous. Your home, and perhaps your furnishings, become more valuable. Family support will be better than usual and family connections will also tend to be helpful.

As we mentioned, this aspect often brings a move and the fortunate purchase or sale of a home. But this need not be taken too literally. Often the existing home is renovated. Perhaps a new extension or a new room is added. This would also fit the symbolism. Often expensive items are purchased for the home. Equally, often there is the purchase of another home (or, you discover that you have access to a second home). The whole effect is 'as if' you had moved, 'as if' the home was enlarged, 'as if' you are in new and better domestic circumstances.

Virgos of childbearing age start to become more fertile from November 8 onwards, and this will be the case for the next two years. Jupiter in the 4th house signals the enlargement of the family circle. Generally this happens through birth or marriage, but sometimes this happens through meeting people who are 'like' family to you. You have this feeling towards them and vice versa.

Renovations or major repairs will go better from January 26 to March 17 and from November 8 onwards. If you're beautifying the home – repainting or redecorating in a cosmetic kind of way – November 22 to December 21 is a good time for this.

Parents or parent figures will probably not move this year. One of the parents is having a very strong love and social year. If he or she is single, there is romance. Siblings and sibling figures are prospering this year. There are some shakeups in the home (probably some repairs) but a move is more likely next year. Children and children figures in your life have probably had multiple moves in recent years. There could be more this year, but they seem ready for more stability, ready to settle down. Grandchildren (if you have them) seem very unsettled and restless. They might not move, but they will live in different places for long periods of time.

Finance and Career

The last two years were banner financial years for you, Virgo. Most of your financial goals (the short-term ones at least) have been attained and you don't seem that focused or concerned about money this year. Your empty money house shows a lot of freedom here, but the focus – the interest – is not there. This tends to the status quo.

This lack of attention is perhaps the major financial weakness these days. But then again, if nothing's wrong why focus?

Jupiter, as we have mentioned, spends most of the year in your 3rd house. This would indicate a new car (and a good one) and new communication equipment (also good quality). It shows the prosperity of siblings and sibling figures in your life. You earn from your communication and intellectual skills. It favours, as we have mentioned, sales, marketing, writing, teaching, blogging, advertising and PR. Trading – buying and selling – would also be favoured.

Venus is your financial planet, and she is an excellent one to have. This is her natural domain and she is strong in this role. But she is a fast-moving planet. In any given year she will move through all the sectors of your Horoscope (although this year, because of her retrograde period, she will only move through 11 of your 12 houses). So there are many short-term financial trends that depend on where Venus is and the aspects she is receiving. These are best covered in the monthly reports.

Venus, because of her retrograde, will spend an unusual amount of time in your money house – from August 7 to September 9 and again from November 11 to December 2. This is a signal for prosperity, but perhaps not as great as you have had in the past two years.

Venus will be retrograde (a rare occurrence compared with the other planets) from October 5 to November 16. This will be a time to put your finances under review. A time to gain clarity on your financial goals and the improvements you want to make. It will not be especially good for making important financial moves.

This is not a particularly strong career year. Most of the long-term planets are below the horizon of your chart. Your 10th house of career is not a house of power and, with the exception of the short-term planets, it is basically empty. The year ahead is more about gaining internal harmony; about feeling right rather than doing right. Doing right will come later on.

With fast-moving Mercury as your career planet, there will be many short-term career trends that depend on where he is and the aspects he receives. This too is best covered in the monthly reports.

Love and Social Life

Neptune, as we have mentioned, has been in your 7th house of love for some years now, and will be there for many more to come. Neptune, the most spiritual and idealistic of all the planets, is not only your love planet, but he is in his own sign and house. Thus he is even more spiritual, more idealistic, than usual. So, you're looking for the ideal love, the perfect love. Your standards are very, very high. It is doubtful that any mortal human could live up to them. There are many loving human beings out there, but the fact that they're human – in mortal bodies – puts some limitation on this. So, these imperfections can create a subtle feeling of dissatisfaction.

Often, with Neptune involved in love, there is a tendency to 'idealize' the partner. To project a perfection that doesn't really exist. This is the psyche's attempt, like Pygmalion, to create the ideal love. But, of course, every now and then reality breaks through and a sense of disappointment comes in. Still, it is fun while the illusion lasts. Everyone more or less knows that romance is 90 per cent magic and only 10 per cent logic. So as long as you can keep the magic going, there is happiness.

Having said all the above, the year ahead is going to be a happy love and social year. You're in the mood for romance. Jupiter is making beautiful aspects to your love planet almost all year – until November 8. So if you're unattached, you're pretty certain to meet someone special – the cosmos will bring the opportunity to you. Singles will date more and attend more parties. Those who are married should have more harmony and romance within the marriage, and they too will be socializing more and making new and significant friends. The family and family connections seem to be playing an important role in the love life – perhaps by playing Cupid.

With Neptune so involved in love, the spiritual connection – the spiritual compatibility – is ultra-important. With spiritual compatibility almost every problem can be worked out. But without it, even little things can be insurmountable. Thus you are attracted to spiritual types of people. You find musicians, poets, psychics, spiritual channels alluring. Romantic opportunities happen in spiritual settings – the prayer meeting, the meditation or spiritual seminar, the charity event or the yoga weekend. If you're running to the bars and clubs in search of love, you're just wasting your time. You might find entertainment in these places, but not love.

Those of you in your second marriage will have the marriage tested this year. Those working towards the third marriage are better off not marrying. The love life will be exciting, but there is no need for commitment. Those in or working on the third marriage will have a stable kind of year. Those who are married will most likely stay married, singles will most likely stay single.

Self-Improvement

There are many dramatic changes happening in your spiritual life this year. A lot of attitudes and opinions will get blasted away. There will be changes in your practice, your teachings and perhaps your teachers. The Sun, your spiritual planet, will get eclipsed three times this year – usually this only happens twice. Further, there will be two eclipses in your 12th house of spirituality – one a Lunar Eclipse the other a Solar. So, four out of the five eclipses this year directly impact here. Realize that these things – these shakeups and changes – are for your good. They will advance you on your path. Often what holds us back are false ideas and concepts of what spirituality is. These things need to be blasted away so that something authentic can come in.

With the Sun as your spiritual planet you would gravitate to the solar-oriented paths – the esoteric side of Christianity would be comfortable. The path of beauty and creativity would also be comfortable. The same laws that go into creating a painting or sculpture – or any other work of art – are the same laws that the Divine used to create the Universe. We learn about the creator by becoming mini-creators.

With spiritual Neptune in your 7th house of love and as your love planet, the path of love and devotion is powerful for you. You feel close to the Divine when you are in love. It is a challenging path, but powerful.

Neptune in your 7th house is not only making you idealistic about romance, but is executing a higher agenda. This is a long-term process. You are being led, step by step, through exaltations and disappointments, to spiritual love. This is above 'romantic' love. This love, when you contact it, will always love you perfectly and always supply every need in love. Every need means just that, no matter what it is. You will always feel like you're on your honeymoon, whether you're in a relationship or not. It is all the same. Each has different joys.

If the love life gets too complicated, or you feel overwhelmed and inadequate, your Horoscope is advising the 'surrender' of the love life to the Divine. Make a complete surrender with no equivocations. If this is done, you will find the whole love situation magically straightening out.

Get right spiritually and you will always have love.

Uranus is making a major move into your 9th house this year. This year it is a brief visit – an announcement of things to come. But next year he will move into your 9th house for the long haul. So, along with all the spiritual changes, there will be philosophical changes – changes (and dramatic ones) in your personal religion and philosophy of life. This relates to your spirituality but is not the same thing. Your belief systems will get tested and many of your beliefs will get shattered. Some of them should get shattered – often what passes for religion is nothing more than superstition.

Since Uranus is your health planet many of your philosophical beliefs about health and disease will get changed. This too is for your good. If you have a worldly perspective on this – the prevailing perspective – then you are subject to all kinds of needless ills. But if you understand the spiritual philosophy of health and disease, you become more immune to things. And, you have more tools at your disposal for when problems do arise.

Month-by-month Forecasts

January

Best Days Overall: 5, 6, 15, 16, 25, 26
Most Stressful Days Overall: 12, 13, 14, 20, 21, 27, 28
Best Days for Love: 1, 2, 5, 6, 10, 11, 15, 16, 20, 21, 27, 28, 29, 30
Best Days for Money: 1, 2, 3, 4, 8, 9, 10, 11, 15, 16, 20, 21, 25, 26, 29, 30
Best Days for Career: 3, 4, 15, 16, 25, 26, 27, 28

Usually Spring is considered the best starting energy of the year, but this year, the way things are working out, the month ahead could be even better. *All* the planets are moving forward this month (which is very rare). Your personal solar cycle is in its growing, waxing phase for another two months, and the universal Solar Cycle entered its waxing phase last month. Personally you have great aspects. If you can choose a day between the 17th and the 30th (when the Moon also waxes) you will have a really optimum time for starting new projects or launching new ventures. There is much cosmic 'oomph' behind your efforts.

The month ahead is happy. You're in the midst of a yearly personal pleasure peak until the 20th. (You will have another one around your birthday.) The holidays are over, but you're still in party mode.

Finances also look good, with your financial planet Venus in the conservative sign of Capricorn until the 18th. The financial judgement is sound, conservative, down-to-earth. Venus in your 5th house indicates happy money: money that is earned in happy ways and that is spent on happy things. The attitude is that 'money is to be enjoyed'. Generally this would show risk taking, but the Capricorn influence would tone this down.

A Lunar Eclipse on 31st basically affects you only mildly, but it won't hurt to take it easy over that period. It might not be so nice for the people around you. This eclipse occurs in your 12th house of spirituality, signalling dramatic changes here – changes of teachings, attitudes and practice. Often these come from interior revelation (which is the correct way to make changes). There are likely to be shakeups and disturbances in a spiritual or charitable organization you're involved with. Guru figures have life-changing dramas. Every Lunar Eclipse affects friendships (rather than romantic attachments), and this one is no different. Friendships get tested. Sometimes the friendship itself is inherently flawed and the eclipse reveals this. Sometimes it's not the relationship itself but dramas that happen in the life of your friend. Your high-tech equipment can get temperamental during this period too. Often it needs repair or replacement. So, make sure your important files are backed up and that your anti-virus, anti-hacking software is up to date.

February

Best Days Overall: 2, 3, 11, 12, 21, 22
Most Stressful Days Overall: 9, 10, 16, 17, 23, 24
Best Days for Love: 4, 5, 6, 7, 16, 17, 25, 26
Best Days for Money: 4, 5, 6, 7, 16, 17, 25, 26
Best Days for Career: 4, 5, 14, 15, 23, 24, 25, 26

Like last month, you still have a very good window for launching new products or projects. All systems are go. All the planets are moving forward and the cosmic and personal solar cycles are waxing. (Avoid the Solar Eclipse of the 15th – but from the 16th to the end of the month is good.) You will see faster progress towards your goals.

The planetary power is all in the Western, social sector of your chart this month. Only the Moon (for half the month) will animate the East. So you're in a strong social period now. It is time to let others have their way, so long as it isn't destructive. Let go of self will and focus more on others. This unselfishness might seem saintly to others (and it does increase your popularity), but really it is just the planetary cycle you're in. Maintain likeability and your own good will come to you in normal and natural ways. Many psychological ills have their origin in too much self-centredness. It is healthy every now and then to take a break from yourself.

A Solar Eclipse on the 15th has a strong impact on you (stronger than last month's eclipse). It occurs in your 6th house, indicating job changes and disturbances in the workplace. These job changes can be with your present company or a new one. If you hire others, there is employee turnover and dramas in the lives of employees. Children and children figures in your life are forced to make dramatic financial changes. Your health is good, but a health scare or new health revelation brings important changes to your health regime. Like last month's eclipse, the spiritual life is affected. No question that major changes are happening in your practice, attitudes and teachings. Once again there are dramas in the lives of guru figures and shakeups in a spiritual or charitable organization you're involved with.

Mercury and Jupiter are hit by this eclipse. Thus the family (Jupiter's domain) is affected, and especially the parents or parent figures in your life. Repairs could be necessary in the home. Family members are likely to be more temperamental this period, so be patient with them. Since Mercury is also the ruler of your Horoscope, there can be a physical detox and a need to redefine yourself – your image and self-concept. This redefining will go on for another six months. If you don't define yourself for yourself, others will do it for you, and this won't be so pleasant.

Aside from the eclipse, love is the major headline this month. On the 18th the Sun enters your 7th house of love and you begin a yearly love and social peak. Next month will be even better.

March

Best Days Overall: 1, 2, 10, 11, 12, 20, 21, 29, 30
Most Stressful Days Overall: 8, 9, 15, 16, 17, 22, 23
Best Days for Love: 6, 7, 8, 15, 16, 17, 18, 19, 24, 25, 26, 27
Best Days for Money: 3, 4, 6, 7, 8, 15, 16, 17, 18, 19, 24, 25, 26, 27, 31
Best Days for Career: 8, 18, 19, 22, 23, 26, 27

You remain in the midst of a yearly love and social peak until the 20th. Love is the main headline of the month ahead and it looks good. Last month (February 24–26) brought a very happy (very idealistic) romantic opportunity for singles. Those of you already attached had more romance with the existing love. There were happy social experiences too. You have a strong attraction for creative, artistic and spiritual types these days. The Sun travelling with Neptune from the 3rd to the 5th brings a meeting with a guru or a spiritual type of lover. (Or both.)

The planetary power is now in the upper half of your chart. Thus the focus is more on the career and outer objectives rather than home and family. However, with Mars in your 4th house until the 17th, it is a good time to make major repairs in the home. Also, this aspect can bring surgery, or near-death kinds of experiences to family members.

There is prosperity this month. The 1st and 2nd look especially good. The ruler of your Horoscope, Mercury, travels with your financial planet, Venus. Both are making beautiful aspects to Jupiter. It should be a nice payday! On the 6th your financial planet moves into your 8th house, indicating that you have a knack for making others rich. By the karmic law, this will enrich you too – in due course. Venus in the 8th house is good for tax planning, and if you are of appropriate age it is good for estate planning too. Tax and tax issues are influencing your financial decision making – more so than usual. This is a good period for paying off debt – and also for making or refinancing old debt (it all depends on your need). If you have smart ideas, this is a good period to approach outside investors. Venus in Aries from the 6th onwards shows allurement to 'fast money'. But her square with Saturn from the 13th to the 15th suggests more caution. Avoid speculations over that period.

Health needs watching (and being a Virgo, you will certainly be on the case) until the 20th. The most important thing is to get enough rest. Enhance the health in the ways mentioned in the yearly report.

April

Best Days Overall: 7, 8, 16, 17, 25, 26
Most Stressful Days Overall: 4, 5, 6, 12, 13, 18, 19
Best Days for Love: 2, 3, 7, 8, 12, 13, 16, 17, 21, 22, 27, 29, 30
Best Days for Money: 1, 2, 3, 7, 8, 12, 13, 16, 17, 21, 22, 27, 28, 29, 30
Best Days for Career: 4, 5, 6, 14, 15, 18, 19, 23, 24

The love life is still excellent this month, though much less active than last month. Family members and family connections are playing an important role in love. It is likely that singles will reconnect with an old flame (or someone who reminds them of the old flame). The problem here is that you might be looking to repeat past happiness rather than looking to the future.

Until the 24th *all* the planets are still in the Western social sector (only the Moon will pass through the East for half the month), so other people are still paramount. Your social skills – your ability to gain the cooperation of others – will bring success to you. Let go of personal desires for a while. If conditions are irksome, make a note of what bothers you, and adapt to the conditions as best you can. The time is soon coming when changes can be made easily.

The power in your 8th house of regeneration (which began last month on the 20th) is still in effect until the 20th of this month. This favours detox regimes, and weight-loss regimes for those who need them. They will tend to be successful. Sexual activity is increased too. Whatever age or stage you are in life, the libido will be stronger than usual. Every now and then it is healthy to get rid of what doesn't belong in your life. The accumulation of the effete over time is staggering. So, detox the body of what doesn't belong there. Detox your possessions too. This will not only have physical effects, but will unclutter the mind as well. If something is not used in your life, if it is just taking up space, sell it or give it to charity. These redundant things have been 'gumming up' the flow of power into your life. There is something very beautiful – and spiritual – about simplicity. You have the opportunity to learn this in the coming month.

Health and energy are good this month. If you feel under the weather, spiritual healing seems very effective until the 21st. You can see a spiritual healer or employ the techniques on your own.

Venus, your financial planet, spends most of the month in Taurus, your 9th house. This is good. The 9th house is a fortunate house. It shows expanded earnings and financial optimism. On the 24th, Venus crosses your Mid-heaven and enters your 10th house of career, bringing the financial favour of bosses, elders, parents and parent figures.

May

Best Days Overall: 4, 5, 14, 15, 22, 23, 31
Most Stressful Days Overall: 2, 3, 9, 10, 16, 17, 29, 30
Best Days for Love: 7, 8, 9, 10, 17, 18, 19, 26, 27
Best Days for Money: 7, 8, 9, 10, 17, 18, 19, 24, 25, 26, 27
Best Days for Career: 2, 3, 13, 14, 16, 17, 22, 23, 31

This is an active, eventful, but nevertheless successful month, Virgo. There is never a dull moment.

Your health planet Uranus makes a major move on the 16th, from your 8th house to your 9th – from Aries into Taurus. For the next few months the neck and throat become important healthwise. You respond better to 'earth-based' therapies – mud packs, mud baths, crystal healing. If you feel under the weather, spend more time in the mountains or old forests – places where the earth energy is strong. You'll feel much better.

On the same day that Uranus moves into Taurus, Mars will move into your 6th house of health and work. So, the head, face, scalp will still be important healthwise. Detox regimes are beneficial. Good muscle tone is important. Surgery could be recommended to you too – only it is usually better to explore detox options first. With health more delicate from the 21st onwards, these things are important. And of course, as always, make sure to get enough rest.

The pace at work gets more hectic after the 16th. Probably there are dramas at the workplace. There can be work-related travel and job opportunities in foreign lands.

On the 21st, as the Sun moves into your 10th house of career, you enter a yearly career peak. There will be much success. The planets in your 10th house are beneficent ones – friendly ones – so there is good fortune here. On the 30th, Mercury, the ruler of your Horoscope, will also enter the 10th house – signalling more good fortune. The important thing is not to over work.

The Sun in your 10th house shows that being involved in charities and altruistic kinds of causes helps the career. You probably get more recognition for these kinds of activities than for your actual professional skills. But when Mercury moves into the career house there is

more personal recognition. Personal appearance and overall demeanour play an important role in the career. It is important that you 'look
the part' of what you're striving for.

Finances are good all month (with a few short-term challenges).
Until the 19th Venus is in your 10th house, showing you have the
financial favour of the authority figures in your life. Often this indicates
pay rises (official or unofficial). Your good professional reputation
leads to more earnings. There is a nice payday on the 31st.

June

Best Days Overall: 1, 2, 10, 11, 18, 19, 28, 29
Most Stressful Days Overall: 5, 6, 7, 12, 13, 25, 26
Best Days for Love: 5, 6, 7, 14, 15, 16, 23, 24
Best Days for Money: 1, 2, 5, 6, 7, 10, 11, 14, 15, 16, 19, 23, 24,
    28, 29
Best Days for Career: 3, 4, 12, 13, 14, 23, 24

Continue to watch the health until the 22nd. Review our discussion of
this from last month. Health and energy will dramatically improve
after the 21st.

You're still in the midst of a yearly career peak until the 21st, so you
can let home and family issues slide for a while. This is a time to reach
– aggressively – for your outer goals. Mercury is still in your 10th
house until the 12th, showing personal success and elevation. You're
seen by others as successful. Others 'look up' to you and aspire to be
like you.

Finances are going well too. Your financial planet is part of a Grand
Trine in Water until the 14th. On the 1st and 2nd she makes beautiful
aspects to Jupiter and Neptune, showing a nice payday and good financial cooperation with the spouse, partner or current love. Mercury will
make nice aspects to Jupiter on the 19th and 20th, bringing another
nice payday and a career boost to boot. On the 14th Venus enters your
12th house of spirituality. It is time to pay attention to intuition, which
Einstein called 'the greatest gift of the gods'. This, as our regular readers know, is the short cut to wealth. An instant of a real intuition is
worth many, many years of hard labour.

Early in the month – from the 1st to the 7th – Venus will be 'out of bounds'. Thus you are earning in ways that are outside your norm. This can also be read as your financial goals pulling you outside your normal comfort zone. However, this does seem profitable.

The love life will sparkle this month too – especially from the 12th onwards. Mercury is in beautiful aspect with your love planet, Neptune, from then on. The 20th and 21st are especially good for love. Singles will have a strong romantic opportunity or meeting then. But romance is likely afterwards as well. The only problem with romance is Neptune's retrograde move on the 18th. This will slow things down a bit but won't stop love. It's probably a good thing too. A dash of caution in love won't hurt.

Last month, on the 21st, the planetary power began to shift. The Western sector of your chart (the social sector) is still dominant, but less so than in previous months. You have more independence than you've had all year. Your challenge now is to balance your personal interests with those of others – not so easy to do.

July

Best Days Overall: 7, 8, 16, 17, 25, 26
Most Stressful Days Overall: 3, 4, 10, 11, 22, 23, 24, 30, 31
Best Days for Love: 3, 4, 5, 6, 12, 13, 16, 20, 21, 25, 26, 30, 31
Best Days for Money: 1, 5, 6, 12, 13, 16, 18, 19, 20, 21, 25, 26, 27, 28, 29
Best Days for Career: 5, 6, 10, 11, 14, 15, 22, 23, 24

Two eclipses are shaking up the world this month, but you seem relatively untouched by them. The cosmic purpose of an eclipse is to blast away the things that are hampering progress, hampering the Divine Plan of your life. In this sense the eclipses are good – though not pleasant.

The Solar Eclipse of the 13th occurs in your 11th house and impacts more on your friends and friendships than on you personally. Friendships get tested. The cosmos only wants the best for you. Anything that falls short of that will go down the tubes. Good friendships will survive this, but the flawed ones are in danger. A parent or parent figure has a financial crisis of some kind and is forced to make dramatic changes. There is chaos and disruption in a charity or spiritual organization you're involved with. Once again you're making changes to the spiritual life – the teachings, practice and attitudes. This is a periodic 'course correction' which is basically healthy. And again, computers, software and high-tech gadgetry get tested. They can be more temperamental this period and often repair or replacement is necessary. Cars and communication equipment will also get tested. Pluto, the ruler of your 3rd house of communication, is affected. It would be a good idea to drive more carefully over this period (best if you can stay off the road altogether, but if you must drive, be more mindful and cautious).

The Lunar Eclipse of 27th occurs in your 6th house and shows once again job changes (either within your company or with another one) and changes in the conditions of work. It also announces dramatic changes in your health regime and approach. Often this comes because of a health scare, but your health looks good and there are other causes for it. Mars is affected here. Thus there can be dreams of death or 'close calls' – perhaps someone dear to you has a close call. The cosmos is forcing you to confront death (usually on a psychological level) so that you get a better understanding of it. The fear of death holds many people back and this needs to be dealt with. The spouse, partner or current love has to make important financial course corrections. Their financial thinking hasn't been realistic. There are dramas in the lives of friends, and once again friendships get tested. High-tech equipment gets tested again too.

August

Best Days Overall: 4, 5, 12, 13, 21, 22, 31
Most Stressful Days Overall: 6, 7, 19, 20, 26, 27
Best Days for Love: 5, 8, 9, 14, 15, 16, 17, 24, 25, 26, 27
Best Days for Money: 5, 8, 9, 14, 15, 16, 17, 24, 25, 26, 27
Best Days for Career: 1, 2, 3, 6, 7, 10, 11, 19, 20, 29, 30

In spite of the eclipses July should have been a prosperous month. Venus moved into your own sign on July 10 and is there until the 7th of this month, bringing financial windfalls and happy opportunities.

You look and feel prosperous. Expensive personal items – clothing or accessories – come to you. On the 7th Venus moves into your money house and stays there for the rest of the month. And so she will be in her own sign and house, and thus stronger on your behalf. She's comfortable in her own home. Earnings should increase.

The Sun moves into your sign on the 22nd and you begin a yearly personal pleasure peak. This is a wonderful time for self-indulgence, for indulging in the pleasures of the body. It is also very good for getting the body and image the way you want it to be.

But we're not yet finished with eclipses. A Solar Eclipse on the 11th occurs in your 12th house of spirituality. Not only that, but the eclipsed planet, the Sun, also happens to be the ruler of your 12th house. So the spiritual life, which has been shaken up multiple times this year, gets shaken up once again. Much ferment is happening here. A further course correction is necessary. Once again there are shakeups and instability in a spiritual or charitable organization you're involved with, and guru figures in your life are still not off the hook. Friends can be having financial crises and have to make important changes. Aunts or uncles (or those who play that role in your life) are having their marriages tested. Parents or parent figures need to drive more carefully.

Happily the health is good this month, and after the 22nd it gets even better. You're entering your period of maximum independence now and should make the changes that need to be made. You might not be having life on your terms completely, but more so than at any other time of the year.

The Sun's move into your sign on the 22nd enhances your spirituality. You have an 'other worldly' kind of glamour. The physical body is more amenable to your will. You're being shown spiritual techniques to mould and sculpt the body. A spiritual guru comes calling and seems devoted to you.

September

Best Days Overall: 1, 9, 17, 18, 19, 27, 28
Most Stressful Days Overall: 2, 3, 15, 16, 22, 23, 24, 29, 30
Best Days for Love: 2, 3, 4, 5, 13, 14, 22, 23, 24
Best Days for Money: 2, 3, 4, 5, 11, 12, 13, 14, 22, 23, 24
Best Days for Career: 2, 3, 9, 18, 19, 29, 30

You're still very much into a yearly personal pleasure period this month. So enjoy life and pamper yourself a little. Be nice to your body. Your 1st house is strong until the 22nd.

Love is a bit more challenging this month. You and the spouse or current love seem very far apart – especially from the 6th to the 22nd. You each seem focused on your own interests and you are seeing things from completely opposite perspectives. This doesn't make one person a saint and the other a demon. You just have opposite perspectives on things. The object is to bridge your differences. Respect the perspective of the other person. See it as 'complementary' to your own. Somewhere there is middle ground. In astrology one's opposite is always the natural marriage partner (if they don't kill each other first). These are considered the strongest partnerships. Each has something the other lacks. They fill each other's gaps. Having said this, it is not that easy to do. It takes some work.

On the 6th, as Mercury moves across your Ascendant and into the lower half of your chart (the night side), the lower half of the Horoscope starts to dominate. Career and outer activities become less important, while home, family and emotional wellness start to become more important. It is time to shift your focus to the home and family.

Mercury serves double duty in your chart. He is the ruler of your Horoscope and also your career planet. His move into your 1st house brings career opportunities to you and there's nothing much that you need to do. These opportunities seek you out. This aspect also indicates that others see you as successful. You look the part. You have the image. Probably you dress the part too.

The month ahead is prosperous – perhaps the most prosperous of the year. On the 22nd the Sun and Mercury move into your money house and you enter a yearly financial peak. You are very focused here.

You take matters into your own hands. You're less likely to delegate financial matters to others and, even if you do, you're watching very carefully. The Sun in your money house brings a wonderful financial intuition. Mercury in the money house brings the financial favour of bosses, elders, parents and parent figures – the authority figures in your life.

Mercury, the ruler of your Horoscope, pauses in the heavens from the 22nd to the 25th – he pauses in his latitudinal motion and then changes direction. So this will most likely happen for you too.

October

Best Days Overall: 6, 7, 15, 16, 25, 26
Most Stressful Days Overall: 1, 12, 13, 14, 20, 21, 27, 28
Best Days for Love: 2, 3, 10, 11, 20, 21, 29, 30
Best Days for Money: 2, 3, 8, 9, 10, 11, 20, 21, 29, 30
Best Days for Career: 1, 9, 10, 20, 21, 27, 28, 29, 30

A happy and prosperous month ahead, Virgo, enjoy! Health and energy are excellent now and there is only one long-term planet in stressful alignment. Many more are in harmonious alignment with you. With increased energy, the moods are better and you're able to achieve more (provided you don't squander your energy on frivolous things). Things that seemed impossible a few months back – and which you perhaps dismissed – are now eminently possible and very doable. Mars is still in your 6th house of health. Thus scalp and face massage are still good. Vigorous physical exercise – according to your age and stage in life – is important. There is still a tendency to surgery. But, as we have mentioned, detox regimes will be very effective.

You're still in the midst of a yearly financial peak until the 23rd. You're being helped by an astute and very reliable financial intuition. Intuition might seem irrational at the time, but in hindsight it is always rational. It is just a higher form of rationality. Mercury is still in the money house and remains there until the 10th. This is always a positive for finance. It shows focus. It shows that you adopt the image of wealth and that others see you this way. You're not projecting 'neediness'. Later in the month (from the 28th to the 30th) Mercury will travel with Jupiter, bringing a nice payday and happy opportunities. The only financial complication is the retrograde of Venus, your financial planet, which begins on the 5th. This won't stop earnings, but it will slow things down a bit. When the financial planet is retrograde, our regular readers know to avoid major purchases or major investments (of course you still shop for groceries and other necessities). But this aspect also shows a need to be more perfect – more correct – in our financial dealings. Little things matter. Cheques should be signed and dated correctly. The envelopes should be addressed correctly. There is no need to make matters worse than they need to be. It is also good to review your finances over this period and see where improvements can be made. When Venus goes forward again next month you can put your plans into action.

By the 23rd your short-term financial goals are basically achieved and you can shift your attention to intellectual interests and communication. Those of you involved in sales, marketing, teaching or writing should have a good month. There is much power in your 3rd house from the 23rd onward. Students, below college level, are focused on their studies and are successful. An excellent period for scoping out a new car or communication equipment (do the research, but don't buy). You have a good feeling for these things now.

November

Best Days Overall: 2, 3, 11, 12, 21, 22, 29, 30
Most Stressful Days Overall: 9, 10, 16, 17, 23, 24
Best Days for Love: 4, 5, 6, 7, 8, 14, 15, 16, 17, 23, 24, 25, 26
Best Days for Money: 4, 5, 8, 14, 15, 19, 23, 24, 27
Best Days for Career: 1, 9, 10, 19, 20, 23, 24, 27, 28

An eventful kind of month with many changes happening, but mostly on an internal level. You will see the external effects later on.

The night side (lower half) of your chart gets very powerful this month and the planetary power is grouped at the nadir (the lowest point) of your Horoscope. Even your career planet, Mercury, spends the month in your 4th house of home and family, far away from his natural home. In a major transit, Jupiter will move into your 4th house on the

8th. This signals, as we have mentioned in the yearly report, the expansion of the family circle, a move or renovation of the existing home and a happy home and family experience. On the 22nd, the Sun will also move into your 4th house. So this is where the action will be this month. You can safely let career matters go (or de-emphasize them) these days. Your mission right now is the home and family.

Siblings and sibling figures in your life have had a prosperous year, and their prosperity will increase even further in the next twelve months (but especially from the 22nd onwards). You seem very involved with this.

Children and children figures in your life begin a highly spiritual kind of year. Things have been tough for them this year and they need 'higher help' – happily this will be very available now.

Love is straightening out, little by little. Last month both of the planets involved with love were retrograde. This month they start to move forward again. Venus (the generic love planet) moves forward on the 16th, while Neptune, your actual love planet, starts moving forward on the 25th. So clarity is finally being gained here (the most important thing). With clarity we will make the correct decisions. Mars moves into your 7th house on the 16th and stays there for the rest of the month, complicating things somewhat. If you can avoid the pitfalls – anger, power struggles, showing dominance – things can work out. If not, a current relationship seems troubled.

Uranus, your health planet, moves back into Aries on the 16th. Avoid making important health decisions (or job decisions) now. Study things further. With your health planet back in your 8th house, enhance the health in the ways mentioned in the yearly report. Health needs more attention from the 22nd onwards.

December

Best Days Overall: 9, 10, 18, 19, 27, 28
Most Stressful Days Overall: 6, 7, 14, 15, 21, 22
Best Days for Love: 2, 3, 4, 5, 14, 15, 23, 24, 31
Best Days for Money: 2, 3, 6, 14, 15, 16, 23, 24, 26, 29, 30
Best Days for Career: 4, 5, 14, 21, 22, 23, 24

Your 4th house of home and family is still very powerful this month. Pay more attention here. December is a family kind of period after all. You can let career matters slide for a while.

The 4th house is the lowest point in your chart. It symbolizes the deepest part of the night – the midnight hour. The body is passive but great activity is happening internally. The body is being prepared for the activities of the next day. So, this is a time to work on your goals by internal rather than external methods – through meditation, visualization and willed dreaming. Imagine yourself being where you want to be in your career, love and financial life. Imagine your body the way you want it to look. Ignore the mirror or your present circumstances. Hold on to your image. Get into the feeling of your image as best you can and stay there for as long as you can. Repeat this every night, or whenever you have spare moments. When the feeling comes to you, your goals are as good as achieved. By the spiritual law they must happen. How they happen is not your business. It is the business of a Higher Power.

This is a month (and a year) for psychological breakthroughs. The psyche is very active these days and close to you. Memories that arise might seem random to the conscious mind, but they are giving deep messages about your present condition. Observe these memories. Write them down. Look at them from your present perspective. Many of them will lose their hold on you as you see them for what they are. When you reinterpret past events – put them in proper perspective – you change the past (in a manner of speaking). Whatever happened, happened, but you see it in a different light. This is great therapy.

Finances look good this month. Venus started to move forward again on November 16, so the financial judgement is realistic and sound once again. On the 2nd she moves into Scorpio, your 3rd house. This shows the importance of sales, marketing, PR and advertising in whatever you're doing. It shows financial opportunities right in your neighbourhood – close to home. Neighbours, siblings or sibling figures are playing an important role in the financial life. There are opportunities to profit from trading – from buying and selling.

Mars remains in your 7th house of love all month. Avoid unnecessary power struggles with the beloved.

Libra

☖

THE SCALES

Birthdays from
23rd September to
22nd October

Personality Profile

LIBRA AT A GLANCE

Element – Air

Ruling Planet – Venus
  Career Planet – Moon
  Love Planet – Mars
  Money Planet – Pluto
  Planet of Communications – Jupiter
  Planet of Health and Work – Neptune
  Planet of Home and Family Life – Saturn
  Planet of Spirituality and Good Fortune – Mercury

Colours – blue, jade green

Colours that promote love, romance and social harmony – carmine, red, scarlet

Colours that promote earning power – burgundy, red-violet, violet

Gems – carnelian, chrysolite, coral, emerald, jade, opal, quartz, white marble

Metal – copper

Scents – almond, rose, vanilla, violet

Quality – cardinal (= activity)

Qualities most needed for balance – a sense of self, self-reliance,
    independence

Strongest virtues – social grace, charm, tact, diplomacy

Deepest needs – love, romance, social harmony

Characteristic to avoid – violating what is right in order to be socially
    accepted

Signs of greatest overall compatibility – Gemini, Aquarius

Signs of greatest overall incompatibility – Aries, Cancer, Capricorn

Sign most helpful to career – Cancer

Sign most helpful for emotional support – Capricorn

Sign most helpful financially – Scorpio

Sign best for marriage and/or partnerships – Aries

Sign most helpful for creative projects – Aquarius

Best Sign to have fun with – Aquarius

Signs most helpful in spiritual matters – Gemini, Virgo

Best day of the week – Friday

Understanding a Libra

In the sign of Libra the universal mind – the soul – expresses its genius for relationships, that is, its power to harmonize diverse elements in a unified, organic way. Libra is the soul's power to express beauty in all of its forms. And where is beauty if not within relationships? Beauty does not exist in isolation. Beauty arises out of comparison – out of the just relationship between different parts. Without a fair and harmonious relationship there is no beauty, whether it in art, manners, ideas or the social or political forum.

There are two faculties humans have that exalt them above the animal kingdom: their rational faculty (expressed in the signs of Gemini and Aquarius) and their aesthetic faculty, exemplified by Libra. Without an aesthetic sense we would be little more than intelligent barbarians. Libra is the civilizing instinct or urge of the soul.

Beauty is the essence of what Librans are all about. They are here to beautify the world. One could discuss Librans' social grace, their sense of balance and fair play, their ability to see and love another person's point of view – but this would be to miss their central asset: their desire for beauty.

No one – no matter how alone he or she seems to be – exists in isolation. The universe is one vast collaboration of beings. Librans, more than most, understand this and understand the spiritual laws that make relationships bearable and enjoyable.

A Libra is always the unconscious (and in some cases conscious) civilizer, harmonizer and artist. This is a Libra's deepest urge and greatest genius. Librans love instinctively to bring people together, and they are uniquely qualified to do so. They have a knack for seeing what unites people – the things that attract and bind rather than separate individuals.

Finance

In financial matters Librans can seem frivolous and illogical to others. This is because Librans appear to be more concerned with earning money for others than for themselves. But there is a logic to this financial attitude. Librans know that everything and everyone is connected and that it is impossible to help another to prosper without also prospering yourself. Since enhancing their partner's income and position tends to strengthen their relationship, Librans choose to do so. What could be more fun than building a relationship? You will rarely find a Libra enriching him- or herself at someone else's expense.

Scorpio is the ruler of Libra's solar 2nd house of money, giving Libra unusual insight into financial matters – and the power to focus on these matters in a way that disguises a seeming indifference. In fact, many other signs come to Librans for financial advice and guidance.

Given their social grace, Librans often spend great sums of money on entertaining and organizing social events. They also like to help others when they are in need. Librans would go out of their way to help a friend in dire straits, even if they have to borrow from others to do so. However, Librans are also very careful to pay back any debts they owe, and like to make sure they never have to be reminded to do so.

Career and Public Image

Publicly, Librans like to appear as nurturers. Their friends and acquaintances are their family and they wield political power in parental ways. They also like bosses who are paternal or maternal.

The sign of Cancer is on Libra's 10th career house cusp; the Moon is Libra's career planet. The Moon is by far the speediest, most changeable planet in the horoscope. It alone among all the planets travels through the entire zodiac – all twelve signs and houses – every month. This is an important key to the way in which Librans approach their careers, and also to what they need to do to maximize their career potential. The Moon is the planet of moods and feelings – Librans need a career in which their emotions can have free expression. This is why so many Librans are involved in the creative arts. Libra's ambitions wax and wane with the Moon. They tend to wield power according to their mood.

The Moon 'rules' the masses – and that is why Libra's highest goal is to achieve a mass kind of acclaim and popularity. Librans who achieve fame cultivate the public as other people cultivate a lover or friend. Librans can be very flexible – and often fickle – in their career and ambitions. On the other hand, they can achieve their ends in a great variety of ways. They are not stuck in one attitude or with one way of doing things.

Love and Relationships

Librans express their true genius in love. In love you could not find a partner more romantic, more seductive or more fair. If there is one thing that is sure to destroy a relationship – sure to block your love from flowing – it is injustice or imbalance between lover and beloved. If one party is giving too much or taking too much, resentment is sure to surface at some time or other. Librans are careful about this. If anything, Librans might err on the side of giving more, but never giving less.

If you are in love with a Libra, make sure you keep the aura of romance alive. Do all the little things – candle-lit dinners, travel to exotic locales, flowers and small gifts. Give things that are beautiful, not necessarily expensive. Send cards. Ring regularly even if you have nothing in particular to say. The niceties are very important to a Libra. Your relationship is a work of art: make it beautiful and your Libran lover will appreciate it. If you are creative about it, he or she will appreciate it even more; for this is how your Libra will behave towards you.

Librans like their partners to be aggressive and even a bit self-willed. They know that these are qualities they sometimes lack and so they like their partners to have them. In relationships, however, Librans can be very aggressive – but always in a subtle and charming way! Librans are determined in their efforts to charm the object of their desire – and this determination can be very pleasant if you are on the receiving end.

Home and Domestic Life

Since Librans are such social creatures, they do not particularly like mundane domestic duties. They like a well-organized home – clean and neat with everything needful present – but housework is a chore and a burden, one of the unpleasant tasks in life that must be done, the quicker the better. If a Libra has enough money – and sometimes even if not – he or she will prefer to pay someone else to take care of the daily household chores. However, Librans like gardening; they love to have flowers and plants in the home.

A Libra's home is modern, and furnished in excellent taste. You will find many paintings and sculptures there. Since Librans like to be with friends and family, they enjoy entertaining at home and they make great hosts.

Capricorn is on the cusp of Libra's 4th solar house of home and family. Saturn, the planet of law, order, limits and discipline, rules Libra's domestic affairs. If Librans want their home life to be supportive and happy they need to develop some of the virtues of Saturn – order, organization and discipline. Librans, being so creative and so intensely in need of harmony, can tend to be too lax in the home and too permissive with their children. Too much of this is not always good; children need freedom but they also need limits.

Horoscope for 2018

Major Trends

There's good news and bad news in the year ahead. First, the good news. After seven years of stressful alignment with you, Uranus is beginning to move away. Instead of being in continuous stressful alignment, he will only be in stressful alignment for approximately half the time. Those of you born early in the sign of Libra (from September 23 to October 2) will hardly even feel Uranus's influence. This move is not only positive healthwise, but it will start to stabilize the love and social life. More on this later.

Jupiter spends most of the year in your money house. Thus the year ahead is going to be very prosperous. More good news.

On November 8 Jupiter will move into your 3rd house of communication and intellectual interests. This is an excellent transit for students not yet at college, for teachers, writers, lecturers, journalists, sales and marketing people. It brings enhanced skills. Students should be successful in their studies.

Neptune has been in your 6th house of health for many years now and will be there for many more to come. This signals the importance of the feet and also the importance of spiritual healing. More on this later.

Now, the bad news (although it's not really bad, just challenging). Saturn, since late December of last year, is now in stressful alignment with you. Uranus is leaving his stressful aspect, but Saturn is replacing him. So your health will still need watching in the year ahead. More on this later.

Saturn's move into your 4th house will impact on the family. Most likely you will have extra family responsibilities to deal with. Emotionally, you will not feel able to express how you're really feeling. This can lead to repression and perhaps depression. There are many things you can do about this, however – more details later.

There will be three Solar Eclipses this year – usually there are only two. Since the Sun rules your 11th house of friends, this indicates turbulence (life-changing kinds of dramas) in the lives of your friends. Computers and other bits of technology might need replacing in the year ahead. We will discuss this more fully in the monthly reports.

Your most important interests this year are finance (until November 8); communication and intellectual interests (from November 8 onwards); home and family; health and work; love and romance (until May 16 and from November 6 onwards); and sex, occult studies and personal transformation (from May 16 to November 6).

Your paths of greatest fulfilment this year are finance (until November 8); communication and intellectual interests (from November 8 onwards); friends, groups and group activities (until November 17); and career (from November 17 onwards).

Health

(Please note that this is an astrological perspective on health and not a medical one. In days of yore there was no difference, both of these perspectives were identical. Now there could be quite a difference. For a medical perspective, please consult your doctor or health practitioner.)

Health, as we mentioned, still needs attention this year. Uranus is leaving a stressful aspect for a while, but Saturn replaces him. Indeed, there will be periods in the year (from January 1 to May 16 and from November 6 onwards) where *both* Saturn and Uranus are in stressful aspect. Moreover, Pluto has been in stressful aspect with you since 2008 and this is still the situation this year. So there are two (and at times three) long-term planets in stressful alignment with you. Overall energy could be a lot better. You will have to try to make sure you maintain high energy levels. This is the first defence against disease. In many cases a good night's sleep – or an afternoon nap – will do more for you than a visit to the doctor's.

The good news is that your 6th house of health is strong this year. This shows focus. You're on the case. You're not going to let little things mushroom into big things. The danger would be if you were not paying attention.

Also, as our regular readers know, there is much you can do to enhance the health and prevent problems from developing. Give more attention to the following – the vulnerable areas of your chart (the reflex points are shown below):

- The heart. This has only become an important area for you, Libra, since 2008 (and even more important since 2011). Learn to replace worry and anxiety with faith.

Important foot reflexology points for the year ahead

Try to massage all of the foot on a regular basis – the top of the foot as well as the bottom – but pay extra attention to the points highlighted on the chart. When you massage, be aware of 'sore spots' as these need special attention. It's also a good idea to massage the ankles and below them.

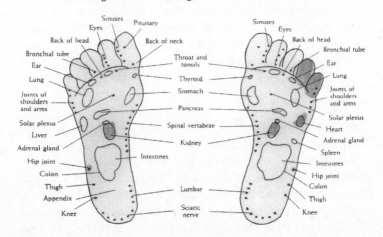

- The kidneys and hips. These are always important for Libra. Regular hip massage (and the buttocks too) should be part of your health regime. This will not only strengthen the kidneys but the lower back as well. A herbal kidney cleanse every now and then – especially if you feel under the weather – would be helpful.
- The feet are another always important area, as Neptune, the planet that rules the feet, is your health planet. They have become even more important since 2012 as Neptune moved into his own sign and into your 6th house. Regular foot massage (see the chart above) should be part of your health regime. Shoes should fit correctly and not unbalance you. Comfort is preferable to fashion, although if you can have both, all the better. There are all kinds of inexpensive gadgets that give foot massage. There are some that even give foot whirlpool treatments. This would be a good investment.

Neptune is the most spiritual of all the planets. These days he is even more so than usual. Thus, you respond well to spiritual-type therapies – meditation, prayer, laying on of hands, reiki and the manipulation of subtle energies. If you feel under the weather, see a spiritual healer.

Neptune rules the oceans and he resides these days in a water sign. Thus you have a special connection to the healing power of the water element. You will find it very beneficial – from the health perspective – to spend more time around water: oceans, rivers and lakes. Swimming, boating, water skiing and water sports are healthy kinds of exercises. If you feel under the weather, soak in the tub for an hour or so and you will feel much better.

Home and Family

The home and your family have been a very important area for you for many years – ever since Pluto moved into your 4th house in 2008. This year it becomes even more important. Pluto is still there and Saturn joins him. Your 4th house is easily the strongest house (overall) in the Horoscope – it is also the most challenging.

Pluto in your 4th house for so long has brought deaths in the family. In some cases these were 'figurative' deaths – the family circle broke up or shifted – in some cases it was 'literal' death, with the actual death of family members. In many cases family members experienced surgery or near-death kinds of experiences. A cosmic detox has been going on in the family and domestic life and these happenings are some of the side-effects. Believe it or not, you are giving birth to your ideal of family life, the Divine Idea of how your family and home should be. The birthing process is seldom easy – generally there's a lot of blood and gore – but the end result is good.

Pluto in your 4th house has also brought major repairs or renovations in the physical home, and more could happen this year too.

Saturn in your 4th house shows a rearrangement of the home and family life. It is getting restructured in a healthier kind of way. This aspect does not favour a move, but a need to make better use of the space that you have. If you feel cramped in your present home – and many of you do – the solution is to rearrange things in a different way. If you do, you will find that you have all the space that you need. A move is more likely next year (though it doesn't seem like a smooth ride) than this year.

Saturn in your 4th house shows that you are taking on more responsibilities at home and with the family. This applies to you and also to a parent or parent figure. He or she seems unduly pessimistic – everything looks black – and this impacts on the family.

There will be a tendency to manage the home and family like a business, in a corporate kind of way. While this will bring efficiency and order (and a little of this is good), it can also put a chill on the family life. Family is about unconditional love and support. The family relationship transcends business.

Pluto is your financial planet. His position in the 4th house shows that you're spending more on the home and family, investing here. It shows earning money through the family and family connections, and good family financial support.

Your financial planet in the 4th house favours making money from home – from a home office or home-based business. Your home is as much an office as it is a home. You can be buying business equipment for the home this year.

Repairs and renovations can happen any time this year (the plumbing especially should be checked), but if you have some free will in the matter, the period from March 17 to May 16 seems best. If you're redecorating or beautifying the home in a cosmetic way, January 1–20 is good.

Siblings and sibling figures in your life are likely to move this year – the opportunity is there. A parent or parent figure has probably moved multiple times in recent years and it could happen this year too. But he or she is getting ready to settle down more. The wanderlust is about over.

Finance and Career

Last year, as Jupiter was in your own sign, was a strong financial year. This year will be even better as Jupiter, as we mentioned, spends most of the year – until early November – in your money house. This is a classic astrological signal of prosperity and good fortune. It shows expanded earnings. It shows that assets you already own are increased in value. Those of you who have stock portfolios will find that they are worth more. Since Jupiter rules your 3rd house of communication and intellectual interests, your intellectual property (your ideas, writings, speeches, lectures, etc.) will be worth more. Jupiter not only increases physical earnings but brings happy financial opportunities as well. For investors, this position favours telecommunications, transportation and media companies. For-profit educational institutions are also favoured. Buying, selling, trading and retailing are favoured as well, and these activities are good for non-investors as well.

There are other things Jupiter brings to the table. There is great financial faith and optimism. There was a book written many years ago entitled *Your Faith Is Your Fortune*, and this is certainly the case for you this year.* You will have inspired financial ideas and a wonderful intuition this year (Neptune is making beautiful aspects to Jupiter for most of the year). Very often it is not money that we need, but an idea – a solution. And these you will have in abundance.

Pluto, your financial planet, has been in your 4th house of home and family for many years, and we have discussed some of this earlier.

---

* *Neville Goddard, Your Faith Is Your Fortune (Martino Publishers, 2011; first published 1941).*

Thus you have a good feeling for residential real estate, the food business, hotels and motels, restaurants and industries that cater to the home. It is an aspect that favours a family kind of business. This could be your family business or a business that is run like a family, with a family kind of atmosphere to it. It shows, as we mentioned, earning from home, from a home office or a home-based business. You're spending more on the home and family as well.

This is a strong financial year, but not an especially strong career year. Career just doesn't seem that important. Wealth is more important than status, prestige or professional recognition. Some years are like that. The cosmos always aims for a balanced development and, over the course of a life, different areas will be emphasized over others.

There are two Lunar Eclipses this year (the normal number) and these always bring career change and 'course corrections'. There will also be a Solar Eclipse in your 10th career house on July 13 that brings more of the same. We will discuss this in the monthly reports.

Your career planet is the Moon – the fastest moving of all the planets. Where the other fast-moving planets (the Sun, Mercury and Venus) need a year to move through all your signs and houses, the Moon will do this every month. Thus there are many short-term career trends depending on where the Moon is and the aspects she receives. We will deal with these in the monthly reports.

Love and Social Life

Uranus, the planet of sudden change – revolutionary change – has been in your 7th house of love for the past seven years. This has tested marriages and serious relationships. Many a Libra has divorced over these past years. Many have broken off serious relationships. For singles this position was not favourable to marriage. Happily this is changing now. Uranus is leaving your 7th house from May 16 to November 6: next year he will move out for the long haul.

Although Uranus is still a factor for approximately half the year, he has more or less done his job now, and the love and social life is becoming more settled. Serious committed relationships have a better chance of survival now.

I don't think you will marry this year – next year would be much better for that – but there will be more stability in love. For the past seven years you have been attracting 'non-serous' kinds of people. Rebel types. Many were geniuses to be sure, but not people interested in commitment. They all seem to have a desire (more like a lust) for personal freedom. Over this long period your whole social circle has changed, probably out of all recognition. By now you have become more or less comfortable with sudden social changes and the insecurities they bring. This was Uranus's whole purpose.

Love will not be as exciting as it has been over these last seven years, but it will be more stable and settled.

As we mentioned, marriage is not likely this year, but singles will still date and have fun. Mars, your love planet, will spend a lot of time – an unusual amount of time – in Aquarius, your 5th house of fun and creativity, this year. On and off, he will be there for approximately five months. This shows a love affair rather than a marriage – and a very complicated one.

Those working in or working on the second marriage have a status quo kind of year. Those of you who are marrieds will tend to stay married, and singles will tend to stay single. Those in or working on the third marriage will have their relationships tested. Three Solar Eclipses will see to that. If the marriage or relationship is basically sound, it will survive. Those working on the fourth marriage shouldn't marry just yet.

Your love planet, Mars, will go retrograde this year – this tends to happen once every two years and will be from June 26 to August 27. This is not a time to make important love decisions one way or another. It is a time to gain clarity.

There seems to be much turmoil and upheaval in your friendships this year as well. Four out of the five eclipses this year impact on them. Thus friends are experiencing life-changing kinds of events and this could affect your relationship.

Self-Improvement

Uranus's move into your 8th house of regeneration shows you're entering an era of sexual experimentation. This is neither good nor bad; it all depends on how you handle it. On the one hand, all the old rule books about sex – the dos and don'ts – get thrown out the window and you learn about what works for you through trial, error and experimentation. Since, as our regular readers know, every person is 'wired up' in a unique way, you can't really make universal rules about this. You learn how you personally function and what works for you. On the other hand, sometimes these experiments can go too far – they can actually be destructive. This should be avoided.

Many of you are involved in personal transformation. It is very trendy these days. You will be more experimental here too.

Saturn will be in your 4th house all year. We have discussed the physical kinds of effects this will have, but this position has a great impact on your emotional life too – on your everyday moods and feelings. Your 4th house is not just about where you live physically, but where you live emotionally. So, a reorganization of the emotional life is happening. You're going to learn to manage your moods the way you manage your physical circumstances. It was never intended that people be 'victims' of mood or emotion. Mood and emotion are intended to serve us.

In this process of managing emotion – and the cosmos will arrange things so that it becomes necessary – mistakes are often made. Self-control, to many, means repression – the stifling of true feelings. (Often this is because you feel unsafe in expressing them.) This can't go on for very long. It is like trying to stifle a yawn. You can do it for a time, but sooner or later, it is going to happen and it will be much stronger than it would have been. Not only that, but holding back your feelings can cause many other problems – depression and even physical illness.

What is needed is a safe, healthy way of expressing negative feeling. Some might find that talking to a trained therapist will be helpful. Some might take refuge in medication (which doesn't cure anything but is merely a scientific form of repression). Talking things out with a good friend would be another option, or writing down your negative feelings on paper. In my book *A Technique for Meditation* we give other ways of getting rid of unwanted feelings (see Chapters 2 and 3).

Spiritual healing has been strong in your chart for many years. So, it has been a great interest. You're going deeper and deeper into it. You already understand much but there's always more to learn.

The important thing in spiritual healing is to acknowledge no other healing force but the Divine. This doesn't mean that a doctor or therapist can't be a help; it means that you seek your healing from the Divine first. The Divine can heal directly or through therapists or doctors. The important thing is to stay open to the moment-by-moment intuition.

Month-by-month Forecasts

January

Best Days Overall: 8, 9, 17, 18, 19, 27, 28
Most Stressful Days Overall: 1, 2, 15, 16, 22, 23, 29, 30
Best Days for Love: 1, 2, 5, 6, 10, 11, 15, 16, 20, 21, 22, 23, 27, 28
Best Days for Money: 1, 2, 5, 6, 10, 11, 15, 16, 20, 21, 25, 26, 29, 30
Best Days for Career: 1, 2, 5, 6, 15, 16, 27, 28, 29, 30

You begin your year with the Western, social sector of your chart dominant. This is your favourite sector. While others are not so comfortable focusing on relationships and the interests of others, you excel at this. No need to give you lectures on consensus and gaining your ends through cooperation – you know all about this and can teach the rest of us.

Though your yearly financial peak will happen later on in the year, this is a good financial month. Jupiter will be in your money house until November 8, and Mars, your love planet, is in the money house until the 27th of this month. Thus there is great focus here, which is 90 per cent of success. Mars in the money house shows the cooperation of friends and social contacts in the financial life, and the support of the spouse, partner or current love. Often with this kind of aspect there are opportunities for business partnerships or joint ventures.

This month you have the chart of a person who likes to do business with friends, with the people you socialize with. You like to socialize – to befriend – the people you do business with as well. A lot of the social activity this month is business related.

For singles this shows an allurement to wealth. Wealth, material gifts and financial support are all romantic turn-ons these days. Romantic opportunities happen as you go about pursuing your financial goals or with people involved in your finances. The ruler of your Horoscope, Venus, will travel with your financial planet from the 8th to the 10th. This shows a nice payday and financial opportunity happening. (The Sun will also be travelling with Pluto in that period, reinforcing what we say here.)

Health needs some attention this month – especially until the 20th. Enhance the health in the ways mentioned in the yearly report.

A Lunar Eclipse on the 31st occurs in your 11th house of friends and tests these things. Often it brings dramas in the lives of friends which complicate your relationship. High-tech gadgets will get tested as well. Don't panic if your computer or smart phone starts acting erratically. Career changes are also happening. A parent or parent figure has to make important financial changes.

February

Best Days Overall: 4, 5, 14, 15, 23, 24
Most Stressful Days Overall: 11, 12, 19, 25, 26
Best Days for Love: 4, 5, 9, 10, 16, 19, 20, 25, 26, 27, 28
Best Days for Money: 2, 3, 6, 7, 11, 12, 16, 17, 21, 22, 25, 26
Best Days for Career: 4, 5, 14, 15, 25, 26

When the Sun entered your 5th house of creativity and fun on January 20 (Venus having entered there on January 18) you began one of your yearly personal pleasure peaks. A fun kind of month ahead. A Solar Eclipse on the 15th also occurs in your 5th house, however, so have fun, but safely. When people are scheduling leisure activities there's a tendency to travel. But this eclipse impacts on the two planets that rule travel – Mercury and Jupiter. So try to avoid travelling during this eclipse period. It will be a good idea to stay off the roads too – unless absolutely necessary. If it is necessary, drive more carefully.

The Solar Eclipse of the 15th affects children and children figures in your life. They should take it easy over this period – there is no need for stressful or daredevil-type activities. A parent or parent figure is forced to make important financial changes. Siblings and sibling figures should also drive more carefully. Children and children figures are forced to redefine themselves now, forced to create a new and better image of themselves over the next six months. They will dress differently, change hairstyles and, in general, present a new look to the world. If they haven't been careful in dietary matters a physical detox could happen. Friendships get tested too. (The eclipsed planet, the Sun, rules your 11th house of friends.) Technological equipment and gadgetry also get tested and often need repair or replacement.

Basically though, this eclipse is benign for you (especially when you compare them to others you've had to deal with in the past). It is just inconvenient.

Health and energy are good this month. With three long-term planets in stressful alignment with you all year, you always need to watch your health, but this is one of your better periods. If you feel under the weather, enhance the health in the ways mentioned in the yearly report.

Your love planet, Mars, spends the month in your 3rd house. Thus love is close to home – in your own neighbourhood. Your neighbourhood, such as it is, has more glamour and romance in it than the finest resorts of the world. Love opportunities for singles happen at educational functions – at school or school functions, at lectures and seminars – perhaps even at the library or bookshop. The gift of the gab attracts you these days. Good intellectual compatibility, good exchanges of ideas, are romantic turn-ons.

March

Best Days Overall: 3, 4, 13, 14, 22, 23, 31
Most Stressful Days Overall: 10, 11, 12, 18, 19, 24, 25
Best Days for Love: 8, 9, 18, 19, 20, 26, 27, 29, 30
Best Days for Money: 1, 2, 6, 7, 10, 11, 12, 15, 16, 17, 20, 21, 24, 25, 29, 30
Best Days for Career: 6, 7, 16, 17, 24, 25, 26

Mars's move into your 4th house on the 17th has multiple meanings for you. It impacts on health in a stressful way. After the 20th there are many planets (70 per cent) in stressful alignment with you, so take it nice and easy from that date onwards. The important thing, as always, is to get enough rest. Energy deficiency is the primal disease. It leaves you open to all kinds of things. Let go of trivialities and focus only on the essential. Do your best every day and refuse to worry – worry might not take you to hell itself, but it will take you to the gates of hell. Enhance the health in the ways mentioned in the yearly report. It will be a good idea to schedule more massages into your week or time at a health spa.

Mars in your 4th house is excellent for doing repairs, renovations or beautification projects in the home. It indicates more entertaining from home and more socializing with the family and extended family. It also shows a shift in the love attitudes. Until the 17th love can be found in the neighbourhood and perhaps with neighbours. After the 17th the home and family itself are the centre for love. Romantic opportunities come from the family or through family connections. The gift of the gab is less important to you, and now you crave emotional intimacy. You like people with whom you can share feelings. There is a tendency to be more nostalgic in love too – a tendency to want to relive the past, to revive past high points. This, of course, is impossible. You might be missing the splendours of the present – of the new and better experiences that await. Often with this aspect you meet up with an old flame from the past (or someone who reminds you of him or her, someone with similar mannerisms or personality). Usually this is not serious but it does have a therapeutic value. You get to resolve old issues.

On the 20th, as the Sun enters your 7th house, you begin a yearly love and social peak. The social life becomes hyperactive. Singles have many opportunities for romance this period. But keep in mind that Uranus in your 7th house is not so great for marriage. Venus will travel with Uranus on the 28th and 29th and your need for freedom increases. The current love can see you as too rebellious.

Finances are better before the 20th than after. After the 20th you have to work harder for earnings than usual.

April

Best Days Overall: 1, 9, 10, 11, 18, 19, 27, 28
Most Stressful Days Overall: 7, 8, 14, 15, 21, 22
Best Days for Love: 7, 8, 14, 15, 16, 17, 25, 26, 27
Best Days for Money: 2, 3, 7, 8, 12, 13, 16, 17, 21, 22, 25, 26, 29, 30
Best Days for Career: 4, 5, 14, 15, 16, 21, 22, 25

Health is improving but still needs keeping an eye on. Review our discussion of this last month. Continue to enhance the health in the ways mentioned in the yearly report. Soaking in a tub when you feel stressed will relax the body and rejuvenate you too. Water-based therapies are good. Health will improve further after the 20th. The worst will be over with.

Mars, your love planet, spends the month in your 4th house. Review our discussion of this last month.

You're still very much in a yearly love and social peak until the 20th, so there is more going out, more parties, more dating. However, with Uranus in your 7th house all of this seems unstable. It is fun, but not likely to be serious.

You're still in a very prosperous year, but finances are a bit slower than usual. Pluto, your financial planet, will begin to go backwards on the 22nd and Jupiter, the occupant of your money house, went retrograde on March 9. This is not the end of the world, but it shows a need for more caution and for a review of finances. Important financial decisions are better made before the 22nd than afterwards. Since these retrogrades will go on for many months, be more careful about the little details of finance. Read the fine print of contracts, credit-card offers and insurance quotes. Make sure cheques are signed and dated correctly. Make sure you address your envelopes correctly. If you're mailing an important document, it might be a good idea to send it special delivery. The point here is not to make things slower than they need to be. Keep copies of all receipts. Be as perfect as possible in your financial dealings. Delays and glitches will probably still occur, but not as often as they could.

The most important thing over the next few months is to gain clarity on your financial picture and strategy. It's a time for study and due diligence.

Your 8th house of regeneration is powerful all month, but especially after the 20th. Venus is in the 8th house until the 24th. Thus there is more sex appeal to the image. It just 'shines out' naturally. In general there is more libido than usual too. Very good for weight-loss and detox regimes.

May

Best Days Overall: 7, 8, 16, 17, 24, 25
Most Stressful Days Overall: 4, 5, 11, 12, 13, 18, 19, 31
Best Days for Love: 4, 5, 7, 8, 11, 12, 13, 15, 16, 17, 24, 26
Best Days for Money: 4, 5, 9, 10, 14, 15, 18, 19, 22, 23, 26, 27, 28
Best Days for Career: 4, 5, 14, 15, 18, 19, 24

If you got through the past two months with health and sanity intact, you're done a great job! Congratulations! The month ahead is infinitely easier than the past two. Mars and Uranus leave their stressful aspects with you on the 16th. Vitality soars (especially compared with the past two months).

The planetary power is now on the day side (upper half) of your Horoscope. This began on March 20 and is in full swing now. Home and family are still very important – an important focus – but now you can shift attention to the career and outer objectives. To really serve your family you need to be successful in your career. You can miss out on a school play or soccer game, but you don't want to miss out on an important deal. You seem successful this month – and you haven't even hit your peak yet. Venus, the ruler of your Horoscope, crosses the Mid-heaven and enters your 10th house of career on the19th (the Moon, your career planet, is also in your 10th house on the 19th). This shows personal success and recognition. It shows elevation. People look up to you. You're above everyone in your world. Physical appearance and overall demeanour play an important role in the career. You need to spend on your image, but don't overspend. There is special success on the 31st.

With your 8th house strong until the 21st it's a good time for 'resurrection' activities. There are areas in your life – perhaps a business, a friendship or project – that seem dead. Now is the time to bring them back to life. Resurrection seems like a miraculous thing, but it is very normal in nature. You can more easily tap into this power now.

This is also a good time for detox and weight-loss regimes. Rid the body (and the emotional life) of what doesn't belong there. You will feel much better.

Uranus's move into your 8th house this month on the 16th shows an experimental attitude to sex and sexual expression. You seem ready to try anything – ready to throw out all the dos and don'ts. This is fine so long as the experiments are not destructive. This also shows that the spouse, partner or current love is entering a period of financial experimentation. He or she is throwing out all the rule books and learning what works financially through trial, error and experiment. Much new knowledge will happen this way.

June

Best Days Overall: 3, 4, 12, 13, 20, 21, 22, 30
Most Stressful Days Overall: 1, 2, 8, 9, 14, 15, 28, 29
Best Days for Love: 3, 4, 6, 7, 8, 9, 12, 13, 16, 20, 21, 22, 23, 24, 30
Best Days for Money: 1, 2, 5, 6, 7, 10, 11, 14, 15, 18, 19, 23, 24, 28, 29
Best Days for Career: 3, 4, 12, 13, 14, 15, 23

A very hectic, but successful month. Health needs watching from the 21st onwards. The good news is that health won't be as challenging as March and April were. (If you got through those months, you'll get through the month ahead.) Still, make sure to get enough rest. Take breaks from work and recharge your batteries. Don't allow yourself to get over tired. Enhance the health in the ways mentioned in the yearly report. Water-based therapies are still powerful.

Your love planet has been in your 5th house since May 16 and will be here for the whole of the coming month. This shows another shift in love and love attitudes. Love should be fun and you're attracted to the people you can have fun with, the ones who can show you a good time, the ones who laugh and have a carefree attitude. This is all well and good, but this aspect doesn't favour serious romance. (Even though, with Uranus out of your 7th house, serious romance is on the table now.) Mars in the 5th house wants love to be a constant honey-moon. It is not ready to deal with the tough times that inevitably happen even in the best of relationships. But this is how you feel now and these are the kinds of people you're attracting.

Venus has been the 'morning star' in your career. On May 19 she announced the rising sun in your career, and now, on the 21st, he appears and you enter a yearly career peak. You have a lot of help from your friends. Networking helps and your technological expertise is important. Your willingness to travel also seems important.

Though the career is going very well, finances are shakier this month, from the 21st onwards. Pluto your financial planet is not only retrograde, but receiving stressful aspects. So you need to work harder to achieve your financial goals. Also, this shows that the career success you seek entails some kind of financial sacrifice. You have to be willing to make it. (This sacrifice seems short term though.)

Your challenge this month – and it won't be easy – is combining a successful career with a successful home and family life. The demands of both are very strong on you. It will be difficult to please everybody, but somehow you'll manage.

July

Best Days Overall: 1, 10, 11, 18, 19, 27, 28, 29
Most Stressful Days Overall: 5, 6, 12, 13, 25, 26
Best Days for Love: 1, 5, 6, 10, 11, 16, 18, 19, 25, 26, 27, 28, 29
Best Days for Money: 1, 7, 8, 12, 13, 16, 17, 20, 21, 25, 26, 27, 28, 29
Best Days for Career: 3, 4, 12, 13, 21, 22

The month ahead is basically happy, but two eclipses will shake the world around you. They will keep you on your toes as well. Don't be lulled by the apparent harmony. Be happy, but also be vigilant.

The Solar Eclipse of the 13th occurs in your 10th house of career, bringing career changes. There are shakeups in your company or industry. There are dramas in the lives of bosses, parents or parent figures. The rules of the game are changing and you're forced to make course corrections in your career. Every Solar Eclipse will test friendships. Sometimes it's the relationship that's the problem. If there are flaws, this is when you learn of them. But often it is not the relationship itself, but the dramas (often life-changing dramas) that happen in the lives of friends that prove testing. As with every Solar Eclipse, your high-tech equipment will get tested. Computers tend to be temperamental, and in many cases you'll find they need repair or replacement. Parents or parent figures in your life are not only having personal crises, but financial ones as well. Important changes have to happen. Your finances also seem affected as this eclipse impacts on your financial planet, Pluto. My feeling is that you have underestimated yourself. Your financial prospects are better than you have planned for and now you have to make adjustments to your thinking.

The Lunar Eclipse of the 27th occurs in your 5th house of creativity and children, and impacts on the children in your life. Once again they need to redefine themselves and create a new image and look for the world. They can have job changes as well. This eclipse also impacts on your career, industry and company – more dramas are happening there. Parents, parent figures and bosses are once again affected. They, too, have to re-imagine themselves over the next six months. Again a parent or parent figure is forced to make important financial changes.

Their thinking hasn't been realistic. This eclipse is more powerful than it appears on the surface. It impacts on two other planets – Mars and Uranus. Thus a current relationship gets tested. Long-repressed grievances come up for resolution. The impact on Uranus shows that high-tech gadgetry will again be tested. Take all necessary safeguards for your files and photos.

August

Best Days Overall: 6, 7, 14, 15, 24, 25
Most Stressful Days Overall: 1, 2, 3, 8, 9, 21, 22, 29, 30
Best Days for Love: 1, 2, 3, 5, 6, 13, 14, 15, 22, 24, 25, 29, 30
Best Days for Money: 4, 5, 8, 9, 12, 13, 16, 17, 21, 22, 26, 27, 31
Best Days for Career: 2, 3, 8, 9, 10, 11, 20, 31

Another Solar Eclipse on the 11th (the third Solar Eclipse of the year) will once again test friendships and your high-tech gadgetry. Even the new stuff you got last month can be more erratic now. Friendships that can endure all these eclipses are indeed good ones. Children and children figures are having their friendships tested too. If they are of appropriate age, their marriages or love relationships are also getting tested. Parents and parent figures need to make more financial adjustments. The changes made last month might not be enough. A family member can be facing surgery or having a near-death kind of experience (this is not necessarily literal death, but psychological encounters).

The good news here is that you're very focused on friendships this month and will most likely overcome the challenges. Also, with the Sun in your 11th house, you have a good feeling for technology, and these challenges will add to your knowledge. If you need to buy new equipment, the purchases will be good.

Your financial planet, Pluto, is still retrograde this month, but Jupiter in your money house is moving forward. After the 23rd, as the Sun moves into Virgo, Pluto will receive beautiful aspects. Prosperity is definitely happening, but at a slower pace. July 27–28 should have been a nice financial period as Venus made beautiful aspects with Pluto.

Love is very complicated this month. First off, your love planet spends the entire month 'out of bounds'. So the search for love is taking you outside your normal social sphere. Singles are meeting people outside their usual circle, so there is more insecurity here. Not only is Mars 'out of bounds' but he is also retrograde all month. This increases the insecurity. It will not be a good idea to make love decisions one way or another these days. The good news is that Mars is in your 5th house, so love isn't that serious this month. It is more about entertainment than commitment. After the 13th Mars retrogrades back into your 4th house. This can once again bring an encounter with an old flame (or someone who reminds you of the old flame). It also shifts your attitudes about love. Family values seem important from the 13th onwards. Though you might be searching far and wide, love is close to home.

September

Best Days Overall: 2, 3, 11, 12, 20, 21, 29, 30
Most Stressful Days Overall: 4, 5, 17, 18, 19, 25, 26
Best Days for Love: 1, 2, 3, 10, 11, 13, 20, 21, 22, 23, 25, 26, 29, 30
Best Days for Money: 1, 4, 5, 9, 10, 13, 14, 18, 19, 22, 23, 24, 27, 28
Best Days for Career: 1, 4, 5, 9, 18, 19, 29

Though the Western, social sector of your chart is still dominant this month, the short-term planets are entering their maximum Eastern position. You can't ignore other people or have your own way entirely, but you have more independence than you've had all year. So now is the time to make any changes that need to be made. Now is the time to take more responsibility for your own happiness. If you wait too long, these things will become more difficult.

The good news here is that you're very comfortable with less independence. You enjoy exercising your social genius. You don't mind getting things done by consensus and negotiation. High-handed independent action is not your style, Libra.

The month ahead is spiritual, a period for internal growth. But this internal growth will translate – by the spiritual law – to external growth. Cherish it. It is the necessary prelude. So, this is a month for spiritual studies, for the study of sacred literature, for attending spiritual seminars or lectures and for more involvement in charities and altruistic activities. With the ruler of the 11th house in your spiritual house, you seem to be exploring the spiritual world in a more scientific and rational way. You're going deeper into the scientific side of the spiritual life. (Mercury in your 12th house from the 6th to the 22nd also favours a more rational approach.) Spirituality is not 'mumbo jumbo' but a science in its own right.

On the 22nd both the Sun and Mercury cross your Ascendant and enter your 1st house. You begin a yearly personal pleasure period. It is time to pamper the body and reward it for its yeoman service all these years. The body is of the animal kingdom and needs rewarding every now and then. If we are kind to animals, we should be kind to our bodies.

The month ahead looks prosperous. Venus, the ruler of your Horoscope, moves into your money house on the 9th, joining Jupiter who has been there all year. So the money house is a house of power this period. You're taking a more active role in your financial life. You're spending on yourself and your image. You're projecting an image of wealth.

October

Best Days Overall: 1, 8, 9, 17, 18, 19, 27, 28
Most Stressful Days Overall: 2, 3, 15, 16, 22, 23, 29, 30
Best Days for Love: 1, 2, 3, 8, 9, 10, 11, 17, 18, 19, 20, 21, 22, 23, 27, 28, 29, 30
Best Days for Money: 2, 3, 6, 7, 10, 11, 15, 16, 20, 21, 25, 26, 29, 30
Best Days for Career: 1, 2, 3, 8, 9, 18, 19, 29, 30

The love life began improving last month. Mars, your love planet, started to move forward again, and he will spend the entire month in your 5th house of fun and entertainment. Moreover, he is back 'in bounds'. You're back in your normal social sphere. As we have said, the love planet in your 5th house is not conducive to serious, committed kinds of relationships. It is more about fun and entertainment. You're not really looking for anything serious: love is just another form of entertainment, like going to the movies or theatre. Venus goes retrograde on the 5th and thus you might be 'backtracking' out of a relationship.

You're still in the midst of a yearly personal pleasure peak until the 23rd. Enjoy! This power in your 1st house is not only good for indulging the body, but also for getting it into the shape that you want.

On the 23rd the Sun will enter the money house and you begin a yearly financial peak. You have a very prosperous month ahead. Your money house is chock-full of planets from the 23rd onwards – and they are beneficent ones as well. Add to this Pluto's resumption of forward motion on the 2nd and you have more signals of prosperity. The financial confidence is back. You have clarity on finances. You know what to do and how to do it.

After the 23rd (and even before that) the short-term planets are making nice aspects to your planet of health and work, Neptune – a good sign for job seekers. And even those of you already employed can have opportunities for overtime or side jobs. (Permanent job offers need more study, however, as Neptune is still retrograde.)

Health is much better this month than last month. Mars's move into Aquarius last month was a positive healthwise. You still have two long-term planets in stressful alignment, but most of the planets are either kind to you or leaving you alone. Health will further improve after the 23rd as Neptune starts to receive positive stimulation. If you feel under the weather, enhance the health in the ways mentioned in the yearly report.

November

Best Days Overall: 4, 5, 14, 15, 23, 24
Most Stressful Days Overall: 11, 12, 19, 20, 25, 26
Best Days for Love: 4, 5, 14, 15, 16, 19, 20, 23, 24, 25, 26
Best Days for Money: 2, 3, 6, 7, 8, 11, 12, 19, 21, 22, 27, 29, 30
Best Days for Career: 6, 7, 8, 16, 17, 25, 26, 27

A lot of change is happening this month as two major long-term planets change signs. On the 6th Uranus retrogrades back into Aries, your 7th house of love, and on the 8th Jupiter leaves your money house and enters your 3rd house of communication. Mercury is 'out of bounds' from the 4th to the 20th as well. Thus you're outside your normal sphere in your religious and spiritual life. You're exploring exotic and perhaps foreign teachings. You can't seem to find the answers you want in your current path. This is OK. It happens very often.

You're still in the midst of a yearly financial peak until the 22nd. So the month ahead is prosperous. But the interest in finance is waning. Jupiter, as we mentioned, leaves the money house on the 8th and the Sun will leave it on the 22nd. I read this as a good thing. Short-term financial goals have been achieved and there's no need to pay special attention anymore. You can move on to other things.

Jupiter's move into your 3rd house will bring a new car and communication equipment in the coming year – and high quality too. This is an excellent aspect for students below college level; they are successful in their studies for the next year. It is especially good for those planning to go to college as success at school will enhance their college prospects. It is also a wonderful aspect for sales and marketing people, for traders, retailers, teachers and writers. They all seem successful in their work.

The love life becomes unstable once again from the 6th onwards. But after seven years of this, you seem comfortable with it. You know how to handle it. You can enjoy the sudden and dramatic changes that happen in your social life. Instability is also exciting. Mars, your love planet, moves from your 5th house into your 6th house on the 16th. This again produces change in the love attitudes. The love planet in Pisces makes you more idealistic. You're attracted to more spiritual types of people – to creative, artistic people. The workplace become a venue for love too. There are love opportunities with co-workers (or through them). The love planet in the 6th house also indicates an attraction to health professionals or for people involved in your health. A visit to the doctor's surgery can become much more than it seems.

Venus spends the month in your own sign. On the 16th she starts moving forward again, increasing self-confidence and self-esteem. You look great these days. Venus enhances the physical beauty, grace and charm. You're attracting the opposite sex this month.

December

Best Days Overall: 2, 3, 11, 12, 21, 22, 29, 30
Most Stressful Days Overall: 9, 10, 16, 17, 23, 24
Best Days for Love: 2, 3, 4, 5, 14, 15, 16, 17, 23, 24, 31
Best Days for Money: 4, 5, 6, 9, 10, 16, 18, 19, 26, 27, 28, 31
Best Days for Career: 6, 7, 17, 23, 24, 27

Though your yearly financial peak has passed, you're having a mini financial peak this month. First off, the Moon will visit your money house twice this month (usually she visits only once). Venus, the ruler of your Horoscope moves into the money house on the 2nd and spends the rest of the month there. And Mercury is in your money house until the 13th. So your money house is strong. You're not delegating financial management to others these days, but you are taking personal charge. Even those of you who have financial planners or accountants are supervising things more closely than usual. You're presenting an image of wealth to the world – dressing, looking and acting the part. The financial intuition is excellent. Hard to imagine you lacking for any needful thing.

You're in a yearly intellectual peak right now. The mental faculties are going to be enhanced for the next twelve months, as Jupiter will be in your 3rd house for most of 2019. But for the month ahead – especially until the 21st – the faculties are exceptionally good. You absorb and comprehend data, information and knowledge easily. You inhale it. Learning is much easier. Students excel in their studies. Teachers, writers, sales and marketing people all communicate better. This is a great period to take courses in subjects that interest you. And if you have expertise in a subject it is a great month to teach it to others, either by the written or spoken word.

The problem with so much power in the 3rd house is that it can be too much of a good thing. The mind can be overstimulated. The thinking, if not kept in check, can get out of control. There can be problems getting to sleep. There is tendency to talk too much. Phone bills can get out of control if you're not careful.

Siblings and sibling figures in your life have had a tough financial year in 2018. But the tide started to turn last month. They are taking on added financial responsibilities, but the wherewithal will be there to handle it. On the 21st, they enter a yearly financial peak.

Health will need more watching after the 21st. So, as always, don't allow yourself to get overtired. Make sure you get enough rest. Enhance the health in the ways mentioned in the yearly report.

The love life looks good. Venus is making nice aspects to your love planet all month. But the current love looks stressed out. (He or she should feel better after the 21st.) There is a happy social or love opportunity from the 5th to the 7th. This can involve a work-related gathering, a co-worker or someone involved in your health.

Scorpio

♏︎

THE SCORPION

Birthdays from
23rd October to
22nd November

Personality Profile

SCORPIO AT A GLANCE

Element – Water

Ruling Planet – Pluto
  Co-ruling Planet – Mars
  Career Planet – Sun
  Love Planet – Venus
  Money Planet – Jupiter
  Planet of Health and Work – Mars
  Planet of Home and Family Life – Uranus

Colour – red-violet

Colour that promotes love, romance and social harmony – green

Colour that promotes earning power – blue

Gems – bloodstone, malachite, topaz

Metals – iron, radium, steel

Scents – cherry blossom, coconut, sandalwood, watermelon

Quality – fixed (= stability)

Quality most needed for balance – a wider view of things

Strongest virtues – loyalty, concentration, determination, courage, depth

Deepest needs – to penetrate and transform

Characteristics to avoid – jealousy, vindictiveness, fanaticism

Signs of greatest overall compatibility – Cancer, Pisces

Signs of greatest overall incompatibility – Taurus, Leo, Aquarius

Sign most helpful to career – Leo

Sign most helpful for emotional support – Aquarius

Sign most helpful financially – Sagittarius

Sign best for marriage and/or partnerships – Taurus

Sign most helpful for creative projects – Pisces

Best Sign to have fun with – Pisces

Signs most helpful in spiritual matters – Cancer, Libra

Best day of the week – Tuesday

Understanding a Scorpio

One symbol of the sign of Scorpio is the phoenix. If you meditate upon the legend of the phoenix you will begin to understand the Scorpio character – his or her powers and abilities, interests and deepest urges.

The phoenix of mythology was a bird that could recreate and reproduce itself. It did so in a most intriguing way: it would seek a fire – usually in a religious temple – fly into it, consume itself in the flames and then emerge a new bird. If this is not the ultimate, most profound transformation, then what is?

Transformation is what Scorpios are all about – in their minds, bodies, affairs and relationships (Scorpios are also society's transformers). To change something in a natural, not an artificial way, involves a transformation from within. This type of change is radical change as opposed to a mere cosmetic make-over. Some people think that change means altering just their appearance, but this is not the kind of thing that interests a Scorpio. Scorpios seek deep, fundamental change. Since real change always proceeds from within, a Scorpio is very interested in – and usually accustomed to – the inner, intimate and philosophical side of life.

Scorpios are people of depth and intellect. If you want to interest them you must present them with more than just a superficial image. You and your interests, projects or business deals must have real substance to them in order to stimulate a Scorpio. If they haven't, he or she will find you out – and that will be the end of the story.

If we observe life – the processes of growth and decay – we see the transformational powers of Scorpio at work all the time. The caterpillar changes itself into a butterfly; the infant grows into a child and then an adult. To Scorpios this definite and perpetual transformation is not something to be feared. They see it as a normal part of life. This acceptance of transformation gives Scorpios the key to understanding the true meaning of life.

Scorpios' understanding of life (including life's weaknesses) makes them powerful warriors – in all senses of the word. Add to this their depth, patience and endurance and you have a powerful personality. Scorpios have good, long memories and can at times be quite vindictive – they can wait years to get their revenge. As a friend, though, there is no one more loyal and true than a Scorpio. Few are willing to make the sacrifices that a Scorpio will make for a true friend.

The results of a transformation are quite obvious, although the process of transformation is invisible and secret. This is why Scorpios are considered secretive in nature. A seed will not grow properly if you keep digging it up and exposing it to the light of day. It must stay buried – invisible – until it starts to grow. In the same manner, Scorpios fear revealing too much about themselves or their hopes to other people. However, they will be more than happy to let you see the finished product – but only when it is completely unwrapped. On the other hand, Scorpios like knowing everyone else's secrets as much as they dislike anyone knowing theirs.

Finance

Love, birth, life as well as death are Nature's most potent transformations; Scorpios are interested in all of these. In our society, money is a transforming power, too, and a Scorpio is interested in money for that reason. To a Scorpio money is power, money causes change, money controls. It is the power of money that fascinates them. But Scorpios can be too materialistic if they are not careful. They can be overly awed by the power of money, to a point where they think that money rules the world.

Even the term 'plutocrat' comes from Pluto, the ruler of the sign of Scorpio. Scorpios will – in one way or another – achieve the financial status they strive for. When they do so they are careful in the way they handle their wealth. Part of this financial carefulness is really a kind of honesty, for Scorpios are usually involved with other people's money – as accountants, lawyers, stockbrokers or corporate managers – and when you handle other people's money you have to be more cautious than when you handle your own.

In order to fulfil their financial goals, Scorpios have important lessons to learn. They need to develop qualities that do not come naturally to them, such as breadth of vision, optimism, faith, trust and, above all, generosity. They need to see the wealth in Nature and in life, as well as in its more obvious forms of money and power. When they develop generosity their financial potential reaches great heights, for Jupiter, the Lord of Opulence and Good Fortune, is Scorpio's money planet.

Career and Public Image

Scorpio's greatest aspiration in life is to be considered by society as a source of light and life. They want to be leaders, to be stars. But they follow a very different road than do Leos, the other stars of the zodiac. A Scorpio arrives at the goal secretly, without ostentation; a Leo pursues it openly. Scorpios seek the glamour and fun of the rich and famous in a restrained, discreet way.

Scorpios are by nature introverted and tend to avoid the limelight. But if they want to attain their highest career goals they need to open up a bit and to express themselves more. They need to stop hiding their light under a bushel and let it shine. Above all, they need to let go of any vindictiveness and small-mindedness. All their gifts and insights were given to them for one important reason – to serve life and to increase the joy of living for others.

Love and Relationships

Scorpio is another zodiac sign that likes committed clearly defined, structured relationships. They are cautious about marriage, but when they do commit to a relationship they tend to be faithful – and heaven help the mate caught or even suspected of infidelity! The jealousy of the Scorpio is legendary. They can be so intense in their jealousy that even the thought or intention of infidelity will be detected and is likely to cause as much of a storm as if the deed had actually been done.

Scorpios tend to settle down with those who are wealthier than they are. They usually have enough intensity for two, so in their partners they seek someone pleasant, hard-working, amiable, stable and easy-going. They want someone they can lean on, someone loyal behind them as they fight the battles of life. To a Scorpio a partner, be it a lover or a friend, is a real partner – not an adversary. Most of all a Scorpio is looking for an ally, not a competitor.

If you are in love with a Scorpio you will need a lot of patience. It takes a long time to get to know Scorpios, because they do not reveal themselves readily. But if you persist and your motives are honourable, you will gradually be allowed into a Scorpio's inner chambers of the mind and heart.

Home and Domestic Life

Uranus is ruler of Scorpio's 4th solar house of home and family. Uranus is the planet of science, technology, changes and democracy. This tells us a lot about a Scorpio's conduct in the home and what he or she needs in order to have a happy, harmonious home life.

Scorpios can sometimes bring their passion, intensity and wilfulness into the home and family, which is not always the place for these qualities. These traits are good for the warrior and the transformer, but not so good for the nurturer and family member. Because of this (and also because of their need for change and transformation) the Scorpio may be prone to sudden changes of residence. If not carefully constrained, the sometimes inflexible Scorpio can produce turmoil and sudden upheavals within the family.

Scorpios need to develop some of the virtues of Aquarius in order to cope better with domestic matters. There is a need to build a team spirit at home, to treat family activities as truly group activities – family members should all have a say in what does and does not get done. For at times a Scorpio can be most dictatorial. When a Scorpio gets dictatorial it is much worse than if a Leo or Capricorn (the two other power signs in the zodiac) does. For the dictatorship of a Scorpio is applied with more zeal, passion, intensity and concentration than is true of either a Leo or Capricorn. Obviously this can be unbearable to family members – especially if they are sensitive types.

In order for a Scorpio to get the full benefit of the emotional support that a family can give, he or she needs to let go of conservatism and be a bit more experimental, to explore new techniques in childrearing, be more democratic with family members and to try to manage things by consensus rather than by autocratic edict.

Horoscope for 2018

Major Trends

Jupiter's move into your sign on October 10 of last year initiated a multi-year cycle of prosperity. He remains in your sign almost all of the year ahead – until November 8 – so the money is rolling in. Jupiter in anyone's sign is a prosperity signal, but for you more so than most. Jupiter is your financial planet. So his impact on finances is much stronger. On November 8 Jupiter will enter your money house – his own sign and house. This brings more prosperity. More on this later.

Pluto has been in your 3rd house for many years now, since 2008. So you've been very interested in communication and intellectual pursuits. This has been very good for students as it shows success in their studies – especially for students below college level. Saturn entered your 3rd house at the end of 2017 and will be there for two more years, signalling that students will now have to work harder in school to achieve their grades. They need more discipline. They can't just coast in their studies – more is being demanded. Teachers, lecturers, writers, journalists, sales and marketing people will all have to work harder too – there are greater demands being placed on them.

Though you will find career activities fulfilling and are likely to succeed, this is not an especially strong career year. There will be many changes here, course corrections and the like in the year ahead. We will have three Solar Eclipses in 2018 (usually there are only two), and two eclipses occur in your 10th house of career. So you can expect change and shakeups this year. More on this later.

Uranus will leave your 6th house of health and work this year – but only for a while. Next year he will leave for the long haul. In the meantime you get an announcement of things to come (from May 16 to November 6). He enters your 7th house of love and starts to test your current marriage or relationship. However, there will be more stability at your place of work and with those you employ (if you do). More details later.

Neptune has been in your 5th house since 2012 and will be there for many more years. This shows that the children and children figures in your life are becoming more spiritual. They seem very idealistic. Those of you in the creative arts will find your work much more inspired. Your taste in entertainment is becoming more refined – more spiritualized.

Your most important interests this year will be the body, image and personal pleasure (until November 8); finance (from November 8 onwards); communication and intellectual interests; children, fun and creativity; health and work (until May 16 and from November 6 onwards); and love, romance and social activities (from May 16 to November 6).

Your paths of greatest fulfilment this year will be the body, image and personal pleasure (until November 8); finance (from November 8 onwards); career (until November 17); and religion, philosophy, higher education and foreign travel (from November 17 onwards).

Health

(Please note that this is an astrological perspective on health and not a medical one. In days of yore there was no difference, both of these perspectives were identical. But now there could be quite a difference. For a medical perspective, please consult your doctor or health practitioner.)

Health looks excellent in the coming year. As the year begins there are no long-term planets in stressful alignment with you. In fact, almost all of them are in harmonious alignment. Only on May 16, as Uranus moves into Taurus, will there be any long-term planet stressing you. And this will only be briefly – until November 6. (And those of you born late in the sign of Scorpio – from October 30 to November 22 – won't feel this too much.) So health and energy will be good this year. Sure, there will be periods in the year where health and energy are 'less easy'. These periods come from the transits of short-term planets. They pass quickly and are not trends for the year.

Your 6th house is strong for about half the year. Uranus moves in and out of there this year so you're focused on health, but the focus is waning (as it should).

With more energy at your disposal, those with pre-existing conditions should feel less. They would tend to be in abeyance as the body has more energy to neutralize them.

Good though your health is you can make it even better. Give more attention to the following - the vulnerable areas of your Horoscope (the reflex points are shown in the chart below):

- The colon, bladder and sexual organs. These are always important for Scorpio. Safe sex and sexual moderation are always issues for you. A herbal colon cleanse every now and then would be a good idea - especially if you're feeling under the weather.
- The head, face and scalp. These too are important for you, as Mars, the ruler of these areas, is your health planet. Scalp and face massages should be part of your regular health regime. Craniosacral therapy will also be effective here.
- The musculature. Another important area for you, as it is also ruled by Mars. A weak or flabby muscle can knock the spine and skeleton out of alignment. Thus, good muscle tone is important. Vigorous physical exercise - according to your age and stage in life - is important.

Important foot reflexology points for the year ahead

Try to massage all of the foot on a regular basis - the top of the foot as well as the bottom - but pay extra attention to the points highlighted on the chart. When you massage, be aware of 'sore spots' as these need special attention - as do the ankles and below them.

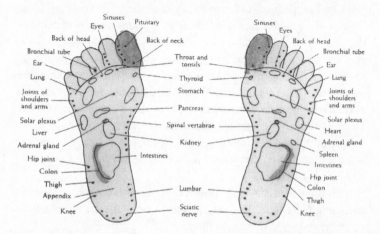

- The adrenals – another area ruled by Mars. Anger and fear – the fight or flight response – stresses the adrenals so avoid these emotions as much as possible. Meditation is a big help here. Ginseng is said to be helpful for the adrenals.
- The ankles and calves. These have only become important in the past seven or so years as Uranus, the ruler of these areas, has occupied your 6th house. They should be regularly massaged, and give the ankles more support when you exercise. Your health planet will spend an unusual amount of time – almost five months – in the sign of Aquarius, the sign that rules these areas. So continue to give attention here this year. Next year, from March 7, when Uranus will leave your 6th house for good these will become less important.

Uranus is your home and family planet, thus good health for you also means good domestic health, good family relations and good emotional health. If problems (God forbid) arise, restore harmony at home and with the family as quickly as possible. It is very important to maintain your emotional harmony. Moods should be kept positive and constructive. Meditation will be a help here.

Jupiter spends most of the year in your 1st house. This is a good thing, but from a health perspective it can lead to weight problems. Enjoy the good life, but there is no need to go overboard here.

Home and Family

This has been a tempestuous area – and challenging – for many years now. You and the family (and one of the parents or parent figures in your life) have been in conflict. Passions have been high. The family as a whole, the parent or parent figures have had surgery or near-death kinds of experiences. Perhaps major repairs have been needed in the home and perhaps numerous times. The good news is that things are getting slightly easier. Uranus has moved away from his square to Pluto (an inharmonious aspect). And he is changing signs this year, from militant Aries to more sedate Taurus. The improvements will be even stronger next year – from March 7 onwards – as your family planet moves into Taurus for the long term.

In spite of improving conditions we still see much change and drama in the home and family. There will two eclipses in your 4th house this year. One, a Solar Eclipse on February 15 and the second a Lunar Eclipse on July 27. Often eclipses here bring repairs to the home and dramas in the lives of family members. We will discuss this further in the monthly reports.

Mars will spend an unusual amount of time in your 4th house – five or so months – on and off. Usually he will spend only a month and a half in a sign. This tends to show conflicts with family members, high passions and perhaps health issues in the family. It often shows a need for major repairs. (Some of you might even decide to build a home during this period.)

Uranus, as we mentioned, moves into Taurus from May 16 to November 6. A parent or parent figure becomes more 'laid back' and easy going. Since Taurus rules your 7th house of love, there will be a desire for more harmony and stability.

For many years now you've been installing health equipment and health gadgets in the home. You've been working to make the home (and the family) more healthy. By now the home is as much a health spa as a home. Soon though, the focus will shift to beautifying the home. You will be more concerned with 'appearance' than usual. You will redecorate and buy objects of beauty. The home will be a place of beauty as well as a home. In some cases people get carried away and the home becomes more like an art gallery or museum than a home, but the root urge is to beautify it.

There is another reason for this urge to decorate and beautify your nest. You will be doing more entertaining from home. The home will be an important social centre and you want it to look good.

Repairs and renovations can happen anytime this year. But, if you have free will in the matters (not always the case), May 16 to August 13 and September 11 to November 15 would be good.

The beautification of the home is most likely to happen from May 16 to November 6. If you need to do this beforehand, January 18 to March 20 is a good time.

A move is not likely this year – though there's nothing against it. Siblings and sibling figures in your life have most likely had serial moves in recent years, but things are starting to calm down. They seem ready to settle down. Children and children figures are having an intensely spiritual kind of year, but the home life seems stable. Looks like they're travelling though.

Scorpios of childbearing age are unusually fertile right now. A pregnancy wouldn't be a surprise.

Finance and Career

You have a very prosperous year ahead, Scorpio. Enjoy.

As we said, Jupiter's move into your sign announces a multi-year cycle of prosperity. Jupiter is your financial planet and his position in your 1st house for most of the year shows financial windfalls coming to you. The money people in your life are supportive and approving of you. They back you.

It also shows that you're living a high lifestyle – living on a higher standard than usual. You're travelling, dressing well, dressing expensively and enjoying the pleasures of the body. More importantly perhaps, you feel prosperous; you look and dress that way, and others see you that way. In the eyes of many in your world you have become the 'money person'.

Your physical appearance and overall demeanour seem a big factor in earnings, and perhaps this is why you're spending on yourself and dressing expensively. Many models and athletes have this kind of aspect. They earn because of their physical attributes.

The beautiful thing about this transit is that there's not much you need to do to attract wealth or financial opportunity. It will find you. Just go about your daily business and it will happen.

Jupiter's wonderful aspect to Neptune most of the year shows a marvellous financial intuition (the short-cut to wealth) and luck in speculations. It shows 'happy money' – money that is earned in pleasurable ways, perhaps while you're at a party or tennis court or some place of entertainment. It also shows someone who is enjoying his or her earnings. Someone who is spending on leisure and fun activities. It is one thing to prosper and quite another to enjoy the fruits of prosperity. This year you have both.

On November 8, Jupiter will move into your money house, bringing more prosperity. Earnings increase. Assets your own –

whether a home, possessions, or your share portfolio – increase in value.

Though you seem successful in your career and seem to be enjoying it (the Moon's north node is in your 10th house of career almost all year, until November 17) this is not an especially strong career year. There is much change and upheaval going on here. Your career planet, the Sun, will get eclipsed three times this year (usually this happens only twice). Not only that. There will be two eclipses – one solar and one lunar – in your 10th house. Consider this: there will be five eclipses this year, and four of them will affect your career. So, there are many changes in your company, your industry and in the rules and regulations concerning your career. You will have to make many 'course corrections' in the year ahead. Your plans are not written in stone.

The Sun is your career planet and he is a fast-moving planet. In any given year he will move through all the signs and houses of your Horoscope, so there are many short-term career trends depending on where the Sun is and the aspects he receives. These are best covered in the monthly reports.

Love and Social Life

This area is starting to become more complicated this year. Complicated, but also very exciting. This will be the trend for many more years as Uranus establishes himself in your 7th house of love.

Those of you in existing relationships are going to have the relationship tested – and severely. I have seen marriages survive a Uranus transit – but not many. Those that did required an enormous amount of work and effort (on both sides). If you are willing to put in the effort, things can work out. But without this, it doesn't look good.

It is very important now to give the spouse, partner or current love as much space as possible – so long as it isn't destructive. Try to do unconventional things as a couple. Things off the beaten track. Inject change and excitement within the current relationship. With a little creativity this can be done. This will give you a fighting chance.

For singles, Uranus's move into your 7th house is not a good marriage indicator. It favours serial kinds of love affairs rather than marriage. Part of the reason is that you seem to be attracting 'non serious' kinds of people. Yes, they are exciting people, genius types, but not serious. It's probably not advisable to marry for a while.

The good news, though, is that you have more freedom in love. You're exploring your social freedom. Love and love opportunities can happen at any time in any place – often when you least expect it, and often when things look darkest. Love appears like a lightning flash in the sky. But, alas, it can disappear just as quickly.

Learning to deal with social instability is one of the main life lessons this year and in coming years.

The family, family connections and a parent or parent figure seem to be playing a big role in the love life. Perhaps they are playing Cupid. Perhaps you meet someone at a family gathering or function. Perhaps all of the above.

By the time Uranus has done his work – in the next seven years – you will be in completely new social circumstances, involved with a new circle of friends.

Venus is your love planet and she is a fast-moving planet. This year she moves through eleven signs and houses of your Horoscope (usually she will move through all of them). Thus there are many short-term love trends that depend on where Venus is at any given time and the kinds of aspects she receives. These are best covered in the monthly reports.

Venus will make one of her rare retrogrades this year – from October 5 to November 16. If love seems to be going backwards instead of forward, or you seem more confused on this issue, don't despair. This is normal when Venus is retrograde. This is not a time for making important love decisions one way or another. It is a time to review, get the facts, gain mental clarity on the issue, and see where improvements can be made. Then you can act when Venus starts moving forward again.

Self-Improvement

Saturn, as we mentioned, is now in your 3rd house. This is a challenging transit for students and intellectual workers. It is good to understand why this is so and the cosmic agenda behind it. Saturn wants to make you a more thorough and deeper thinker. There is an internal need for 'depth' – for deep understanding of a subject. So the thought process is slower, but deeper. Saturn says, 'better to slow down and get it right than to make snap, superficial judgements'. Most schools favour the superficial approach – memorize the facts and spew them out in a test. So, this transit makes things more difficult for students. It will not satisfy you these days. You'll spend more time on your studies (and in digesting information in general), but what you learn will be understood in a deep way.

The speech will also slow down – even for those of you who are verbally gifted. Circumstances will be arranged where you have to know what you're talking about before you speak. You'll have to do your homework. You will speak less, but when you do, you'll have something to say – something valid.

The children and children figures in your life are becoming ever more spiritual. They are under intense spiritual influences. Their bodies are more sensitive as well. They have a lower tolerance for drugs or alcohol and should avoid these things. Young people in general tend to be idealistic, but this is different. Many are having deep spiritual experiences. They are having prophetic kinds of dreams and experiencing all kinds of supernatural phenomena. Don't 'pooh-pooh' these things. If the child tells you of a dream experience, listen without making a judgement. Some of these dreams can be hidden messages to you and your financial circumstances. 'Out of the mouth of babes' goes the saying.

Uranus's move into your 7th house tends to destabilize the love and social life, but this is not punishment – though at times it can feel this way. There are attitudes (and perhaps people) that need shaking up – that need to be changed. Perhaps you've felt imprisoned by a certain set of friends or by your current relationship. You might not feel strong enough to break the bonds. So, the cosmos, through Uranus – the great over-turner – has to come in and do the job for you. If your prayers are to be answered you must allow this 'shakeup' to happen.

Month-by-month Forecasts

January

Best Days Overall: 1, 2, 10, 11, 20, 21, 29, 30
Most Stressful Days Overall: 3, 4, 17, 18, 25, 26, 31
Best Days for Love: 5, 6, 15, 16, 25, 26, 27, 28
Best Days for Money: 1, 2, 10, 11, 12, 13, 14, 20, 21, 29, 30
Best Days for Career: 3, 4, 5, 6, 15, 16, 27, 28, 31

Get ready for a very prosperous year. Though you had your yearly financial peak last month, the month ahead still looks very prosperous. Mercury in the money house until the 11th favours paying off debts and becoming more tax efficient. This position is also good for refinancing existing debt or borrowing, if you need to. Investments in technology seem good. On the 27th Mars enters your money house. This shows earning from work. Generally overtime or side/second jobs are available. Mars travels with Jupiter from the 4th to the 9th which reinforces the above. It also shows very happy job opportunities coming.

There is a Lunar Eclipse on the 31st that occurs in your 10th house of career. Thus course corrections are necessary here. These can come from shakeups in your company or industry. A parent or parent figure has personal dramas. The marriage of parents or parent figures (and of bosses) gets tested. There are shakeups in your place of worship – some chaos going on there. Religious figures in your life are having personal dramas. Your personal religious beliefs get tested too. This is a good thing: some will have to be modified, some will have to be discarded. These kinds of changes have a great impact. Avoid foreign travel (if possible) during the eclipse period.

The month ahead is an excellent time for starting a new project or launching a new product. *All* the planets are moving forward. Your personal solar cycle is waxing (growing) and the universal solar cycle began waxing last month. This will give a lot of forward momentum to your project and you should see fast progress. If you can choose a day between the 17th and 30th, when the Moon is also waxing, you will have the premier time for launching new ventures.

As the month begins, most of the planets are in the independent Eastern sector – the sector of self (though this is soon to change). If there are conditions that irk you, you still have time to make any changes, although if you wait too long, it will become more difficult.

Love is in the neighbourhood – close to home – this month. Later in the month, it is actually at home. Love opportunities come via the family and family connections.

February

Best Days Overall: 6, 7, 16, 17, 25, 26
Most Stressful Days Overall: 14, 15, 21, 22, 27, 28
Best Days for Love: 4, 5, 16, 21, 22, 25, 26
Best Days for Money: 6, 7, 9, 10, 16, 17, 25, 26
Best Days for Career: 4, 5, 14, 15, 25, 27, 28

Last month, on the 20th, the planetary power began to shift from the East to the West – from the sector of self to the sector of others. The planets are now moving towards others and their interests – and so should you. It is time to be more social and less personally assertive. If conditions irk you, adapt to them as best you can. It will be easier to change things to your liking in about six months' time, as the planetary power starts moving towards you again.

Home and family is the main focus this month. The 4th house is where the power is this month. This is a time to get this area in right order, so that you're ready for your next career push in a few months. All the planets (very unusually) are below the horizon now – the night side of your chart. You're behaving like a 'night person' rather than a day person. The night side of your personality is stronger. This aspect favours getting into emotional harmony and pursuing your goals by the methods of the night, rather than the day. Meditation, visualization, putting yourself emotionally in the place you want to be – these are the methods that work best now. It is about changing your inner condition and letting the outer condition change in natural ways – by the spiritual law.

Your 4th house is further emphasized by a Solar Eclipse on the 15th, which occurs in that house, impacting on the family and family members. The family can be having personal dramas. They are apt to be more temperamental this period (even before the eclipse happens), so be more patient with them. Often repairs are needed in the home. The dream life is likely to be hyperactive and perhaps disturbing, but pay it no mind. It is not a portent of the future and has very little personal significance. It's just the psyche responding to emotional flotsam stirred up by the eclipse. Siblings and sibling figures are forced to make important financial changes. Mothers and fathers – or those who play this role in your life – are affected here. Career changes are likely and you might see this down the road. Once again the marriages of parents, parent figures and bosses are being tested. Jupiter, your financial planet, is affected by this eclipse, so you need a financial course correction. Your thinking hasn't been realistic. This eclipse affects you strongly, so take it easy over that period. Spend more time quietly at home. You need to rest and relax more anyway until the 18th, but especially during the eclipse period.

March

Best Days Overall: 6, 7, 15, 16, 17, 24, 25
Most Stressful Days Overall: 13, 14, 20, 21, 26, 27
Best Days for Love: 8, 18, 19, 20, 21, 26, 27
Best Days for Money: 6, 7, 8, 9, 15, 16, 17, 24, 25
Best Days for Career: 6, 7, 16, 17, 26, 27

Your financial planet Jupiter goes retrograde on the 9th for a few months. You don't stop your life because of a retrograde, of course. You shop for your necessities, and do what is necessary. It's the major purchases, the major financial decisions that are better being postponed. Nor will Jupiter's retrograde not stop earnings, only slow things down a bit (and often this is a good thing). The important thing over the next few months is to attain clarity on your finances – your strategy and thinking. With Jupiter retrograde, things are not what they seem.

Money still comes from work until the 17th. The health field looks like an interesting investment for those of you who invest. Financial opportunities are coming to you all the time, still – only now they need studying rather more. With Jupiter in your sign the money people in your life are very supportive. And, in many cases, you are the money person in your life. This is how people see you.

Your 5th house of fun and creativity became powerful on February 18, and remains so until the 20th. Half of the planets are either there or moving through there this month. This is a lot of power. A great month for the children and children figures in your life. They have confidence, self-esteem and prosperity – especially after the 20th. This cosmic vacation will bring all kinds of solutions to you. Very often the mind is blocked by too much focus on one thing. Focusing on fun and creative pursuits instead allows solutions to come naturally, with little effort. This period will recharge the batteries and give you a zest for more work later on – after the 20th.

Health is good this month. If you like you can enhance it further through thigh massage and liver cleanses (until the 17th). After the 17th enhance the health through back and knee massage. Good dental hygiene becomes more important then, too.

On the 20th the Sun enters your 6th house of health and work. Since health is good, there's no need to overly focus here. Focus on your work. The authority figures in your life are impressed with your good work ethic.

April

Best Days Overall: 2, 3, 12, 13, 21, 22, 29
Most Stressful Days Overall: 9, 10, 11, 16, 17, 23, 24
Best Days for Love: 7, 8, 16, 17, 27
Best Days for Money: 2, 3, 4, 5, 6, 12, 13, 21, 22, 29, 30
Best Days for Career: 4, 5, 14, 15, 16, 23, 24, 25

This is a very good month for job seekers. There are at least three job opportunities available, and Mars in the 3rd house suggests that they are in the neighbourhood, close to home. Those already employed have opportunities for overtime or side jobs.

Health and energy continue to be good. Though, after the 20th, the health will need more attention. This is a short-term issue. Enhance the health in the ways mentioned in the yearly report. This month also pay more attention to the spine, knees, bones, teeth, skeleton and overall skeletal alignment. Regular back massage will be good (especially from the 1st to the 3rd).

Pluto, the ruler of your Horoscope, goes retrograde on the 22nd. (This happens just around the time that you enter a yearly social peak.) This tends to weaken self-confidence and self-esteem. In your case this is probably a good thing. With your Western, social sector so strong – and soon to be even stronger – too much self-confidence – too much self-assertion – is not such a good thing. When in doubt, defer to others and let them have their way (so long as it isn't destructive). Since you're in a period where the social skills are being cultivated, personal will and desires are less important.

All of this will help the love life, which gets stronger from the 20th onwards. You're in the mood for love. Venus, your love planet, spends most of the month in your 7th house and the Sun enters there on the 20th. While marriage is unlikely for singles, there are still happy romantic opportunities and meetings (especially on the 17th and 18th). The career planet (the Sun) in the 7th house shows that you're mixing with high and mighty people these days – people above you in status and power. You're romantically attracted to power and prestige. You find people who have the power to help you careerwise alluring. A lot of your socializing seems business or career related.

You're still very much in a prosperity year, but this month – especially after the 20th – finances are temporarily stressful. You need to work harder for earnings. The focus on love and career might be distracting you from finance. Also, Jupiter is still retrograde.

May

Best Days Overall: 9, 10, 18, 19, 26, 27, 28
Most Stressful Days Overall: 7, 8, 14, 15, 20, 21
Best Days for Love: 7, 8, 14, 15, 17, 26
Best Days for Money: 2, 3, 9, 10, 18, 19, 26, 27, 29, 30
Best Days for Career: 4, 5, 14, 15, 20, 21, 24

You're still in the midst of a yearly love and social peak until the 21st, so the social life is active and happy. But new complications are developing in love. Uranus makes a major move into your 7th house on the

16th. This will make the love life more exciting – you never know what's going to happen next. But it also destabilizes the social life. Most of you won't feel it just yet (you will feel it in future years), but those of you born early in the sign of Scorpio (October 23–25) will certainly feel this. On the 19th, as your love planet moves into Cancer, she moves in opposition to Saturn and Pluto. This shows that you and the beloved are seeing things in opposite ways. You are far apart from each other (mentally and emotionally, if not physically). Your challenge is to bridge your differences. Sometimes this aspect shows a temporary separation (either you or the beloved are travelling). The Horoscope shows much distance between you.

Health still needs watching until the 21st. This is nothing serious, just that overall energy is not up to its usual standards. You can enhance the health in the ways mentioned in the yearly report. Until the 16th back and knee massage is helpful. After the 16th give more attention to the ankles and calves. Massage them regularly.

Uranus is your family planet. His move into your 7th house shows more socializing with the family or with family connections. And, it shows that a parent or parent figure in your life is very involved in your love life. Perhaps he or she is playing Cupid.

Mars moving into your 4th house on the 16th makes it a good time for home repairs or construction.

The planetary power begins to shift dramatically from the night side (lower half) of your Horoscope to the day side (the upper half). Thus dawn is breaking in your year. You need to act like your 'daytime' self. The career and outer goals are now becoming ever more important. Until the 21st it is good to pursue career goals by social means – by hosting or attending the right kind of parties and gatherings. After the 21st, your gift of the gab – your sales and marketing skills – become very important. It will be good to purge your career goals of extraneous, unnecessary baggage – ideas and opinions that are not useful. Perhaps your approach is wasteful or lacking in focus? Now is the time to detox these things.

June

Best Days Overall: 5, 6, 7, 14, 15, 23, 24
Most Stressful Days Overall: 3, 4, 10, 11, 16, 17, 30
Best Days for Love: 6, 7, 10, 11, 16, 23, 24
Best Days for Money: 5, 6, 7, 14, 15, 23, 24, 25, 26
Best Days for Career: 3, 4, 12, 13, 16, 17, 23

A happy and prosperous month ahead, Scorpio. Enjoy.

There is a happy romantic opportunity on the 1st or the 2nd. Venus will be 'out of bounds' then (from the 1st to the 7th), which suggests that this meeting is with someone outside your normal social sphere. This can also involve a business partnership or joint venture.

Last month, on the 21st, your 8th house of regeneration (your favourite house) became powerful, and remains so this month until the 21st. This is a comfortable situation for you, for, by nature, you are an 8th-house kind of personality. The libido is more active now, and detox regimes of all kinds go well. Your personal financial interest is stronger than usual this year, but now it is good to think about other people's financial interests too. This is a good month for tax and insurance planning and, if you are of appropriate age, for estate planning. A good month to get rid of the unnecessary from your life and possessions.

There are a few bumps on the road in the career, but these are short-term issues and pass quickly. There are some problems or delays from the 26th to the 28th – short-term setbacks – but, basically, the career is going well. On the 14th your love planet Venus crosses your Mid-heaven and enters your 10th house. This favours a social approach to the career. It favours attending or hosting the right kind of parties or gatherings. It shows that you're meeting (on a social level) the kind of people who can be helpful in the career. Likeability seems more important than professional skills. Venus's move into your 10th house is also good for the love life. It shows focus. Love is high on your agenda. Perhaps it is the most important thing. The spouse, partner or current love is successful and supporting your career. On a romantic level, singles will be attracted to the power people, the people of high status and position. Singles have opportunities for office romances – with bosses or those in authority. However, with Uranus in your 7th house all month, the stability of these things is in question.

Mercury crosses your Mid-heaven on the 29th – also a positive career transit. It reinforces the social approach and the importance of likeability to your career. It also shows that your technological expertise and online presence is important careerwise. Your career planet in your 9th house from the 21st onwards shows that a willingness to travel is important.

July

Best Days Overall: 3, 4, 12, 13, 20, 21, 30, 31
Most Stressful Days Overall: 1, 7, 8, 14, 15, 27, 28, 29
Best Days for Love: 5, 6, 7, 8, 16, 25, 26
Best Days for Money: 1, 12, 13, 20, 21, 22, 23, 24, 27, 28, 29
Best Days for Career: 3, 4, 12, 13, 14, 15, 21, 22

You're entering the best career period of your year on the 22nd. The career is going to be active – and also hectic. A Solar Eclipse of the 13th will also impact the career.

This month's Solar Eclipse will open career doors for you. It occurs in your 9th house but the eclipsed planet, the Sun, is your career planet. Since this happens before your career peak, it seems like a preparation for success. Barriers are being blown away. The chess board is being rearranged. There are shakeups in your company or industry. There are dramas in the lives of bosses. The rules of the game are changing and you need to make a course correction in the career (you will have this same issue next month too). There is a tendency to business-related travel until the 22nd, but try to avoid the eclipse period. Try to schedule your trips around it. Bosses, parents and parent figures in your life are having their marriages tested. They are having all kinds of personal dramas. There are shakeups in your place of worship and in the lives of worship leaders. College students are forced to make important educational changes – often they change schools or courses. Your personal religious and philosophical beliefs will get tested. This is generally a good thing; some of these beliefs will be modified and some will get discarded. Only a true belief can withstand 'reality checks'. This eclipse impacts on Pluto, the ruler of your Horoscope, which means it has a strong effect on you. Spend more time quietly at home. Often the eclipse will trigger a detox of the body (especially if you haven't been careful in dietary matters), but this is not sickness (though the symptoms can be similar). It will also provoke a period of self-redefinition and re-evaluation. The events of the eclipse force this. Over the next six months you will be adopting a new look – a new image.

There is a second eclipse this month. The Lunar Eclipse of the 27th also affects you strongly. You need be take a more relaxed schedule from the 22nd onwards anyway, but especially during the eclipse period. This eclipse occurs in your 4th house and impacts on the ruler of the 4th house, Uranus. So family is affected here. There can be dramas in the family circle. Often repairs are needed in the home. There can be a health scare – either personal or with a family member. Since Mars is impacted here, job changes are likely – this can be within your present situation or with another company. Your health regime will change over the next few months.

August

Best Days Overall: 8, 9, 16, 17, 26, 27
Most Stressful Days Overall: 4, 5, 10, 11, 24, 25, 31
Best Days for Love: 4, 5, 14, 15, 24, 25, 31
Best Days for Money: 8, 9, 16, 17, 19, 20, 26, 27
Best Days for Career: 2, 3, 10, 11, 20, 31

Another Solar Eclipse on the 11th (the third one this year) shakes up the career and creates dramas in the lives of people involved in your career. More course corrections are necessary. The changes you make will be good ones, but are generally not pleasant while they're happening. You're going to feel the effects of this eclipse for the next six months or so. Parents and parent figure are again affected, and are forced to redefine themselves (the same is true for bosses). Often what happens is that they get slandered – competitors attempt to define them in a negative way – and they have to define themselves for themselves. This involves taking stock and forming a clear self-conception.

Health still needs watching this month, especially until the 22nd. Yes, you're busy out there in the world and you're working hard, but make sure you get enough rest. If you cut out the inessentials in your life you should have time for work and rest. Mars, your health planet, is behaving unusually this month. For a start, he spends the month 'out of bounds'. Secondly, he is making one of his rare retrograde moves. This suggests that in health matters you are exploring therapies that are 'outside' the mainstream (and outside your own personal mainstream). (Your job can also be taking you out of your normal sphere.) His retrograde suggests that you should avoid making dramatic health changes unless you have done your research well. Enhance the health in the ways mentioned in the yearly report. Until the 13th, calf and ankle massage is good. After the 13th (as Mars retrogrades back into Capricorn) regular back and knee massage will be beneficial.

Venus, your love planet, has her solstice this month. From the 5th to the 9th she pauses in the heavens (in her latitudinal motion) and then reverses direction. This suggests a need to take a breather in your love life and then reverse direction.

Finances are much improved now (although they've been good all year). Jupiter started to move forward on July 10 and is forward for the rest of the year. There is good financial confidence. Stalled deals and projects start moving forward again. There is clarity in financial matters. After the 22nd, finances will be even better than before.

September

Best Days Overall: 4, 5, 13, 14, 22, 23, 24
Most Stressful Days Overall: 1, 7, 20, 21, 27, 28
Best Days for Love: 1, 2, 3, 13, 22, 23, 27, 28
Best Days for Money: 4, 5, 13, 14, 15, 16, 22, 23, 24
Best Days for Career: 1, 7, 9, 18, 19, 29

On July 22 the planetary power began to shift from the West to the East – from the sector of others to the sector of the self. This trend is in full swing now. You have more personal independence now, and it is time to think about yourself and your own interests. Other people are always important, but now number one is important. Your happiness is in your hands. The planetary power supports you. By now, after six months of compromise and consensus and of putting other people first, you know what conditions need changing. Now and for the next few months is the time to make these changes. They will happen much easier. It's time to start having things your way. Your happiness is just as important as anyone else's. This is the cycle you're in right now.

The month ahead is very social. It is more about friendships, groups and group activities rather than romance, but romance is happening too and it looks happy. On the 9th your love planet crosses your Ascendant and enters your 1st house. This gives many messages. The spouse, partner or current love is very dedicated to you. Your interest comes before his or her own. This aspect shows someone who is having his or her way in love – having love on your terms. Love and romance pursue you rather than the other way round. In a man's chart this signals young women in your personal sphere. In a woman's chart it indicates more beauty and grace in the image – more physical beauty.

Yes, you're having things your way this month, but with Pluto still retrograde, you're not yet sure what your way is! This is the only challenge.

Health is much better than last month. You can enhance it further through back and knee massage until the 11th, and through ankle and calf massage from the 11th onwards. Now that Mars is moving forward again it is safer to go 'out of bounds' in your health regime and treatments. There seem to be no answers within your normal sphere.

On the 22nd, as the Sun enters your 12th house, you enter a strongly spiritual period. Your spiritual understanding and insights (which are good in their own right) will also benefit the career. A good period to boost the career through charitable activities or by involvement with causes that you believe in.

October

Best Days Overall: 2, 3, 10, 11, 20, 21, 29, 30
Most Stressful Days Overall: 4, 5, 17, 18, 19, 25, 26, 31
Best Days for Love: 2, 3, 10, 11, 20, 21, 25, 26, 29, 30
Best Days for Money: 2, 3, 10, 11, 12, 13, 14, 20, 21, 29, 30
Best Days for Career: 1, 4, 5, 8, 9, 18, 19, 29, 31

A happy and prosperous month, Scorpio. Enjoy.

The planetary power is now in its maximum Eastern position this month. Keep in mind our discussion of this last month. Personal initiative matters now. Make yourself happy and the world becomes a happier place. Personal independence was strong last month, but it is even stronger now. On the 2nd Pluto, the ruler of your Horoscope, starts to move forward, so you gain more clarity about your goals. On the 23rd the Sun moves into your own sign. Your 1st house is easily the strongest in the Horoscope this month and you are in one of your yearly personal pleasure peaks. It is time to reward your most faithful servant – your body – and pamper it a little. (Of course don't overdo this, or the weight will balloon.)

Health is excellent this month. Only two planets are in stressful alignment with you. The overwhelming majority are either making nice aspects or leaving you alone. If you feel under the weather, enhance the health through ankle and calf massage. Your health planet in the sign of Aquarius indicates an experimental approach to health. New and untried therapies attract you and could work for you.

The Sun's move into your 1st house brings happy career opportunities to you. There's nothing much you need to do to benefit – they will find you. Also, you look successful. You have this image and people see you this way.

Venus, like last month, is still in your own sign. This is wonderful for love. Like last month love pursues you. You just have to be yourself and go about your daily business. The only complication is Venus's retrograde, beginning on the 5th. This won't stop love and social activities but it could slow things down.

Personal appearance is excellent this month, Scorpio, and the opposite sex takes notice. Venus in your sign gives beauty and glamour. The

Sun in your sign gives charisma and star power and, in your chart, a sense of gravitas. You're a person of substance. Jupiter in your sign gives the image of wealth; the Sun gives an image of success.

Prosperity is strong this month, but will get even stronger next month (and next year will be even stronger than the past year).

November

Best Days Overall: 6, 7, 8, 16, 17, 25, 26
Most Stressful Days Overall: 1, 14, 15, 21, 22, 27, 28
Best Days for Love: 4, 5, 14, 15, 21, 22, 23, 24
Best Days for Money: 8, 9, 10, 19, 27
Best Days for Career: 1, 6, 7, 8, 16, 17, 27, 28

An eventful but happy and prosperous month. Uranus moves backwards out of your 7th house on the 6th, bringing more stability to the love and social life. Boring is sometimes beautiful. Things are more predictable. It is much easier to make long-range social plans. Enjoy this while it lasts. Come next year Uranus will move into your 7th house again and will stay for many years. In the meantime, enjoy. Venus, your love planet, will start to move forward on the 16th, which will also improve the love life. A relationship that was going backwards now starts moving forward again. There is more ground to cover before it becomes the way it was, but at least things are moving in the right direction.

Venus spends the month in your 12th house of spirituality. Thus, love opportunities happen in spiritual-type settings. It's not at the clubs or nightspots these days, it's at the spiritual lecture or seminar, the prayer meeting, the charity event, or as you get involved in altruistic causes. Love is idealistic this month. Spiritual compatibility is as important as physical compatibility these days.

Perhaps the main headline this month is Jupiter's move into your money house on the 8th. Here he will be in his own sign and house. He is at home, so to speak. Comfortable. Powerful. The king is in his castle. Earning power and financial acumen are greatly increased. You can look forward to another prosperous twelve months.

You're still in a yearly personal pleasure peak until the 20th, so keep in mind our discussion of this from last month. Career opportunities are coming to you. Just be who you are and go about your business. Bosses, elders, parents and parent figures in your life seem devoted to you and supportive. You have their favour.

Health is even better than last month. The two planets that were stressing you out are moving away from their stressful aspects. Uranus moves away on the 6th and Mars on the 16th. So you have plenty of energy – energy to burn. Your challenge is to use this to good effect, to advance your goals.

On the 22nd the Sun enters your money house and you begin a yearly financial peak. A very prosperous period. The 24th to the 28th, as the Sun travels with Jupiter, looks especially prosperous. Now (from the 22nd onwards) you have the financial favour of bosses, elders, parents and parent figures. They are favourably disposed to your financial goals.

December

Best Days Overall: 4, 5, 14, 15, 23, 24, 31
Most Stressful Days Overall: 11, 12, 18, 19, 25, 26
Best Days for Love: 2, 3, 14, 15, 18, 19, 23, 24
Best Days for Money: 6, 7, 16, 26
Best Days for Career: 6, 7, 17, 25, 26, 27

Another happy and prosperous month, Scorpio.

You're still very much in a yearly financial peak – until the 21st. (There is prosperity afterwards too, but the trend is stronger until the 21st.) Many of the financial trends we mentioned last month are still in effect. You still have the financial favour of bosses, elders, parents and parent figures. Your good professional reputation is important in your finances. Investors have a good feeling for publishing, travel agencies, airlines and for-profit colleges. You're a big spender – and perhaps an impulsive spender – these days, but you don't seem to mind. Earnings come easily and are spent easily. You will give more and receive more this holiday season.

Love improved last month and gets even better this month. On the 2nd Venus once again (this time moving forward) crosses your Ascendant and enters your 1st house. She brings a social magnetism to the image – grace, glamour and charm. Love pursues you once again, without you having to do anything special. The current love is very devoted to you.

With Venus in your own sign love is passionate, intense and generally possessive. This has good points and bad points. The passions are high, but if jealousy enters the picture you'll have to look out.

Health is even better than last month. There are no planets in stressful alignment with you. Only the Moon will occasionally make stressful aspects, but these pass very quickly and even her stressful aspects are overwhelmed by the good aspect. Like last month, your challenge is to put all this extra energy to good use. Even though health is good, you can make it even better by giving more attention to the feet. Foot massage is especially powerful this month.

The planetary power is now below the horizon of your chart. It is on the night side, the lower half of your Horoscope. Thus you're in the 'night time' of your year. Career and outer objectives can be de-emphasized. It is time to focus on the family and your emotional wellness. Feeling right – feeling good – is more important than doing good. Right feeling will lead to right doing further down the road. Now is the time to gather your forces and set the stage for your next career push in six or so months' time.

Sagittarius

THE ARCHER

Birthdays from
23rd November to
20th December

Personality Profile

SAGITTARIUS AT A GLANCE

Element – Fire

Ruling Planet – Jupiter
  Career Planet – Mercury
  Love Planet – Mercury
  Money Planet – Saturn
  Planet of Health and Work – Venus
  Planet of Home and Family Life – Neptune
  Planet of Spirituality – Pluto

Colours – blue, dark blue

Colours that promote love, romance and social harmony – yellow,
  yellow-orange

Colours that promote earning power – black, indigo

Gems – carbuncle, turquoise

Metal – tin

Scents – carnation, jasmine, myrrh

Quality – mutable (= flexibility)

Qualities most needed for balance – attention to detail, administrative and organizational skills

Strongest virtues – generosity, honesty, broad-mindedness, tremendous vision

Deepest need – to expand mentally

Characteristics to avoid – over-optimism, exaggeration, being too generous with other people's money

Signs of greatest overall compatibility – Aries, Leo

Signs of greatest overall incompatibility – Gemini, Virgo, Pisces

Sign most helpful to career – Virgo

Sign most helpful for emotional support – Pisces

Sign most helpful financially – Capricorn

Sign best for marriage and/or partnerships – Gemini

Sign most helpful for creative projects – Aries

Best Sign to have fun with – Aries

Signs most helpful in spiritual matters – Leo, Scorpio

Best day of the week – Thursday

Understanding a Sagittarius

If you look at the symbol of the archer you will gain a good, intuitive understanding of a person born under this astrological sign. The development of archery was humanity's first refinement of the power to hunt and wage war. The ability to shoot an arrow far beyond the ordinary range of a spear extended humanity's horizons, wealth, personal will and power.

Today, instead of using bows and arrows we project our power with fuels and mighty engines, but the essential reason for using these new powers remains the same. These powers represent our ability to extend our personal sphere of influence – and this is what Sagittarius is all about. Sagittarians are always seeking to expand their horizons, to cover more territory and increase their range and scope. This applies to all aspects of their lives: economic, social and intellectual.

Sagittarians are noted for the development of the mind – the higher intellect – which understands philosophical and spiritual concepts. This mind represents the higher part of the psychic nature and is motivated not by self-centred considerations but by the light and grace of a Higher Power. Thus, Sagittarians love higher education of all kinds. They might be bored with formal schooling but they love to study on their own and in their own way. A love of foreign travel and interest in places far away from home are also noteworthy characteristics of the Sagittarian type.

If you give some thought to all these Sagittarian attributes you will see that they spring from the inner Sagittarian desire to develop. To travel more is to know more, to know more is to be more, to cultivate the higher mind is to grow and to reach more. All these traits tend to broaden the intellectual – and indirectly, the economic and material – horizons of the Sagittarian.

The generosity of the Sagittarian is legendary. There are many reasons for this. One is that Sagittarians seem to have an inborn consciousness of wealth. They feel that they are rich, that they are lucky, that they can attain any financial goal – and so they feel that they can afford to be generous. Sagittarians do not carry the burdens of want and limitation which stop most other people from giving generously. Another reason for their generosity is their religious and philosophical idealism, derived from the higher mind. This higher mind is by nature generous because it is unaffected by material circumstances. Still another reason is that the act of giving tends to enhance their emotional nature. Every act of giving seems to be enriching, and this is reward enough for the Sagittarian.

Finance

Sagittarians generally entice wealth. They either attract it or create it. They have the ideas, energy and talent to make their vision of paradise on Earth a reality. However, mere wealth is not enough. Sagittarians want luxury – earning a comfortable living seems small and insignificant to them.

In order for Sagittarians to attain their true earning potential they must develop better managerial and organizational skills. They must learn to set limits, to arrive at their goals through a series of attainable sub-goals or objectives. It is very rare that a person goes from rags to riches overnight. But a long-drawn-out process is difficult for Sagittarians. Like Leos, they want to achieve wealth and success quickly and impressively. They must be aware, however, that this over-optimism can lead to unrealistic financial ventures and disappointing losses. Of course, no zodiac sign can bounce back as quickly as Sagittarius, but only needless heartache will be caused by this attitude. Sagittarians need to maintain their vision – never letting it go – but they must also work towards it in practical and efficient ways.

Career and Public Image

Sagittarians are big thinkers. They want it all: money, fame, glamour, prestige, public acclaim and a place in history. They often go after all these goals. Some attain them, some do not – much depends on each individual's personal horoscope. But if Sagittarians want to attain public and professional status they must understand that these things are not conferred to enhance one's ego but as rewards for the amount of service that one does for the whole of humanity. If and when they figure out ways to serve more, Sagittarians can rise to the top.

The ego of the Sagittarian is gigantic – and perhaps rightly so. They have much to be proud of. If they want public acclaim, however, they will have to learn to tone down the ego a bit, to become more humble and self-effacing, without falling into the trap of self-denial and self-abasement. They must also learn to master the details of life, which can sometimes elude them.

At their jobs Sagittarians are hard workers who like to please their bosses and co-workers. They are dependable, trustworthy and enjoy a challenge. Sagittarians are friendly to work with and helpful to their colleagues. They usually contribute intelligent ideas or new methods that improve the work environment for everyone. Sagittarians always look for challenging positions and careers that develop their intellect, even if they have to work very hard in order to succeed. They also work well under the supervision of others, although by nature they would rather be the supervisors and increase their sphere of influence. Sagittarians excel at professions that allow them to be in contact with many different people and to travel to new and exciting locations.

Love and Relationships

Sagittarians love freedom for themselves and will readily grant it to their partners. They like their relationships to be fluid and ever-changing. Sagittarians tend to be fickle in love and to change their minds about their partners quite frequently.

Sagittarians feel threatened by a clearly defined, well-structured relationship, as they feel this limits their freedom. The Sagittarian tends to marry more than once in life.

Sagittarians in love are passionate, generous, open, benevolent and very active. They demonstrate their affections very openly. However, just like an Aries they tend to be egocentric in the way they relate to their partners. Sagittarians should develop the ability to see others' points of view, not just their own. They need to develop some objectivity and cool intellectual clarity in their relationships so that they can develop better two-way communication with their partners. Sagittarians tend to be overly idealistic about their partners and about love in general. A cool and rational attitude will help them to perceive reality more clearly and enable them to avoid disappointment.

Home and Domestic Life

Sagittarians tend to grant a lot of freedom to their family. They like big homes and many children and are one of the most fertile signs of the zodiac. However, when it comes to their children Sagittarians generally err on the side of allowing them too much freedom. Sometimes their children get the idea that there are no limits. However, allowing freedom in the home is basically a positive thing – so long as some measure of balance is maintained – for it enables all family members to develop as they should.

Horoscope for 2018

Major Trends

Jupiter in your 12th house since October of last year shows a spiritual year ahead. This brings internal growth, invisible to the outside world. But you can feel it. On November 8, as Jupiter crosses your Ascendant, others will see it too. You've been in a prosperity period for two years now, and Jupiter's move into your 1st house is going to prolong and accelerate it. Jupiter, the ruler of your Horoscope, in your 1st house will make you even more of a Sagittarius than you are now. All the typical Sagittarian qualities will be accentuated. There will be more than usual travel, more than usual interest in religion, philosophy and higher learning, more than usual ebullience and optimism. There's more on this later on.

Your money house is unusually strong this year. Saturn, your financial planet, moved in here late last year and will be there for the next two years. This shows great financial focus and, with that, success. More on this later.

Neptune has been in your 4th house of home and family since 2012. This shows the 'spiritualization' of the family, and especially of parents or parent figures. The whole family life is becoming more elevated and refined. More details later.

Uranus has been in your 5th house for seven years now. At last this is about to change as he moves into your 6th house from May 16 to November 6. Children and children figures in your life have been more difficult to handle. They have been rebellious and unsettled. This is still the case in the year ahead but things are getting easier. Uranus in your 6th house shows changes in the job situation – and in coming years there will be multiple job changes. This aspect also brings important changes in your health regime and health attitudes. More on this later.

There is much turmoil and change happening in your 9th house of religion and intellectual pursuits. Four out of the five eclipses this year impact here. There are three Solar Eclipses (one more than usual) and two eclipses that actually occur in your 9th house. So college students are making dramatic changes to their educational plans. They can change schools, or courses, or make other important changes. Many of you are changing your place of worship as well.

Your most important areas of interest this year will be finance; home and family; children, fun and creativity (until May 16 and from November 6 onwards); health and work (from May 16 to November 6); spirituality (until November 8); and the body, image and personal pleasure (from November 8 onwards).

Your paths of greatest fulfilment this year will be spirituality (until November 8); the body, image and personal pleasure (from November 8 onwards); religion, philosophy, higher education and foreign travel (until November 17); and sex, occult studies and personal transformation (from November 17 onwards).

Health

(Please note that this is an astrological perspective on health and not a medical one. In days of yore there was no difference, both of these perspectives were identical. But now there could be quite a difference. For a medical perspective, please consult your doctor or health practitioner.)

Health should be good this year. There is only one long-term planet – Neptune – afflicting you. All the others are either in harmonious aspect or leaving you alone. You will feel this in your overall health and energy levels. You had a vulnerable health year in 2016, although 2017 was a little better. If you got through those years, you will sail through the year ahead. The aspects are so much easier now.

With more energy all kinds of vistas open up to you. Projects that you might not have even considered in the past two years now become eminently 'doable'.

Good though your health is, you can make it even better. Give more attention to the following – the vulnerable areas of your chart. This will tend to prevent problems from developing, and even in cases where they can't be totally prevented, they can be softened when they happen. They need not be devastating. (The appropriate reflex points are shown in the chart below.)

- The liver and thighs are always important for you, as these areas are ruled by your sign. Thigh massage should be a regular part of your health regime. This will not only strengthen the liver and thighs, but the lower back as well. It is also said to benefit the colon. A herbal liver cleanse every now and then, but especially when you feel under the weather, might be a good idea.
- The neck and throat. These too are always important for you. Regular neck massage should also be part of your regular regime.

Important foot reflexology points for the year ahead

Try to massage all of the foot on a regular basis – the top of the foot as well as the bottom – but pay extra attention to the points highlighted on the chart. When you massage, be aware of 'sore spots' as these need special attention. It's also a good idea to massage the ankles and below them.

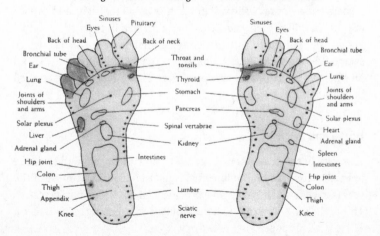

Check for tension in the muscles there and release them. Craniosacral therapy is good for these areas too.

- The ankles and calves. These are only just beginning to gain importance this year – from May 16 to November 7 – as Uranus enters your 6th house of health. But from next March onwards, for the next seven years, these will be important for your health. So massage the ankles and calves. Feel for any sore spots and massage them out. The shin bone should also be massaged (often there are tender points that we're unaware of except when we massage). Give the ankles more support when exercising.

Jupiter's move into your own sign on November 8 will make Sagittarians of childbearing age much more fertile. There will also be a tendency (usually because of the increased good life) to put on weight. This should be monitored as well.

Uranus is the ruler of your 3rd house of communication. His position in your health house indicates the importance of good mental health. Avoid over-using the communication faculties – talking too much. Avoid thinking too much. Turn the mind off when it's not in use. Give the mind the exercise and digestion it needs – read good books and mull them over. Strive for intellectual purity. (This is always a good thing, but now it's becoming a health issue.)

Venus, your health planet, is a fast-moving planet, as our regular readers know. Usually she will move through all the signs and houses of your chart in a given year. (This year, however, because of her retrograde, she will move through eleven rather than the usual twelve sectors.) So, there are many short-term trends in health that depend on where Venus is and the aspects she receives. These are best covered in the monthly reports.

Home and Family

This has been an important area for some years now and will be important for many more to come. Jupiter in Scorpio for most of the year is in beautiful aspect with Neptune, your home and family planet. This is showing harmony with the family. You're getting on with them. There is good cooperation between you.

This aspect favours a move or the enlargement of the present home. It shows the fortunate purchase or sale of a home. In many cases people buy additional homes (or have access to additional homes). It shows the enlargement of your family circle as well. Often this happens in the normal ways – through birth or marriage – but it can also happen through meeting people who play the role of family in your life, people who give you the unconditional emotional support that family should give.

The home, as we mentioned, is becoming more spiritualized. Thus there are probably more religious or esoteric symbols or artworks in the home. Perhaps there are more crystals, gongs, drums or other psychic paraphernalia there. The home – and we have seen this in past years too – is perhaps being used as a meeting place for spiritual activities – prayer meetings, spiritual lectures or seminars, things of this nature.

With Neptune in your 4th house (and as the ruler of your 4th house) it is imperative to keep the home 'psychically' pure. It's not enough to have clean floors and rugs, etc. (though this is a good thing). The thought atmosphere – the emotional atmosphere – needs to be kept clean. This is a year to learn how to get rid of 'ghosts' and discarnate entities. There are people who specialize in this sort of thing. I believe they call it 'space clearing'. Through various techniques (some use incense, sage, sound, prayer or banishing rites to achieve their aims) they come in and purify the psychic energy of a home. If there are problems in the home (and these pests can cause all sorts of problems – psychological or physical) this might be a good idea this year.

After November 8, as Jupiter moves into your own sign, you will have to work harder to achieve family harmony than before. You seem in disagreement with a parent or parent figure.

A house renovation can happen any time this year. But if you have free will in the matter, from November 15 onwards seems good. If you're redecorating, repainting or buying art objects for the home, February 11 to March 7 looks like a good time.

A sibling or sibling figure in your life is very successful careerwise this year but seems emotionally unsettled. He or she can have multiple moves in the coming years. The parents or parent figures are travelling more this year. One of them seems likely to move. It can happen after November 8 or next year. Children and children figures have a stable year. Grandchildren (if you have them) are likely to move. If they are of childbearing age, they are more fertile this year.

Finance and Career

The year ahead, as we mentioned, is prosperous – a continuation of the last two years. Saturn, your financial planet, is now in your money house, in his own sign of Capricorn and in his own house. Thus he is both 'celestially and terrestrially' strong. He is operating with maximum power. This spells higher earnings.

His move into Capricorn late last year is another good signal. Saturn, in his own sign and house, will give sound financial judgement. Last year you might have been more speculative and risk taking. No longer. You are now taking a methodical, step-by-step approach to wealth. You have a long-term view. Quick money – the fast buck – is actually abhorrent right now. You will build your wealth over time in solid kinds of ways.

The financial planet in Capricorn favours gaining control over your finances, rather than letting them control you. It favours budgeting and long-term savings and investment plans, disciplined, daily financial regimes. If you stick to them – and it is likely you will over the next few years – wealth will happen naturally, with little stress or strain. The biggest strain will probably be sticking to your plan. Regularity and discipline is more important for an investment plan than luck. There are always temptations to slack off, but stick to it.

For investors, Saturn in Capricorn favours the commercial real estate industry and the 'blue chip' sector of the market – the old school, traditional large companies listed on Wall Street or the London Stock Exchange. Conservative kinds of investments – but quality ones.

For non-investors, this position favours a business or managerial position in the corporate world. Your managements skills – and they are strong this year – are very marketable. Pluto has been in your money house for many years now and he will remain there for many more to come. Pluto rules debt, and his position favours bonds and the bond market (preferably of the kinds of companies mentioned above).

He also rules taxes. Thus the message of the Horoscope is that good tax planning – tax efficiency – is important in finances.

Those of you of appropriate age are probably doing estate planning these days. Others are either inheriting money or are involved in some administrative way with an estate.

This is not an especially strong career year. Some years are like that. The cosmos aims for a balanced kind of development and so different areas are emphasized in different years. By the time one has reached middle age, there will be development and experience in all the sectors.

Mercury is your career planet. Next to the Moon he is the fastest moving of all the planets. Every year he will move through every sign and house of your chart. Thus there are many short-term career trends that depend on where Mercury is and the aspects he receives. These are best covered in the monthly reports.

Love and Social Life

Saturn in your own sign for the past two years has not helped your love life. Probably, unbeknownst to you, you have come across as cold, brusque, business-like and aloof. These are great qualities in a manager or corporate executive, but not so great for social success. Sagittarians are not cold people by nature, yet, this is how others saw you and reacted to you. Subconsciously these kinds of vibrations were being sent out.

Happily Saturn is now out of your sign, and you're behaving more like your sunny, carefree Sagittarian self. Your native warmth comes through and you will see a big improvement in your love life.

Your 7th house is not prominent this year so love and romance are not big issues. You have no need to make major changes here. The cosmos doesn't push you one way or another. It tends to the status quo. Those who are marrieds will most likely stay married and singles will stay single.

Mercury is your love planet (as well as your career planet). As our regular readers know, he is a fast-moving and erratic kind of planet. Sometimes he moves very fast – he speeds through three signs and houses in a month. Sometimes he moves slowly and sedately. And sometimes he goes backwards. Doesn't this describe your love life well? Because of this there are many short-term trends in love that depend on where Mercury is at any given time and the kind of aspects he receives. These are best dealt with in the monthly reports.

Mercury will go retrograde three times this year. This is another reason why we see improvements in the love life – in the past two years he went retrograde four times. These retrogrades tend to weaken the social confidence. Social judgement is not what it should be. Thus it is not a good time for making important decisions in love, one way or another. It is a time to gain facts, to gain mental clarity on things, to see where improvements can be made. Then, when Mercury moves forward again, you can act on your plans.

Last year was a great year for friendships and group activities. You made new and important friendships. This year, you're not that active here. Again, it's a status quo kind of year.

Co-workers and employees (if you have them) are having a strong social year. Singles are getting involved in serious relationships. Friends and partners are also having a good social year from November 8 onwards. The spouse, partner or current love will also have a banner social year after November 8. He or she is making new and important friendships. Siblings and sibling figures in your life are having their marriages or relationships tested. The good ones will survive, but the flawed ones are likely to end. Children and Children figures are having a quiet, stable love year. Last year was much better.

Self-Improvement

Perhaps there is no sign that understands the spiritual dimensions of wealth better than Sagittarius. It is innate to you. Hardwired, as the saying goes. With your spiritual planet Pluto in your 2nd money house since 2008, the tendency is even stronger. Intuition guides you and you prosper. Financial guidance will often come in dreams, through psychics, seers, astrologers or spiritual channels.

The affluence of the Divine is not at all concerned with what we call 'practical factors'. It is not concerned with the state of the economy, the market or with how much you have in the bank. It creates conditions. It creates wealth. Often it will reveal wealth where you didn't think it existed. With intuition we tend to ignore what some call 'reality' – the material reality – and focus on the spiritual realities of unlimited supply.

But now a new factor has entered the picture. Saturn is now in your money house. He is the most practical of all the planets, the most worldly, the most focused on the 'visible conditions'. Saturn would tend to view the spiritual approach as 'cloud cuckoo land' – a dangerous chimera. Saturn looks at how much you have in the bank, calculates market conditions and future earning power, and makes plans accordingly. Such an approach is totally opposite to the ways of spiritual affluence.

So there are two opposite forces at work in your financial life, one very spiritual, the other ultra-worldly and practical. The spiritual side says, 'give and it shall be given unto you'. Saturn says, 'give only when you can afford to give'.

These two forces argue with each other. It is like having two minds in one body. If you go with your intuition, Saturn, the practical side, is fearful and perhaps even angry. If you go with your practical side, your spiritual side is unsatisfied. Somehow or other – and there are no rules to this – you have to merge these two forces. Unite them. Make them work together.

Perhaps you follow intuition to make money and then use Saturn's practicality to manage and invest it properly. Some might earn in the conventional ways and invest intuitively.

Sometimes this shows someone who is in a management position of a non-profit or charitable organization. The goals are idealistic and spiritual, but the day-to-day management is practical.

Month-by-month Forecasts

January

> Best Days Overall: 3, 4, 12, 13, 14, 22, 23, 31
> Most Stressful Days Overall: 5, 6, 20, 21, 27, 28
> Best Days for Love: 3, 4, 5, 6, 15, 16, 25, 26, 27, 28
> Best Days for Money: 1, 2, 5, 10, 11, 15, 16, 20, 21, 25, 29, 30
> Best Days for Career: 3, 4, 5, 6, 15, 16, 25, 26

Because your birthday was so recent, you're in a waxing personal solar cycle. Last month – on the winter solstice – the universal solar cycle began waxing too. Moreover, *all* the planets are moving forward this month (which is very rare). So, you're in a great period – next month too – for launching new ventures or products into the world. The 17th to the 30th – when the Moon is also waxing – is the best time of the month to do this. There is much cosmic momentum behind you and you should see fast progress.

You begin your year with the Eastern sector (the sector of self) most dominant. This is soon to change but this month you are still in an independent kind of period. So if you haven't made the changes that need to be made, this is the time to make them. Later on (from next month onwards) it will be more difficult to do.

The night side of your chart (the bottom half) is strongest this month and will get even stronger over the next few months. So you're more of a 'night person' now. This is a time for handling home, family and issues of emotional wellness. This is the time to build up the internal energies for the next career push, which will begin in June. This is a time for preparation rather than overt doing.

A Lunar Eclipse on the 31st seems to affect you strongly. It occurs in your 9th house of intellectual pursuits and foreign travel. Sagittarians are big travellers, but avoid the eclipse period if possible. College students make important educational changes. There are shakeups in your place of worship and dramas in the lives of worship leaders. The eclipsed planet, the Moon, rules your 8th house of regeneration. So there can be near-death kinds of experiences. Usually these are psychological confrontations with death rather than literal death.

(Lunar Eclipses happen twice a year and you've gone through many of these things.) Often you have dreams of death. Often you're affected by some grisly crime or terrorist attack – you read about them or are in their vicinity. The cosmos forces you to go deeper into this issue. Venus is impacted (although not directly) by this eclipse. Thus job changes can happen. Sometimes there are disruptions in the workplace. There are dramas in the lives of friends. A parent or parent figure has to make important financial changes.

February

Best Days Overall: 9, 10, 19, 27, 28
Most Stressful Days Overall: 2, 3, 16, 17, 23, 24
Best Days for Love: 4, 5, 14, 15, 16, 23, 24, 25, 26
Best Days for Money: 2, 6, 7, 11, 12, 16, 17, 21, 25, 26
Best Days for Career: 2, 3, 4, 5, 14, 15, 25, 26

A Solar Eclipse on the 15th occurs in your 3rd house of communication and impacts on siblings, sibling figures and neighbours. There are dramas in their lives. They are forced to redefine themselves. Often there are dramatic changes in the neighbourhood – major construction and things of this nature. Students below college level make important educational changes. Often they change schools. There are disruptions and shakeups in their school. Cars and communication equipment get tested. It would be a good idea to drive more carefully over this period, and if you don't need to drive, better to stay off the road. Minimize your time on the road as much as possible. For example, better to go to a local store or restaurant than one that is further away.

The eclipsed planet, the Sun, rules your 9th house, and so foreign travel is not advisable during this period (like last month). If you must travel, schedule it around the eclipse period if possible. Once again, college students make changes to their educational plans. There is more chaos at your place of worship and in the lives of worship leaders. Mercury and Jupiter – two very important planets in your chart – are impacted here. So the love life is affected – there is disturbance in a current relationship – and the career is also affected. Course corrections are necessary now. The impact on Jupiter is more personal. You're forced to make changes in your image and overall look – your presenta-tion to the world. (This will work itself out over five or six months.) Take it easy over the eclipse period – the few days before and after it.

On the 18th both the Sun and Mercury enter your 4th house, making this house of home and family very strong. Your career planet in the 4th house gives a very simple message – the home and family are your career – your mission – this period. Much of your outer career activities can be handled from home. Your work planet, Venus, is also in the 4th house from the 11th onwards – another message to work more from home. Be there for the family.

Mars, your family planet, moved into your 1st house on January 27 and will be there for the rest of the month ahead. Another message to focus on the family.

March

Best Days Overall: 8, 9, 18, 19, 26, 27
Most Stressful Days Overall: 1, 2, 15, 16, 17, 22, 23, 29, 30
Best Days for Love: 8, 18, 19, 22, 23, 26, 27
Best Days for Money: 1, 6, 7, 10, 11, 12, 15, 16, 17, 20, 24, 25, 29
Best Days for Career: 1, 2, 8, 18, 19, 26, 27, 29, 30

Home and family issues are still very important until the 20th. But power in the 4th house has other meanings besides home and family. It is about your emotional life in general. When the 4th house is strong there are opportunities for psychological breakthroughs. These things will happen whether or not you're in formal therapy. Old memories from the past will spontaneously arise so that you can look at them from your present perspective. You're not going to rewrite history – whatever happened, happened. But history will be reinterpreted in a better way. What was terrifying to a three-year-old only brings smiles to an adult. You will be able to see the origins of many likes, dislikes and phobias – and that is the beginning of healing. You need not carry these traumas around with you for the rest of your life.

Finances are basically good this month, but better before the 20th than afterwards. Afterwards you have to work harder for earnings.

Mars, moving into your money house on the 17th, shows that you're willing to put in the work, and so the month ahead seems prosperous. There is good family support. Family and family connections (or the family business) seems important in finances.

Your 5th house of fun and creativity becomes very strong from the 20th onwards. You're entering a yearly personal pleasure peak. It is time to have fun. Time to recharge the batteries through leisure activities. Love seems happy, as your love planet Mercury spends most of the month (from the 6th onwards) in your 5th house. Love is happy but not serious. It is more about entertainment than real romance. Enjoy it for what it is. Existing relationships can be improved through having more fun together as a couple. On the 28th Mercury will go retrograde, which starts to complicate the love life. There is a lack of clarity on this issue. Social judgement is not up to its usual standard.

Mercury in your 5th house also affects the career. There are a few ways to read this. One, that it is important that you enjoy your career. Find creative ways to inject fun into it. Another way to read this is that career gets boosted through fun activities – perhaps you meet an important contact while out at a restaurant or on a theatre visit. Perhaps you further the career by showing important customers a good time. There are many scenarios here.

April

Best Days Overall: 4, 5, 6, 14, 15, 23, 24
Most Stressful Days Overall: 12, 13, 18, 19, 25, 26
Best Days for Love: 4, 5, 6, 7, 8, 14, 15, 16, 17, 18, 19, 23, 24, 27
Best Days for Money: 2, 3, 7, 8, 12, 13, 16, 21, 22, 25, 29, 30
Best Days for Career: 4, 5, 6, 14, 15, 23, 24, 25, 26

The Western, social sector of your chart (the sector of the 'other') has become much stronger ever since February 18. It doesn't completely dominate – you still have many planets in the East – but is the strongest it will be for the current year. So personal independence is not absent, but it is less strong than usual. There is a need to balance your own personal interests with those of others. This is not a chart of someone who defers to others completely (like we see with some of the other signs), but a chart of someone sometimes leaning their way, sometimes deferring to others. A seesaw situation. Sometimes you get your way, sometimes you let others have their way.

By the 20th you're more or less partied out. You're now in the mood for work. It's not a question of having to work. You want to. And this is when work projects go best. Those of you who are unemployed have good job prospects then (there are at least two). Those of you already employed have opportunities for overtime or second jobs.

The retrograde of your love planet, Mercury, doesn't stop love, but it does slow things down – basically a good thing. You need more caution in love until the 15th. Mercury will spend the month in your 5th house of fun and entertainment, which reveals your attitude in love these days. This is where singles are likely to find romantic opportunities – at parties, resorts, night spots – places of entertainment. On the 24th Venus enters your 7th house of love. This signals an opportunity for an office romance – romance with a co-worker. It shows more social-izing at the workplace too. Love, though, doesn't seem serious. More or less the same as last month, love is about fun. It's just another form of entertainment, like going to the movies or the theatre.

The money house is powerful this month. One of the strongest in your Horoscope. Mars will spend the entire month here. Like last month this indicates good family support and the importance of family connections in finance. You're probably spending more on the home and family too.

Health is good this month. This should be considered another form of wealth. You can enhance it further by giving more attention to the neck and throat until the 24th (neck massage is excellent), and to the arms and shoulders from the 24th onwards.

May

Best Days Overall: 2, 3, 11, 12, 13, 20, 21, 29, 30
Most Stressful Days Overall: 9, 10, 16, 17, 22, 23
Best Days for Love: 2, 3, 7, 8, 13, 14, 16, 17, 22, 23, 26, 31
Best Days for Money: 4, 5, 9, 10, 14, 18, 19, 22, 26, 27, 31
Best Days for Career: 2, 3, 13, 14, 22, 23, 31

A lot of interesting changes are happening this month. On the 16th, Uranus makes a major move, from your 5th house to your 6th house of health and work, bringing instability to the job situation. This will go on for a few more months. The good news is that job opportunities can happen in a flash – in the most unexpected ways. This year, you're feeling only the beginnings of this trend. But next year – and for seven more years – it will be more pronounced. The cosmos wants you to learn to be comfortable with job insecurity. This move also brings changes – perhaps multiple changes – to your health regime and to your whole attitude to health. You become more experimental here. Again, this will be more pronounced in future years.

On the 21st the planetary power starts shifting to the day side of your Horoscope – the upper half. So, figuratively speaking, dawn is breaking in your year. You're now becoming (and this month is just the beginning) more of a day person than a night person. It is time to start focusing on your outer life and goals.

Love and social activities are more pronounced (and happier) this month. Your love planet, Mercury, is moving forward and very swiftly. This shows social confidence. Singles are dating more. The social grace is stronger than usual. On the 21st, as the Sun enters your 7th house of love, you begin a yearly love and social peak. You're in the mood for love (which makes all the difference), in the mood for romance. You're socializing with many different kinds of people and seem to get on with various types. This month you more or less get on with everyone.

Finances are excellent all month, but especially until the 21st. On the 1st, the Sun makes nice aspects to your financial planet, Saturn, bringing a nice payday and/or financial opportunity. On the 18th and 19th Mercury makes nice aspects to Saturn, bringing more of the same. You have the financial favour of the spouse, partner or current love and of bosses, parents or parent figures.

Venus spends most of the month 'out of bounds', thus your job can be taking you outside your normal sphere. It can also show that in questions of health and therapeutics you're searching for answers outside mainstream avenues.

June

  Best Days Overall: 8, 9, 16, 17, 25, 26
  Most Stressful Days Overall: 5, 6, 7, 12, 13, 18, 19
  Best Days for Love: 3, 4, 6, 7, 12, 13, 14, 16, 23, 24
  Best Days for Money: 1, 2, 5, 6, 7, 10, 14, 15, 18, 23, 24, 28, 29
  Best Days for Career: 3, 4, 14, 18, 19, 23, 24

Since May 21 health has needed more attention. There's nothing cata-
strophic here, only the stresses of short-term planets. Still, overall
energy is not what it was even a month ago. It's good to understand
these things. As always, make sure to get enough rest. If you feel tired
take a nap or a break. You can enhance the health through a correct
diet until the 14th. Good emotional health is important. Give more
attention to the stomach. After the 14th give more attention to the
heart. Chest massage will be good. Watch how health and energy
levels rebound from the 21st onwards. It is as if a giant cosmic switch
was turned back on and your energy flows normally.

You're still in a yearly love and social peak until the 21st. Foreigners
are always alluring to you, and this month even more so than usual.
There are romantic (and social) opportunities in foreign lands, educational settings and at your place of worship. The social confidence
looks strong now. Mercury is not only moving forward but rather
speedily at that. You're covering a lot of social territory these days.

Finances are bit more stressful this month. There's nothing cata-
strophic here either, they are just slower than usual. Saturn, your
financial planet, is retrograde and receiving stressful aspects. You just
have to work harder for earnings and deal with more delays. You can
avoid making matters worse than they need to be by paying more
attention to the little financial details. Small mistakes can cause big
delays.

Venus makes nice aspects to Jupiter on the 1st and 2nd. This brings
success at the job and happy job opportunities. There is some good
news on the health front. Children or children figures in your life have
a nice payday.

On the 19th and 20th Mercury makes beautiful aspects to both
Jupiter and Neptune. This brings happy career opportunities (and

success) and social happiness. Singles have happy romantic meetings. Family members seem supportive of your career.

With the Western, social side of your Horoscope still strong, and with Jupiter retrograde all month, it is probably best to defer to others this month. Let them have their way so long as it isn't destructive. Too much self will is not conducive to romance, and this is a romantic kind of month.

July

Best Days Overall: 5, 6, 14, 15, 22, 23, 24
Most Stressful Days Overall: 3, 4, 10, 11, 16, 17, 30, 31
Best Days for Love: 5, 6, 10, 11, 14, 15, 22, 23, 24
Best Days for Money: 1, 7, 8, 12, 13, 16, 20, 21, 25, 26, 27, 28, 29
Best Days for Career: 5, 6, 14, 15, 16, 17, 22, 23, 24

Two eclipses this month practically guarantee an eventful, disruptive kind of month. Never a dull moment. You've gone though much worse eclipses in your life, but it won't hurt to take it easy during these periods.

The Solar Eclipse of the 13th occurs in your 8th house – which means that it has a strong impact on you. It can bring near-death kinds of experiences and psychological encounters with death – however, generally it is not literal death. (For this one needs to study the actual Horoscope cast for your date, time and place of birth.) There is no need to tempt the scythe carrier; spend more time quietly at home during this period. The spouse, partner or current love has a financial crisis – a disturbance – and will have to make dramatic financial changes. You can have issues with the tax authorities or with insurance companies. If you are of appropriate age you will make changes to your will. The eclipsed planet, the Sun, rules the 9th house. Once again (as we saw in the earlier eclipses in January and February) there are shakeups in your place of worship and dramas in the lives of worship leaders. College students (or those bound for college) are making important educational changes. Your religious and philosophical beliefs get tested. Your faith gets tested. Pluto, your spiritual planet, is affected pretty directly. This brings shakeups – a period of chaos – in a charity or spiritual organization you're involved with. Guru figures in your life have dramas. The dream life is likely to be hyperactive (and probably negative) this period, but pay no heed. These are not messages from above but astral flotsam and jetsam stirred up by the eclipse.

The Lunar Eclipse of the 27th occurs in your 3rd house but brings more of the same that the Solar Eclipse brought. There can be near-death experiences, or psychological encounters with death. There can be problems with the tax authorities or with insurance claims. Limit your driving to only when absolutely necessary and do your best to stay off the roads. Cars and communication equipment will get tested now, and will often need replacement or repair. Siblings, sibling figures and neighbours have personal dramas. The neighbourhood could be under-going radical change. This eclipse affects students below college level. There are disruptions at school and changes in educational plans.

August

Best Days Overall: 1, 2, 3, 10, 11, 19, 20, 29, 30
Most Stressful Days Overall: 6, 7, 12, 13, 26, 27
Best Days for Love: 1, 2, 3, 5, 6, 7, 10, 11, 14, 15, 19, 20, 24, 25, 29, 30
Best Days for Money: 4, 8, 9, 12, 16, 17, 21, 22, 26, 27, 31
Best Days for Career: 1, 2, 3, 6, 7, 10, 11, 19, 20, 29, 30

Another eclipse on the 11th (the third Solar Eclipse of the year) keeps the pot boiling this month. It is more or less a repeat of the Solar Eclipse we had last month. This one occurs in your 9th house and again impacts on college students, your place of worship and worship leaders. There is still much chaos here. This eclipse happens when 60 per cent of the planets are going backwards (the maximum number for the year) and thus can have delayed reactions. But over the course of the next six months you will see the changes and dramas we mention. You're a traveller by nature, and especially so this month with your 9th house so strong. However, avoid travelling during the eclipse period. Siblings and sibling figures in your life are having their marriages tested (if they are of appropriate age).

In spite of the eclipse, the month ahead is successful. Your career planet, Mercury, starts moving forward on the 19th, and on the 22nd the Sun enters your 10th house of career. You begin a yearly career peak. Your work ethic and friends in the right places are a help until the 7th. Your willingness to travel is also a plus (only avoid the eclipse period if possible).

Prosperity is strong this month but especially after the 22nd. A promotion or pay rise wouldn't be a surprise. (Sometimes these things happen unofficially.) Foreign companies, foreign investments and foreigners in general are favourably disposed to you. The only issue is the retrograde of your financial planet. Prosperity can happen, but more slowly than you expect.

Mercury, your love planet, spends the month in your 9th house, signalling increased social activity and an attraction to foreigners, religious ministers and professors. You have this allurement by birth, but now it is much stronger. Mercury's retrograde until the 19th suggests more caution in love. By nature you are a 'love at first sight' kind of person – a leaper into relationships. And this, too, is stronger this month. But until the 19th more caution is called for. (After the 19th it is a different story.)

Health needs watching from the 22nd onwards. Again there is nothing major afoot here, just less energy than usual. You can enhance the health through arm and shoulder massage until the 7th, and through hip massage after the 7th.

September

Best Days Overall: 7, 15, 16, 25, 26
Most Stressful Days Overall: 2, 3, 9, 22, 23, 24, 29, 30
Best Days for Love: 2, 3, 9, 13, 18, 19, 22, 23, 29, 30
Best Days for Money: 1, 4, 5, 8, 9, 13, 14, 17, 18, 19, 22, 23, 24, 27
Best Days for Career: 9, 18, 19, 29

Last month on the 22nd, the planetary power began to shift back to the Eastern sector of self. This month, on the 6th, as Mercury crossed from the West to the East, the shift gets even stronger – at least 80 per cent (and sometimes 90 per cent) of the planets are now in the East. You've never really lost your independence this year, but now it is stronger than ever. Be respectful of others but go your own way. Take responsibility for your own happiness. It is your personal merit that matters now and not your likeability or social skills.

Health still needs some attention until the 22nd. So, as always, make sure to get enough rest. Enhance the health with hip massage, and perhaps a herbal kidney cleanse, until the 9th. After the 9th give more attention to the colon, bladder and sexual organs. Sexual moderation is called for. You also respond very well to spiritual therapies from the 9th onwards. If you feel under the weather, see a spiritual healer. Health and energy will rebound beautifully after the 22nd. This is just a short-term issue.

You're still in the midst of a yearly career peak and much of what we said last month applies now. Be willing to travel, to take courses that enhance the career, and be willing to mentor others. From the 6th to the 22nd you have friends in high places and they seem supportive. You're successful this month. The spouse, partner or current love also seems successful.

Love should go well this month. Marriage might not be on the cards, but love is. Your love planet, Mercury, will be in your career house from the 6th to the 22nd. This shows that love is high on your agenda. It is perhaps your real career – your mission. You need to be there for the beloved and for friends. It also shows romantic opportunities as you pursue your career goals and with people involved in your career. You're attracted to successful, high-status people these days – and you will meet up with such people. A good part of your social life this month (from the 6th to the 22nd) seems career and business related.

October

Best Days Overall: 4, 5, 12, 13, 14, 22, 23, 31
Most Stressful Days Overall: 1, 6, 7, 20, 21, 27, 28
Best Days for Love: 1, 2, 3, 9, 10, 11, 20, 21, 27, 28, 29, 30
Best Days for Money: 2, 3, 6, 10, 11, 15, 16, 20, 21, 24, 25, 29, 30
Best Days for Career: 1, 6, 7, 9, 10, 20, 21, 29, 30

The cosmic chess board is being rearranged for prosperity this month. Last month, on the 9th, your financial planet Saturn started to move forward; Pluto, in your money house, moves forward on the 2nd. Saturn and Pluto in parallel aspect (they occupy the same degree of latitude) signals an excellent financial intuition. (They've been parallel for a few months, but they were retrograde. Now they move forward and are more reliable.) There is financial clarity and direction now. You're thinking straight and have good intuition. When the Sun moves into Scorpio on the 23rd, watch the earnings soar. (They are OK before that date, but you have to work harder to achieve them.)

Health and energy are super this month. There are no short-term planets in stressful alignment, and only one long-term planet, Neptune, is stressing you – and you've been dealing with this for many years now. With energy, things that previously seemed impossible are now possible. Your health planet, Venus, makes one of her rare retrogrades on the 5th, so don't be so quick to make changes to the diet or health regime. These changes need a lot more study. Venus in your 12th house of spirituality all month, shows that you respond well to spiritual therapies. And with your spiritual 12th house so strong this month (from the 23rd onwards) this is a great period to go deeper into spiritual healing.

Jupiter has been in your 12th house all year, and this month the 12th house is easily the strongest in the Horoscope. It is a period for internal growth. You're seeing (and this has been so all year) that things have to happen 'through you' before they can happen 'to' you. The internal precedes the external. So this internal growth is going to manifest as external growth in the coming months.

Mercury, your love and career planet, spends most of the month – from the 10th onwards – in your 12th house. The message of the Horoscope is, stay right spiritually and everything else – health, career, love and finance – will just fall into place. These things will take care of themselves.

November

Best Days Overall: 1, 9, 10, 19, 20, 27, 28
Most Stressful Days Overall: 2, 3, 16, 17, 23, 24, 29, 30
Best Days for Love: 1, 4, 5, 9, 10, 14, 15, 19, 20, 23, 24, 27, 28
Best Days for Money: 2, 8, 10, 11, 12, 19, 21, 27
Best Days for Career: 1, 2, 3, 9, 10, 19, 20, 27, 28, 29, 30

A happy and prosperous month. The future looks so bright you need sun glasses to gaze upon it. On the 8th Jupiter, the ruler of your Horoscope, crosses your Ascendant and enters your 1st house. He is now in his own sign and house. He is home. He is more powerful on your behalf. This will initiate, as we have mentioned, a multi-year cycle of prosperity. You're a traveller by nature, but now even more so. Shall we fly to Argentina for the soccer match? Or Germany? Your bags are packed. Shall we have lunch in Paris and dinner in London? Your bags are packed. You tend to live a high lifestyle in general, but now these urges are revved up. These days you're a Sagittarius on steroids.

On the 6th Uranus retrogrades back into your 5th house and the job situation becomes temporarily more stable. The experimentalism in health matters also stabilizes.

Avoid making important changes to the health regime until the 16th, when Venus starts to move forward again. Health is still excellent. Even Mars's move into stressful alignment on the 16th will not materially affect the health. Most planets are in harmonious relationship with you. You can enhance your already good health by giving more attention to the hips and kidneys this month. Hip massage will not only strengthen the kidneys but the lower back as well.

The love life is good, albeit more complicated this month. Mercury, your love planet, spends the month in your 1st house. This shows that love seeks you out – pursues you – is always right where you are. You do not have to do anything special. Also it shows someone who has love on his or her terms. Others seem eager to please. But Mercury goes retrograde on the 17th and this can cause delays or glitches. Love blooms on the 27th and 28th as Mercury travels with Jupiter. It brings a happy romantic meeting for singles and happy social experiences for others. It also brings career elevation and success. (But there can be delayed reactions here.)

Career is becoming less important now. By the 22nd there will be only one planet (with the exception of the Moon) above the horizon. The night side of the Horoscope is very dominant now – and will be dominant for months to come. You seem to have achieved your short-term career goals. People see you as successful. You look the part. There's no need to run after career opportunities – they run after you. After the 17th, with Mercury travelling backwards, study these things more closely.

December

Best Days Overall: 6, 7, 16, 17, 25, 26
Most Stressful Days Overall: 14, 15, 21, 22, 27, 28
Best Days for Love: 2, 3, 4, 5, 13, 14, 15, 21, 22, 23, 24
Best Days for Money: 6, 8, 9, 10, 16, 18, 26, 27
Best Days for Career: 4, 5, 14, 23, 24, 27, 28

Another happy and prosperous month ahead, Sagittarius. Enjoy.

The planetary power is now in its maximum Eastern position and you are in your period of maximum personal independence. There is only one planet in the West (the sector of others) – except for the Moon (and her presence in the West is only for half the month). This is a classic indicator of someone who is having life on his or her terms. You're having things your way. This is a mixed blessing, however. If your way is 'unenlightened' this can bring big karmic problems later on. However, if your way is enlightened, not intending harm for others, it's a great blessing.

Health and energy are excellent. Your health planet's move into your 12th house on the 2nd shows that you respond well to spiritual healing methods. Many of you will expand your knowledge of these. You're still very much in a yearly personal pleasure peak. It is time to treat the body well. Your tendency could be to overdo this, and if you do there is a price to pay down the road. Your weight could mushroom.

Jupiter in your sign (along with the Sun) makes those of you of child-bearing age much more fertile this month. This tendency will last for the next twelve months.

On the 21st the Sun enters your already strong money house and makes it even stronger. You begin a yearly financial peak. The Sun will be travelling with Saturn from the 25th to the 31st, increasing earnings. This aspect favours money from foreign countries, foreign companies and foreigners in general.

The love life starts to improve on the 6th as Mercury starts to move forward again. It gets really good from the 13th onwards as Mercury moves back into your 1st house. Like last month, it shows someone who is having love on his or her own terms. The spouse, partner or current love (and others in general) are eager to please. Singles need not do much to attract love. It will find you. Just go about your daily business. Since Mercury is also your career planet, his move into your 1st house brings happy career opportunities. Like last month it indicates someone who has attained their career goals (the short-term ones at least) and looks the part. People see you as successful, and this is how you feel.

Capricorn

♑

THE GOAT

Birthdays from
21st December to
19th January

Personality Profile

CAPRICORN AT A GLANCE

Element – Earth

Ruling Planet – Saturn
  Career Planet – Venus
  Love Planet – Moon
  Money Planet – Uranus
  Planet of Communications – Neptune
  Planet of Health and Work – Mercury
  Planet of Home and Family Life – Mars
  Planet of Spirituality – Jupiter

Colours – black, indigo

Colours that promote love, romance and social harmony – puce, silver

Colour that promotes earning power – ultramarine blue

Gem – black onyx

Metal – lead

Scents – magnolia, pine, sweet pea, wintergreen

Quality – cardinal (= activity)

Qualities most needed for balance – warmth, spontaneity, a sense of fun

Strongest virtues – sense of duty, organization, perseverance, patience, ability to take the long-term view

Deepest needs – to manage, take charge and administrate

Characteristics to avoid – pessimism, depression, undue materialism and undue conservatism

Signs of greatest overall compatibility – Taurus, Virgo

Signs of greatest overall incompatibility – Aries, Cancer, Libra

Sign most helpful to career – Libra

Sign most helpful for emotional support – Aries

Sign most helpful financially – Aquarius

Sign best for marriage and/or partnerships – Cancer

Sign most helpful for creative projects – Taurus

Best Sign to have fun with – Taurus

Signs most helpful in spiritual matters – Virgo, Sagittarius

Best day of the week – Saturday

Understanding a Capricorn

The virtues of Capricorns are such that there will always be people for and against them. Many admire them, many dislike them. Why? It seems to be because of Capricorn's power urges. A well-developed Capricorn has his or her eyes set on the heights of power, prestige and authority. In the sign of Capricorn, ambition is not a fatal flaw, but rather the highest virtue.

Capricorns are not frightened by the resentment their authority may sometimes breed. In Capricorn's cool, calculated, organized mind all the dangers are already factored into the equation – the unpopularity, the animosity, the misunderstandings, even the outright slander – and a plan is always in place for dealing with these things in the most efficient way. To the Capricorn, situations that would terrify an ordinary mind are merely problems to be managed, bumps on the road to ever-growing power, effectiveness and prestige.

Some people attribute pessimism to the Capricorn sign, but this is a bit deceptive. It is true that Capricorns like to take into account the negative side of things. It is also true that they love to imagine the worst possible scenario in every undertaking. Other people might find such analyses depressing, but Capricorns only do these things so that they can formulate a way out – an escape route.

Capricorns will argue with success. They will show you that you are not doing as well as you think you are. Capricorns do this to themselves as well as to others. They do not mean to discourage you but rather to root out any impediments to your greater success. A Capricorn boss or supervisor feels that no matter how good the performance there is always room for improvement. This explains why Capricorn supervisors are difficult to handle and even infuriating at times. Their actions are, however, quite often effective – they can get their subordinates to improve and become better at their jobs.

Capricorn is a born manager and administrator. Leo is better at being king or queen, but Capricorn is better at being prime minister – the person actually wielding power.

Capricorn is interested in the virtues that last, in the things that will stand the test of time and trials of circumstance. Temporary fads and fashions mean little to a Capricorn – except as things to be used for profit or power. Capricorns apply this attitude to business, love, to their thinking and even to their philosophy and religion.

Finance

Capricorns generally attain wealth and they usually earn it. They are willing to work long and hard for what they want. They are quite amenable to foregoing a short-term gain in favour of long-term benefits. Financially, they come into their own later in life.

However, if Capricorns are to attain their financial goals they must shed some of their strong conservatism. Perhaps this is the least desirable trait of the Capricorn. They can resist anything new merely because it is new and untried. They are afraid of experimentation. Capricorns need to be willing to take a few risks. They should be more eager to market new products or explore different managerial techniques. Otherwise, progress will leave them behind. If necessary, Capricorns must be ready to change with the times, to discard old methods that no longer work.

Very often this experimentation will mean that Capricorns have to break with existing authority. They might even consider changing their present position or starting their own ventures. If so, they should be willing to accept all the risks and just get on with it. Only then will a Capricorn be on the road to highest financial gains.

Career and Public Image

A Capricorn's ambition and quest for power are evident. It is perhaps the most ambitious sign of the zodiac – and usually the most successful in a worldly sense. However, there are lessons Capricorns need to learn in order to fulfil their highest aspirations.

Intelligence, hard work, cool efficiency and organization will take them a certain distance, but will not carry them to the very top. Capricorns need to cultivate their social graces, to develop a social style, along with charm and an ability to get along with people. They need to bring beauty into their lives and to cultivate the right social contacts. They must learn to wield power gracefully, so that people love them for it – a very delicate art. They also need to learn how to bring people together in order to fulfil certain objectives. In short, Capricorns require some of the gifts – the social graces – of Libra to get to the top.

Once they have learned this, Capricorns will be successful in their careers. They are ambitious hard workers who are not afraid of putting in the required time and effort. Capricorns take their time in getting the job done – in order to do it well – and they like moving up the corporate ladder slowly but surely. Being so driven by success, Capricorns are generally liked by their bosses, who respect and trust them.

Love and Relationships

Like Scorpio and Pisces, Capricorn is a difficult sign to get to know. They are deep, introverted and like to keep their own counsel. Capricorns do not like to reveal their innermost thoughts. If you are in love with a Capricorn, be patient and take your time. Little by little you will get to understand him or her.

Capricorns have a deep romantic nature, but they do not show it straightaway. They are cool, matter of fact and not especially emotional. They will often show their love in practical ways.

It takes time for a Capricorn – male or female – to fall in love. They are not the love-at-first-sight kind. If a Capricorn is involved with a Leo or Aries, these Fire types will be totally mystified – to them the Capricorn will seem cold, unfeeling, unaffectionate and not very spontaneous. Of course none of this is true; it is just that Capricorn likes to take things slowly. They like to be sure of their ground before making any demonstrations of love or commitment.

Even in love affairs Capricorns are deliberate. They need more time to make decisions than is true of the other signs of the zodiac, but given this time they become just as passionate. Capricorns like a relationship to be structured, committed, well regulated, well defined, predictable and even routine. They prefer partners who are nurturers, and they in turn like to nurture their partners. This is their basic psychology. Whether such a relationship is good for them is another issue altogether. Capricorns have enough routine in their lives as it is. They might be better off in relationships that are a bit more stimulating, changeable and fluctuating.

Home and Domestic Life

The home of a Capricorn – as with a Virgo – is going to be tidy and well organized. Capricorns tend to manage their families in the same way they manage their businesses. Capricorns are often so career-driven that they find little time for the home and family. They should try to get more actively involved in their family and domestic life. Capricorns do, however, take their children very seriously and are very proud parents – particularly should their children grow up to become respected members of society.

Horoscope for 2018

Major Trends

There has been a lot of internal, spiritual growth in the past two years, as the ruler of your Horoscope, Saturn, was moving through your 12th house, and there will be more later on in the year as Jupiter moves into this house on November 8. But now, your internal growth becomes visible to the world and to other people. Saturn has moved into your sign and will stay there for the next two years. Most people are uncomfortable with a Saturn transit, but for you it is good. Saturn will make you even more of a Capricorn than you already are. You will be even more organized, more structured, more of the manager than you have ever been.

Pluto, your planet of friends, has been in your sign for many years now. So, you have been attracting friends. They seem to come to you naturally without much effort on your part. This year, with Jupiter in your 11th house, there are even more friendships happening. These seem to be more on a spiritual type of level than usual.

Uranus has been in your 4th house of home and family for the past seven years, bringing much change and instability in the family circle. Happily, this is beginning to reduce a bit this year. Uranus moves out of your 4th house on May 16 and enters the 5th house of fun, creativity and children. This is a nice financial signal, as Uranus is your financial planet. It is also a good transit for your health. More on this later on.

Neptune has been in your 3rd house for many years now, and will be there for many more to come. Your intellectual interests are becoming more refined and spiritualized. You would enjoy poetry and spiritual literature. Siblings and sibling figures in your life are under strong spiritual influences too. Students below college level need to be careful of 'mind wandering' or daydreaming during class or study. Keep your focus on your studies.

Your most important interests this year are the body, image and personal pleasure; communication and intellectual interests; home and family (until May 16 and from November 6 onwards); children, fun and creativity (from May 16 to November 6); friends, groups and group activities (all year but especially until November 8); and spirituality (from November 8 onwards).

Your paths of greatest fulfilment this year are friends, groups and group activities (until November 8); spirituality (from November 8 onwards); sex, occult studies and personal transformation (until November 17); and love and romance (from November 17 onwards).

Health

(Please note that this is an astrological perspective on health and not a medical one. In days of yore there was no difference, both of these perspectives were identical. But now there could be quite a difference. For a medical perspective, please consult your doctor or health practitioner.)

Health is much improved this year, and it will get even better in the coming years. Uranus, which was in stressful aspect with you for the last seven years, is now moving into harmonious alignment. This year it is only in this new alignment for part of the year, but next year – from March onwards – it will be for the long haul. Saturn in a person's sign is generally not a good health indicator, but for you, Capricorn, it is. He is the ruler of your chart, and always 'friendly' to you. Your empty 6th house is another positive health indicator. You have little need to focus here as there is nothing wrong. You sort of take good health for granted.

Good though your health is, it can be made even better. Give more attention to the following – the vulnerable areas of your chart (the reflex points are shown overleaf). This is where problems are most likely to happen and by keeping these areas in good shape problems can mostly be forestalled (and even in cases where you can't completely prevent a problem, it can be softened considerably; it need not be devastating).

- The heart. This has only recently become an important area this year (really from late last month), but it will be important next year too. Worry and anxiety are said by spiritual healers to be the root cause of heart problems. Meditation will help you to avoid these emotions and, eventually, to transform them.
- The spine, knees, teeth, bones, skin and overall skeletal alignment. These areas are always important for Capricorn, as your sign rules these areas. Regular back and knee massages should be a part of your normal health regime. Regular visits to the chiropractor or osteopath would be beneficial. The vertebrae need to be kept in alignment. Therapies such as Alexander Technique, Rolfing and Feldenkrais are good for the spine. The

Important foot reflexology points for the year ahead

Try to massage all of the foot on a regular basis – the top of the foot as well as the bottom – but pay extra attention to the points highlighted on the chart. When you massage, be aware of 'sore spots' as these need special attention. It's also a good idea to massage the ankles and below them.

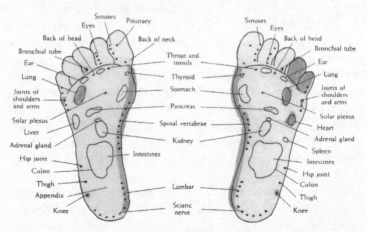

Alexander Technique, which educates the muscles in right posture, is an especially good preventive therapy. Good dental hygiene and regular check-ups are advisable. If you're out in the sun, use a good sun screen.

- The lungs, arms, shoulders and respiratory system. These are also always important for Capricorn, as Mercury, the planet that rules these areas, is your health planet. Arms and shoulders should be regularly massaged. Tension tends to collect in the shoulders and needs to be released.

Capricorn tends to physical leanness. But if you are one of the rare ones that need to lose weight this is a good year for it. Your efforts will be supported by the cosmos.

This is a good year for getting the image and body the way you want it to be on the 'appearance' level – the cosmetic level. We can liken the ruler of your Horoscope to your personal trainer. Saturn is concerned with your outer image. The ruler of your health house, Mercury, plays the role of your 'personal physician'. He is concerned with your health and wellbeing more than with your outer look.

Mercury, is a fast-moving and often erratic planet. Sometimes he moves very fast, sometimes very slow, sometimes he's stationary and sometimes he moves backwards. So there are a lot of short-term health issues that depend on Mercury's status at a given time. These trends are best dealt with in the monthly reports.

Home and Family

As we mentioned, this has been an important – and volatile – area for at least seven years. Probably there have been multiple moves and renovations of the home over this period. You have the profile (and I know people like this) who upgrade and renovate their home and then sell it (at a profit). Then they move and repeat the process again and again. It's a constant upgrading and moving. They upgrade the home the way you upgrade your computer and software. It goes on and on and on. In many cases it shows the search for the 'dream home' or the 'dream domestic situation'. Every time you think 'this is it, I've got it' a new idea comes to you and you move on.

In many cases, there have been break-ups of the family unit, rifts in the family. Sometimes there has been a divorce, sometimes quarrels and realignments in new ways. The whole family situation is vastly different than it was a mere seven years ago.

You also have the profile of someone who is installing all the latest technical gadgetry in the home – smart alarm systems, video cameras connected to the internet, smart toasters and appliances. Anything high-tech is alluring. You've been spending a lot on the home and family – it's been expensive. But the good news is that you earn from this area as well. Uranus, your financial planet, in the 4th house signals earning from home – perhaps in the form of a home office or home-based business. Your home is as much an economic centre as it is a home.

These trends are still in effect this year, but they are much weaker than they have been. The urge to move and renovate and upgrade is lessening. Uranus moves out of your 4th house on May 16 for several months, and by March of next year he will be out of the 4th house for good. So a lot of instability in the home and family life will subside. You're probably settled in your current home for the long haul.

Uranus's move into your 5th house between May 16 and November 6 is a harbinger of things to come. The focus will be less on the physical home and more on the children and children figures in your life. They will be more difficult to handle too. You can't be your normal authoritarian self with them. They won't accept it. You will have to explain – rationally – why such and such has to be done. You will have to appeal to their reason.

Uranus in your 5th house shows that the children and children figures in your life are going through many personal changes. For the next seven years they will be constantly redefining themselves and their image, constantly changing their 'look' and self-concept, constantly upgrading their image and personality. Every month or so it will be like you're dealing with a 'new person'.

Children and children figures will become more experimental with their bodies. They want to test its limits. This is basically good, but it needs to be done consciously and mindfully – not in daredevil type ways. Yoga, tai chi and the martial arts are safe ways to do this.

Finance and Career

Very important financial changes are happening in your life this year (and this is only the beginning), with your financial planet's move out of your 4th house and into your 5th house. As we have said, this year it is only from May 16 to November 6. But next year, Uranus will move in for the long term.

So, you're still spending and earning from the home, from the family and family connections this year. But as Uranus enters your 5th house there will be a financial shift too. With Uranus in Aries these past years, you were perhaps a bit impulsive in your financial decision making – perhaps too reckless. Perhaps you lusted after the 'quick buck' and got burned a few times. Uranus's move into Taurus will bring a more conservative kind of outlook. The financial judgement will improve. And since Uranus will make beautiful aspects to Saturn, the ruler of your chart, there will be prosperity this year. (Next year looks even better.)

The financial planet in Taurus favours investments in copper, land, cattle and agricultural products. Companies that supply farmers are interesting investments.

The financial planet in the 5th house is a very fortunate aspect. There are various ways to read this and all could apply. The act of making money becomes enjoyable, a form of entertainment. You enjoy it as much as some people enjoy video games or the theatre. Making money is not just 'necessity' but a form of leisure. (I know many people who feel this way.) Another way to read this is as someone who enjoys his or her wealth – someone who spends more on leisure and fun activities. The symbolism here is of 'happy' money. This position favours the youth market – industries such as music and entertainment that cater to them. It shows spending more on the children and children figures in your life – perhaps investing in them. The children can be a source of income as well. Much depends on their age and stage in life. Those of appropriate age can be financially supportive. Younger children often have inspired ideas. And often they are the motivating force behind one's earnings.

The financial planet in the 5th house makes you more speculative. But it will be different than it was over the past seven years. It will be more 'controlled' speculation – well thought out. It will not be rash and impulsive.

You're coming out of a strong career year. You were very successful in 2017. This year, career is not a big deal. Most likely you've achieved your important career goals (the short-term ones at least) and have no need to focus here. Your 10th house is mostly empty: only short-term planets move through here. So in the career it is a stable year.

Since Venus, a fast-moving planet, is your career planet, there are many short-term career trends depending on where she is and the aspects she receives. These are best dealt with in the monthly reports.

Love and Social Life

Your 7th house of love is not a house of power this year. It is basically empty with only short-term planets moving through there. It is not a major focus (though there is fulfilment here after November 17). This tends to the status quo. You seem content with things as they are and have no pressing need to make changes. Those who are married will tend to stay married, and singles will tend to stay single.

There is one complication though. Saturn is now in your sign. While this is great for your business and management skills, it is not so great for love. Capricorns are cool customers as it is. Saturn in your sign can make you even cooler – cold – aloof – business-like – lacking in warmth and love. Someone who just wants to get the job done and get on with it. This can be a turn-off to many people, and especially to the current spouse, partner or romantic interest. You need to lighten up a bit and show more affection. Show more positive feeling. You will need to make this a goal. Every night before going to bed project love and warmth to others. One can be a good manager and still be a warm person.

Three eclipses will test your current relationship this year. There will be two Lunar Eclipses, which always test love (the Moon is your love planet). Then there will be a Solar Eclipse on July 13 that occurs in your 7th house of love. So three out of the five eclipses this year impact on your love life. Good relationships will survive, it's the flawed ones that are endangered. We will discuss this more fully in the monthly reports.

For singles this is more a year for love affairs rather than marriage. This is especially so from May 16 to November 6. You're attracted to 'money people' or to people involved in your finances.

If you are in or working on your second marriage, the year ahead is a stable one, but those working on the third marriage have romance this year – perhaps even a marriage. Those working on their fourth marriage also have a stable kind of year.

Parents and parent figures have endured severe testing of their marriages in recent years. It's very unlikely that the relationship has survived. The testing is about over now; it is getting easier although the testing is still going on. If they are single, marriage is not advisable just yet. Siblings and sibling figures have a quiet romantic year. Children and children figures in your life are having an excellent social year. If they are of appropriate age there is serious romance. The only issue is the stability of this. They don't seem ready for marriage commitment.

For all Capricorns this is a wonderful year for friendships and group activities – a happy area of life. New (and spiritual) friends are coming into the picture. It would be good to join spiritual-type groups this year. But groups involved in charities or altruistic kinds of activities would also fit the symbolism. You seem very active in the online social networking scene – a good source for making new friends.

Self-Improvement

Saturn in your sign is going to bring many wonderful things, as we have mentioned. It will strengthen your already strong sense of duty and responsibility. It will strengthen your management skills too. But there is a down side to this that you need to be aware of. Even without Saturn in your sign, you tend to look at the dark side of things. You like to contemplate the 'worst case' scenario in every situation, so that you can plan an escape route. But now Saturn is going to accentuate these tendencies. You can become overly focused on the dark side, overly pessimistic. Everything can look black. Often one feels older, much older than one's years. And this will be true even for young Capricorns. If you overdo this, you can lose all hope, and thus extinguish any desire for improvement.

If you find yourself in this condition, break out of it as soon as possible. Don't hang out in this negative psychic space. You might think that you're just being 'realistic', but it's not so. Meditation will be a big help here. Turn your focus to the Divine or to what you would like to achieve. Imagine yourself in this state. Live in where you would like to be, rather than what your feelings are telling you at the moment.

Jupiter, your spiritual planet, is making beautiful aspects to Neptune, the generic spiritual planet. So in the year ahead there will be many spiritual experiences – prophetic dreams, synchronicities, enhanced ESP abilities and a strong intuition. The dream life will be significant this year and you should record your dreams in a journal. If you have trouble remembering them, give yourself the suggestion before going to sleep that 'I will remember my dreams'.

Those of you who are writers will be very inspired this year.

When Jupiter moves into your spiritual 12th house on November 8, he will make stressful aspects with Neptune, which can create some conflict between your path and the 'general spiritual trend' that's around. It might seem to you that you're being led 'counter' to the spiritual teachings that are popular. But this is only an appearance. The spiritual path is a very personal thing. Each person is, ultimately, his or her own path. It may take some time to see, but you'll find that there's no contradiction. What's being taught publicly is true, and so are your personal guidance and personal path.

Month-by-month Forecasts

January

Best Days Overall: 5, 6, 15, 16, 25, 26
Most Stressful Days Overall: 1, 2, 8, 9, 22, 23, 29, 30
Best Days for Love: 1, 2, 5, 6, 15, 16, 27, 28, 29, 30
Best Days for Money: 1, 2, 4, 10, 11, 13, 14, 17, 18, 19, 20, 21, 23, 24, 29, 30, 31
Best Days for Career: 5, 6, 8, 9, 15, 16, 27, 28

There are many planets in your sign this month: 60 per cent of the planets are either there or moving through there this month. This is a lot of Capricorn energy. These days you're not just a Capricorn but a mega-Capricorn, with all the good and bad points accentuated. On the positive side, your management and organizational skills are greatly enhanced. So is your work ethic and legendary patience. On the negative side, you can be seen as too cold, aloof and business-like. This can hamper the social life. Sometimes too much practicality can become 'impractical' – it has consequences that can defeat what you're trying to do. But you will work this out.

Health is good this month. You have plenty of energy and, being a Capricorn, you will use it wisely. Health this month (especially after the 11th) is as much about 'looking good' as it is about health. The good news is that the personal appearance shines. In your low-key, subdued way, you exude charisma and star power. There is more grace and elegance to the image. Your sense of style (especially until the 18th) is impeccable. There is no problem in attracting the opposite sex – except for the ones we mentioned. You need to warm up a bit – show love and warmth to others.

At least 80 per cent (and sometimes 90 per cent) of the planets are in the independent Eastern sector of your chart. Right now you're in your period of maximum independence. You can and should have things your way. You can and should have life on your terms. If there are conditions that irk you or that are less than perfect, now is the time to make any necessary changes. Later on, as the planets shift to the West in a few months' time, these changes will be more difficult to make. Your happiness is up to you.

Your personal solar cycle will be in its waxing (growing) phase this month (from your birthday onwards). The universal solar cycle began to wax last month December 21, and *all* of the planets are moving forward this month. Thus you're in a really good period for launching new ventures or products into the world. The 17th to the 30th (as the Moon waxes) is the absolute optimum time for this.

A Lunar Eclipse on the 31st occurs in your 8th house of regeneration, so avoid dangerous situations at that time. The spouse, partner or current love could be having a financial or personal crisis and needs to make changes. Your current relationship gets tested.

February

Best Days Overall: 2, 3, 11, 12, 21, 22
Most Stressful Days Overall: 4, 5, 19, 25, 26
Best Days for Love: 4, 5, 14, 15, 16, 25, 26
Best Days for Money: 6, 7, 10, 14, 15, 16, 17, 19, 20, 25, 26, 28
Best Days for Career: 4, 5, 16, 25, 26

Last month's Lunar Eclipse brought financial changes for the spouse, partner or current love. This month's Solar Eclipse of the 15th brings more of the same – but you are also forced to make important financial changes as this eclipse occurs in your money house. These changes are likely to be good – you're in the midst of a yearly financial peak – but can be uncomfortable while they happen. People often change banks, brokers, financial planners or investments under this kind of eclipse. There are dramas in the lives of the money people in your life and they could be having their marriages or relationships tested. Both last month's eclipse and this month's can bring near-death kinds of experiences – brushes with death. So no need to make matters worse – avoid dangerous or potentially stressful situations this period.

In spite of the shakeups caused by the eclipse, the month ahead seems prosperous. You're in the midst of a yearly financial peak as we've said. The money house is strong and thus earning power is strong. It is a good month for paying off debts or taking on loans – according to your need. There is good financial cooperation between you and the spouse, partner or current love.

Love doesn't seem a big issue this month. Once the excitement of last month's Lunar Eclipse passes and you deal with the grievances in your relationship, things should settle down.

Health and energy continue to be good. You can enhance it further in the ways mentioned in the yearly report, but also through calf and ankle massage until the 18th, and through foot massage from the 18th onwards.

This is another excellent month for starting new projects or ventures, if you haven't already done so. You're in a waxing (growing) personal and universal solar cycle, and all the planets are still moving forward, thus you should see fast progress. Avoid the eclipse period, but from the 16th onwards, as the Moon waxes, is the best time of the month for these things.

The planetary power is now in the night side (lower half) of your Horoscope. So you are more the night person than the day person now. You are always ambitious, but your ambitions will go better if the home and family are solid. Tending to your emotional wellness will help the career later on.

March

Best Days Overall: 1, 2, 10, 11, 12, 20, 21, 29, 30
Most Stressful Days Overall: 3, 4, 18, 19, 24, 25, 31
Best Days for Love: 6, 7, 8, 16, 17, 18, 19, 24, 25, 26, 27
Best Days for Money: 6, 7, 9, 13, 14, 15, 16, 17, 18, 19, 24, 25, 27
Best Days for Career: 3, 4, 8, 18, 19, 26, 27, 31

Home and family is the main headline of the month ahead. The focus is here. Anyone who has ever owned a home knows that there is always something to do there – screws need tightening, appliances need tweaking or repair, paint peels and needs retouching, the hot water heater shorts out ... it goes on and on and on. Now is the time to deal with these things.

Your 4th house becomes very powerful from the 20th onwards (and you'll feel the planetary power here even before). Add to this that Mars, the ruler of the 4th house, enters your own sign on the 17th and the focus is greatly magnified.

The ruler of the 4th house moving into your 1st house shows good family support. It shows the devotion (stronger than usual) of a parent or parent figure. Sometimes it shows that he or she is coming to stay for a while.

Venus, your career planet will be in the 4th house from the 6th onwards, signalling that your real career at the moment is the home and family. All roads lead to Rome in this month's chart. The message of the Horoscope is, get into emotional harmony, get the family situation right, and the career and finances will more or less fall into place.

The month ahead, while not a financial peak, is prosperous (next month will also be prosperous). Your financial planet, Uranus, is receiving positive stimulation. Venus travels with Uranus on the 28th and 29th, showing luck in speculations and happy money. You can earn easily and are probably spending on fun kinds of things. Both Venus and Mercury make nice aspects to Jupiter, showing happy job opportunities and prosperity for children and children figures in your life.

Your health will need more attention from the 20th onwards. As always the most important thing is to get enough rest. Don't allow yourself to get over tired. Low energy is the primal disease. Enhance the health through head, face and scalp massage from the 6th onwards. This will not only strengthen those areas, but the entire body. Exercise seems important too. You need good muscle tone. Heat-oriented therapies – hot tubs, saunas or steam rooms – are good. Above all, maintain good emotional health. Keep the moods positive and constructive. Avoid depression like the plague.

April

Best Days Overall: 7, 8, 16, 17, 25, 26
Most Stressful Days Overall: 1, 14, 15, 21, 22, 27, 28
Best Days for Love: 4, 5, 7, 8, 14, 15, 16, 17, 21, 22, 25, 27
Best Days for Money: 2, 3, 6, 9, 10, 11, 12, 13, 15, 21, 22, 24, 29, 30
Best Days for Career: 1, 7, 8, 16, 17, 27, 28

Continue to give attention to your health this month. Do your best to maintain high energy levels. Enhance the health in the ways we discussed last month – head, face and scalp massages are good, as is physical exercise and heat-oriented therapies. If you feel under the weather, plain old sunshine will help. Health and energy will improve dramatically after the 20th. It's like magic.

Mars in your sign all month shows family devotion and interest. Capricorns are rarely rash, but these days you are more so than usual. Impatience can be a problem. You want things done in a hurry (preferably yesterday), and this sense of rush can lead to accidents or injury. Be mindful on the physical plane. Watch the temper.

Your 4th house of home and family remains very strong until the 20th, so continue to pay more attention here. Your career planet, Venus, will spend most of the month (until the 24th) in your 5th house. This shows a devotion to the children or children figures in your life, and that a creative approach is needed in the career. The ideas will come to you.

With the night side of your chart still dominant this month, pursue the career by the methods of night rather than by the methods of day. Visualize, meditate, put yourself emotionally where you want to be. Overt actions will happen naturally and at the right time – nothing can stop your image from manifesting except your own inner denials.

This is a prosperous month. The Sun travels with your financial planet from the 17th to the 19th. This brings financial increase and opportunity to you and to the spouse, partner or current love. There is good financial cooperation between you.

Love is not a big issue this month. Basically this is a good thing as it tends to the status quo. It shows a satisfaction with what is. However, if love problems arise it will probably be due to a lack of attention, a lack of focus. In general, love will go better from the 16th to the 29th as the Moon waxes. It gives more energy and enthusiasm for social matters. Your social grace is stronger. The 20th, with the Moon at her perigee (her closest distance to Earth), should also be a good social day.

May

Best Days Overall: 4, 5, 14, 15, 22, 23, 31
Most Stressful Days Overall: 11, 12, 13, 18, 19, 24, 25
Best Days for Love: 4, 5, 7, 8, 14, 15, 17, 18, 19, 24, 26
Best Days for Money: 3, 7, 8, 9, 10, 13, 18, 19, 22, 26, 27, 31
Best Days for Career: 7, 8, 17, 24, 25, 26

On April 20 you entered one of your yearly personal pleasure peaks. Having fun and enjoying life is not laziness (if one doesn't overdo it – and you're not likely to do so). On the contrary, it will lead to more productivity later on in the month. The leisure – the happy-go-lucky attitude – will recharge the batteries so that work will go smoother later on. This is a very good time to go on holiday, if it is possible – if you have the free will. If not, make your month a mini-vacation right where you are. Fun and happiness will actually enhance your health this month – especially after the 13th.

On the 16th your financial planet, Uranus, makes a major move into your 5th house, so, leisure, fun, personal creativity (a form of fun) will be profitable too. A great financial idea or insight can happen at the leisure park, football field or theatre. Perhaps you make an important financial connection here. For the next few months you're going to enjoy your wealth more – and this is as it should be.

The planetary power has begun to shift to the Western, social sector of your chart, although there are still plenty of planets in the Eastern sector of self. The social sector is far from dominant, but it is stronger than it's been all year. So begin to cultivate more of the social skills. Lighten up a bit. Project love and warmth to others. Your challenge now is to balance your interests with those of others. It's not going to be all your own way the way it was at the beginning of the year. Sometimes you will have to yield to others, sometimes you'll go with your personal interest. And when you do go with your personal interest you do it with more grace now, with the least amount of offense to others.

On the 21st, as the Sun enters your 6th house of health and work, you've got the fun out of your system and are in the mood for work. You work now because you want to, not because you have to. So it is good to achieve work-oriented goals now.

Health is good this month. Mars leaving your sign on the 16th further improves it. Until the 13th enhance the health through scalp, head and face massage. Good muscle tone is still important, so keep up the exercise. On the 13th, as your health planet Mercury moves into Taurus, give more attention to the neck and throat. Don't allow tension to build up in the neck muscles. Release it through regular massage.

June

Best Days Overall: 1, 2, 10, 11, 18, 19, 28, 29
Most Stressful Days Overall: 8, 9, 14, 15, 20, 21, 22
Best Days for Love: 3, 4, 6, 7, 12, 13, 14, 15, 16, 23, 24
Best Days for Money: 1, 3, 4, 5, 6, 7, 10, 14, 15, 18, 23, 24, 28, 30
Best Days for Career: 6, 7, 16, 20, 21, 22, 23, 24

Self-will and self-assertion have been strong all year, but now with Saturn retrograde (since April 18) and with many planets in the Western (social) sector of your chart, these qualities are toned down. A good thing. You're entering a yearly love and social peak on the 22nd and you want to cultivate your social skills more.

The power in your 6th house since May 21 is excellent for job seekers. It is also good for those who employ others. Children and children figures in your life are having a strong financial month. Your emphasis on health this period (until the 22nd) will stand you in good stead for after that date when your health becomes more delicate. Until the 12th enhance the health through arm and shoulder massage (as we mention in the yearly report). After the 12th pay more attention to the diet – the stomach seems more sensitive. After the 12th good social health – a healthy marriage and love life – is part of your sense of health. Do your best to keep the social harmony.

Those of you already in a relationship will see the spouse, partner or current love prosper this month, especially after the 22nd. For singles there is an attraction to money people, to good earners. Wealth is a romantic turn-on. There is also an allurement to power people – people of high status and position. You are meeting these kinds of people this month. For singles there are three important relationships. In general, love will go better from the 13th to the 23rd, as the Moon, your love planet, waxes. The 14th is especially good in that the love planet is at her closest to the Earth (her perigee).

Finances are good this month. Your financial planet is still in your 5th house so be creative in your finances. The financial life should not only be abundant, but a 'thing of beauty' – a work of art. Take an artistic kind of approach to it. Those of you working in the creative arts find your work more marketable these days. Your financial planet makes beautiful aspects to Saturn all month – another indicator of prosperity. You're earning in agreeable and comfortable ways. Mars's position in your money house all month indicates more aggressiveness in finance, but it also shows good family support. Often with this position one earns money from home – a home office or home-based business.

July

Best Days Overall: 7, 8, 16, 17, 25, 26
Most Stressful Days Overall: 5, 6, 12, 13, 18, 19
Best Days for Love: 3, 4, 5, 6, 12, 13, 16, 21, 22, 25, 26
Best Days for Money: 1, 7, 12, 13, 16, 20, 21, 25, 27, 28, 29
Best Days for Career: 5, 6, 16, 18, 19, 25, 26

Your yearly love and social peak is in full swing this month. You are meeting all kinds of new people. So, it is understandable that these new (and some existing) relationships get tested. The Solar Eclipse of the 13th will perform this function.

This eclipse occurs in your 7th house of love and has a strong impact on you, so reduce your schedule over that period. Good relationships – relationships that are inherently sound – will survive the eclipse and get even better. But generally it is not pleasant when dirty laundry comes up for an airing. This eclipse is not only testing love relationships, but friendships as well. Pluto, your planet of friends, is affected here. The testing of relationships can happen in many ways. In some cases it is due to the dynamics of the relationship itself. In other cases it is because of personal dramas in the lives of the beloved or of friends. This eclipse also impacts on the finances of the spouse, partner or current love. More course corrections are necessary here. We saw this with the Solar Eclipse of February 15 too. The finances of a parent or parent figure also need a course correction. Computers and high-tech gadgetry are temperamental and often need repair or replacement. Since the eclipsed planet, the Sun, rules your 8th house there can be near-death experiences or other psychological encounters with death. (Another reason to take it easy this period.) Life in the body is not guaranteed. It can end at any time. The cosmos reminds you (in its own inimitable way) to get serious about life and do what you came here to do.

The Lunar Eclipse of the 27th impacts on your personal finances; it occurs in your money house. Events happen that show your financial thinking and strategies to be amiss or unrealistic. Changes are necessary and often these changes are dramatic ones. This eclipse also tests love. The Moon, the eclipsed planet, is your love planet. So, the spouse, partner or current love should also take it easier during this period. He or she could also have encounters with the scythe carrier. Since Mars is affected too, there are dramas at home, and perhaps unexpected repairs are needed to the home. Family members are more temperamental this period, and more patience with them is needed.

August

Best Days Overall: 4, 5, 12, 13, 21, 22, 31
Most Stressful Days Overall: 1, 2, 3, 8, 9, 14, 15, 29, 30
Best Days for Love: 2, 3, 5, 8, 9, 10, 11, 14, 15, 20, 24, 25, 31
Best Days for Money: 4, 8, 9, 12, 16, 17, 21, 24, 25, 26, 27, 31
Best Days for Career: 5, 14, 15, 24, 25

Just when you thought all the excitement was over with, another Solar Eclipse (the third this year) hits on the 11th. Because it occurs in your 8th house of regeneration (and of course impacts on the Sun, the ruler of that house) death, and encounters with death, are the main themes. You are (most likely) not going to die physically, but you will most probably have psychological encounters with death. Apparently, the cosmos, in its wisdom, deems it necessary to remind you about this subject again. Life on Earth is short. It can end at any time. Get down to the business that you were born to do. Get on with your real mission in life. Don't keep putting it off. Now is the time. Death (or encounters with it) has a magical way of cutting through all the frivolities that occupy us. It gets one focused on life's essence. This is the object here. In addition, once again a change is needed in the finances of the spouse, partner or current love. More dramatic financial change is happening. (These changes seem good since he or she is in a yearly financial peak this month.)

Health is good this month, and will get even better after the 22nd. You can enhance it even further by giving more attention to the heart. Massage the reflex points to the heart. Chest massage and heat-oriented therapies are good. Detox regimes also seem unusually effective.

Your financial planet, Uranus, goes retrograde on the 7th for many months. Earnings are good but perhaps slower than usual. There are more delays involved. This is a good time to review the financial life and gain mental clarity here. You can't stop your financial life for many months, but if you must make important investments or financial decisions, study the matter carefully. Things are not what they seem. Resolve all doubts first (as best you can).

Venus has her solstice from the 5th to the 9th. She pauses in the heavens (in her latitudinal motion) and then changes direction. Children or children figures could be doing the same. A pause and a change of direction is happening in your career too.

The day side of your Horoscope is very strong now – approaching its noon position (this will happen next month). So it's good to focus on the career and let home and family issues go for a while.

September

Best Days Overall: 1, 9, 17, 18, 19, 27, 28
Most Stressful Days Overall: 4, 5, 11, 12, 25, 26
Best Days for Love: 1, 2, 3, 4, 5, 9, 13, 18, 19, 22, 23, 29
Best Days for Money: 1, 4, 5, 8, 9, 13, 14, 17, 20, 21, 22, 23, 24, 27
Best Days for Career: 2, 3, 11, 12, 13, 22, 23

Your financial planet is still retrograde this month but prosperity is still happening; there are delays and glitches but it is happening. Keep in mind our discussion of this from last month. Mars will move back into your money house on the 11th, signalling the importance of family support and family connections in finance. You can be spending more on the home and family but also earning through these avenues.

The Sun, the ruler of your 8th house of regeneration, will be in your 9th house until the 22nd. Thus a healthy detox is happening in your religious and philosophical life, a purging of beliefs and superstitions that never belonged there. It would be beneficial to cooperate with this process. False beliefs – a false perspective on life – impacts on every area of life and creates all kinds of problems.

The main headline this month is the career. Venus is in your 10th house until the 9th. She is in her own sign and house and thus is more powerful on your behalf. On the 22nd both Mercury and the Sun enter your 10th house and you begin a yearly career peak. The month ahead looks successful.

Mercury in your 10th house indicates a good work ethic. It shows the need to work harder on career goals. The Sun in your 10th house gives star quality to the career. It also indicates that bosses, parents or parent figures are having surgery or near-death kinds of experiences. You face near-death experiences in the career. But, as our regular readers know, after death comes resurrection, and conditions that are better than before. So there are career 'scares' this month, followed by new highs.

Health needs more attention being paid to it after the 22nd, and the good news is that you're on the case. Your health planet is at the top of the chart and health is high on your priorities. Enhance your health in the ways mentioned in the yearly report, but we can add a few things this month. Until the 6th continue with chest massage and focus on the heart. From the 6th to the 22nd, the small intestine is important. Massage the reflex to it regularly. Earth-based therapies are powerful during that time – mud baths, mud packs, clay treatments and the like. And after the 22nd give more attention to the hips and kidneys.

October

Best Days Overall: 6, 7, 15, 16, 25, 26
Most Stressful Days Overall: 2, 3, 8, 9, 22, 23, 29, 30
Best Days for Love: 1, 2, 3, 8, 9, 10, 11, 18, 19, 20, 21, 29, 30
Best Days for Money: 2, 3, 6, 10, 11, 15, 17, 18, 19, 20, 21, 24, 25, 29, 30
Best Days for Career: 2, 3, 8, 9, 10, 11, 20, 21, 29, 30

The social life – especially the area of friendships – has been strong all year, with Jupiter being in your 11th house since late 2017. But now this area becomes even stronger – more pronounced – and happier. Venus will spend the month in your 11th house. On the 10th Mercury moves in, and on the 23rd the Sun enters this house too. This is a lot of power. Add to this Saturn and Pluto parallel* to each other (this was so last month too) and we get more indication of social happiness. The love life is quiet, but friendships are very satisfying. You seem very popular with groups and organizations.

The 11th house is where 'fondest hopes and wishes' come true. So you're going to experience much of this in the month ahead. (You've probably experienced this in the past year too.) But, human nature being what it is, as soon as these are fulfilled a new set of 'fondest hopes and wishes' will be born. It goes on and on and on.

You're still in a yearly career peak until the 23rd, so good career progress is being made. By the 23rd, however, your short-term career goals have been achieved, and your focus shifts to friendships – the fruit of career success.

Finances are a bit tricky this month. On the one hand Uranus, your financial planet, is still retrograde and in the cautious sign of Taurus. This suggests going slow and steady in finance. Yet, Mars, the planet of action and risk taking, spends the month in your money house. Mars is not very patient. He wants everything now. So you will have to balance these two urges. Action – and perhaps some risk taking – might be called for, but only after you've done your due diligence

---

They occupy the same degree of latitude. This shows that they are working together.

checks and resolved your doubts. If you're going to take risks, do so with less than you intended – perhaps half or a quarter of the original sum. Hedge your risks.

Health still needs some attention until the 23rd, but will improve dramatically afterwards. You will feel the difference. There was nothing actually wrong with you in the first place. It was just a lack of energy caused by the planetary movements.

November

Best Days Overall: 2, 3, 11, 12, 21, 22, 29, 30
Most Stressful Days Overall: 4, 5, 19, 20, 25, 26
Best Days for Love: 4, 5, 6, 7, 8, 14, 15, 16, 17, 23, 24, 25, 26, 27
Best Days for Money: 2, 8, 10, 14, 15, 19, 20, 27, 28
Best Days for Career: 4, 5, 14, 15, 23, 24

Spiritual interests were strong in 2016 and 2017. This year less so. But now, as Jupiter moves into your spiritual 12th house on the 8th, the spiritual interests are renewed, perhaps even amplified. On the 22nd, the Sun will also enter the spiritual 12th house, making this area even stronger. Spiritual breakthroughs – rapturous experiences when they happen – are likely this month (and in the next twelve months). Your ESP faculties will be enhanced and your dream life will become more active. It is a month for internal growth. And, by the spiritual law, internal growth translates to external growth. You will see this next month. A parent or parent figure is also having a more spiritual month, from the 16th onwards.

Uranus, your financial planet, is still retrograde, suggesting caution in your financial life. This month on the 6th he moves back into Aries again, favouring earning money from the home and from home offices or home-based businesses once more. Family and family connections play a huge role in finances again. (Mars, your family planet, is in the money house until the 16th, reinforcing this.) With Uranus in Aries and Mars in the 2nd house, the tendency is to throw caution to the winds – to go for the 'quick buck'. Be careful here. Uranus is still retrograde.

Venus started to travel backwards on October 5 and continues to do so until the 16th, complicating career issues. Avoid making major career decisions until after the 16th. The object now is to gain mental clarity on this. Venus will spend the month in your 10th house of career, which is good for the career. But after the 16th is much better than before.

Health and energy are greatly improved over last month but could use more monitoring from the 6th onwards. As always, do your best to keep your energy levels high – this is the first defence against disease. With Mercury, your health planet, in your spiritual 12th house all month you respond well to spiritual-type therapies – meditation, reiki, the laying on of hands, the invocation of the Higher Power and the manipulation of subtle energies. If you feel under the weather, a visit to a spiritual healer could be just the ticket. It would be beneficial too to give more attention to the liver and thighs. Massage the thighs regularly, and perhaps give the liver a herbal detox. Heat-oriented therapies are good this month – saunas, steam rooms or hot tubs.

December

Best Days Overall: 9, 10, 18, 19, 27, 28
Most Stressful Days Overall: 2, 3, 16, 17, 23, 24, 29, 30
Best Days for Love: 2, 3, 6, 7, 14, 15, 17, 23, 24, 27
Best Days for Money: 6, 7, 11, 12, 16, 17, 26
Best Days for Career: 2, 3, 14, 15, 23, 24, 29, 30

Capricorns are not prone to excess. They tend to be slim and trim (although the personal Horoscope cast for your exact date, time and place of birth could modify this). Saturn and Pluto in your sign promote slimness too. But in the rare cases of those who need it, the Sun's entry into your sign on the 21st favours weight-loss and detox regimes.

The planetary power is now overwhelmingly in the independent Eastern sector of your chart. You are in (and for January too) the most independent part of your year. Now at least 80 per cent (and sometimes 90 per cent) of the planets are in the East so you're having things your way now. Other people should always be respected, but you're not in need of their approval. This is not a time for 'people pleasing' but about pleasing yourself. You have the power now to create pleasant and happy conditions for yourself. You should take the opportunity.

Love is not a big issue this month (though friendship and group activities are still strong). Love is more or less stable. Your social magnetism and enthusiasm will be strongest from the 7th to the 22nd as the Moon, your love planet, waxes. The 24th is an especially good love day (in spite of the waning Moon) as the Moon will be at her perigee (her closest distance to earth) – *and* she will be in your 7th house of love.

You're still in a very strong spiritual period until the 21st, so you should review our discussion of this last month. A parent or parent figure has a spiritual breakthrough between the 5th and the 7th. Their consciousness of this depends on their status on the spiritual path. Often these things happen without conscious awareness – but they do still happen.

Health is much improved over last month. Spiritual therapies are powerful from the 13th onwards – as we discussed last month. This is a good period to delve deeper into the spiritual dimensions of health. Until the 13th detox regimes are good. More attention should be given to the colon, bladder and sexual organs. Safe sex and sexual moderation are important.

Family members – and especially a parent or parent figure – should be more mindful on the physical plane from the 5th to the 7th. They should keep focused on what they're doing.

Aquarius

~~~

THE WATER-BEARER

Birthdays from
20th January to
18th February

Personality Profile

AQUARIUS AT A GLANCE

Element – Air

Ruling Planet – Uranus
  Career Planet – Pluto
  Love Planet – Sun
  Money Planet – Neptune
  Planet of Health and Work – Moon
  Planet of Home and Family Life – Venus
  Planet of Spirituality – Saturn

Colours – electric blue, grey, ultramarine blue

Colours that promote love, romance and social harmony – gold, orange

Colour that promotes earning power – aqua

Gems – black pearl, obsidian, opal, sapphire

Metal – lead

Scents – azalea, gardenia

Quality – fixed (= stability)

Qualities most needed for balance – warmth, feeling and emotion

Strongest virtues – great intellectual power, the ability to communicate and to form and understand abstract concepts, love for the new and avant-garde

Deepest needs – to know and to bring in the new

Characteristics to avoid – coldness, rebelliousness for its own sake, fixed ideas

Signs of greatest overall compatibility – Gemini, Libra

Signs of greatest overall incompatibility – Taurus, Leo, Scorpio

Sign most helpful to career – Scorpio

Sign most helpful for emotional support – Taurus

Sign most helpful financially – Pisces

Sign best for marriage and/or partnerships – Leo

Sign most helpful for creative projects – Gemini

Best Sign to have fun with – Gemini

Signs most helpful in spiritual matters – Libra, Capricorn

Best day of the week – Saturday

Understanding an Aquarius

In the Aquarius-born, intellectual faculties are perhaps the most highly developed of any sign in the zodiac. Aquarians are clear, scientific thinkers. They have the ability to think abstractly and to formulate laws, theories and clear concepts from masses of observed facts. Geminis might be very good at gathering information, but Aquarians take this a step further, excelling at interpreting the information gathered.

Practical people – men and women of the world – mistakenly consider abstract thinking as impractical. It is true that the realm of abstract thought takes us out of the physical world, but the discoveries made in this realm generally end up having tremendous practical consequences. All real scientific inventions and breakthroughs come from this abstract realm.

Aquarians, more so than most, are ideally suited to explore these abstract dimensions. Those who have explored these regions know that there is little feeling or emotion there. In fact, emotions are a hindrance to functioning in these dimensions; thus Aquarians seem – at times – cold and emotionless to others. It is not that Aquarians haven't got feelings and deep emotions, it is just that too much feeling clouds their ability to think and invent. The concept of 'too much feeling' cannot be tolerated or even understood by some of the other signs. Nevertheless, this Aquarian objectivity is ideal for science, communication and friendship.

Aquarians are very friendly people, but they do not make a big show about it. They do the right thing by their friends, even if sometimes they do it without passion or excitement.

Aquarians have a deep passion for clear thinking. Second in importance, but related, is their passion for breaking with the establishment and traditional authority. Aquarians delight in this, because for them rebellion is like a great game or challenge. Very often they will rebel strictly for the fun of rebelling, regardless of whether the authority they defy is right or wrong. Right or wrong has little to do with the rebellious actions of an Aquarian, because to a true Aquarian authority and power must be challenged as a matter of principle.

Where Capricorn or Taurus will err on the side of tradition and the status quo, an Aquarian will err on the side of the new. Without this virtue it is doubtful whether any progress would be made in the world. The conservative-minded would obstruct progress. Originality and invention imply an ability to break barriers; every new discovery represents the toppling of an impediment to thought. Aquarians are very interested in breaking barriers and making walls tumble – scientifically, socially and politically. Other zodiac signs, such as Capricorn, also have scientific talents. But Aquarians are particularly excellent in the social sciences and humanities.

Finance

In financial matters Aquarians tend to be idealistic and humanitarian – to the point of self-sacrifice. They are usually generous contributors to social and political causes. When they contribute it differs from when a Capricorn or Taurus contributes. A Capricorn or Taurus may expect some favour or return for a gift; an Aquarian contributes selflessly.

Aquarians tend to be as cool and rational about money as they are about most things in life. Money is something they need and they set about acquiring it scientifically. No need for fuss; they get on with it in the most rational and scientific ways available.

Money to the Aquarian is especially nice for what it can do, not for the status it may bring (as is the case for other signs). Aquarians are neither big spenders nor penny-pinchers and use their finances in practical ways, for example to facilitate progress for themselves, their families, or even for strangers.

However, if Aquarians want to reach their fullest financial potential they will have to explore their intuitive nature. If they follow only their financial theories – or what they believe to be theoretically correct – they may suffer some losses and disappointments. Instead, Aquarians should call on their intuition, which knows without thinking. For Aquarians, intuition is the short-cut to financial success.

Career and Public Image

Aquarians like to be perceived not only as the breakers of barriers but also as the transformers of society and the world. They long to be seen in this light and to play this role. They also look up to and respect other people in this position and even expect their superiors to act this way.

Aquarians prefer jobs that have a bit of idealism attached to them – careers with a philosophical basis. Aquarians need to be creative at work, to have access to new techniques and methods. They like to keep busy and enjoy getting down to business straightaway, without wasting any time. They are often the quickest workers and usually have suggestions for improvements that will benefit their employers. Aquarians are also very helpful with their co-workers and welcome responsibility, preferring this to having to take orders from others.

If Aquarians want to reach their highest career goals they have to develop more emotional sensitivity, depth of feeling and passion. They need to learn to narrow their focus on the essentials and concentrate more on the job in hand. Aquarians need 'a fire in the belly' – a consuming passion and desire – in order to rise to the very top. Once this passion exists they will succeed easily in whatever they attempt.

Love and Relationships

Aquarians are good at friendships, but a bit weak when it comes to love. Of course they fall in love, but their lovers always get the impression that they are more best friends than paramours.

Like Capricorns, they are cool customers. They are not prone to displays of passion or to outward demonstrations of their affections. In fact, they feel uncomfortable when their other half hugs and touches them too much. This does not mean that they do not love their partners. They do, only they show it in other ways. Curiously enough, in relationships they tend to attract the very things that they feel uncomfortable with. They seem to attract hot, passionate, romantic, demonstrative people. Perhaps they know instinctively that these people have qualities they lack and so seek them out. In any event, these relationships do seem to work, Aquarian coolness calming the more passionate partner while the fires of passion warm the cold-blooded Aquarius.

The qualities Aquarians need to develop in their love life are warmth, generosity, passion and fun. Aquarians love relationships of the mind. Here they excel. If the intellectual factor is missing in a relationship an Aquarian will soon become bored or feel unfulfilled.

Home and Domestic Life

In family and domestic matters Aquarians can have a tendency to be too non-conformist, changeable and unstable. They are as willing to break the barriers of family constraints as they are those of other areas of life.

Even so, Aquarians are very sociable people. They like to have a nice home where they can entertain family and friends. Their house is usually decorated in a modern style and full of state-of-the-art appliances and gadgets – an environment Aquarians find absolutely necessary.

If their home life is to be healthy and fulfilling Aquarians need to inject it with a quality of stability – yes, even some conservatism. They need at least one area of life to be enduring and steady; this area is usually their home and family life.

Venus, the generic planet of love, rules the Aquarian's 4th solar house of home and family, which means that when it comes to the family and child-rearing, theories, cool thinking and intellect are not always enough. Aquarians need to bring love into the equation in order to have a great domestic life.

Horoscope for 2018

Major Trends

The year ahead is going to be very successful, but also fraught with much change and drama. Perhaps it is the success that is causing all the drama – it changes the family and social dynamic – or perhaps it's the other way around: the changes in the social and family dynamic set you free for more success. Both scenarios could apply here.

Jupiter spends most of the year in your 10th house of career. This is a classic signal of career success and expansion. A signal for promotion, for elevation in your company or professional status. Jupiter remains in your 10th house until November 8.

The change and drama come from the eclipses this year. Four out of five of these impact on the love life. Two eclipses affect you personally – your image and personal goals. They occur in your 1st house. We will discuss this further later on.

Your 12th house of spirituality has been strong for many years, with Pluto residing there since 2008. This year Saturn joins the party and will be here for the next two years. So the year ahead is especially spiritual – more so than in the last few years. More on this later.

The year ahead also looks very prosperous. Jupiter will be making beautiful aspects to Neptune, your financial planet, almost all year. Career success is translating to increased earnings. More details later. Moreover, Neptune has been in your money house – his own sign and house – since 2012. This makes him stronger on your behalf. Another indicator of increased earnings.

Uranus, the ruler of your Horoscope, is making a major move this year, from your 3rd house to your 4th. This only happens every seven years or so. The transit will not be complete this year – it is really only a flirtation with your 4th house from May 16 to November 6. But next year, from March onwards, he will enter your 4th house for the long term. So, long-term changes and upheavals are brewing in the family and the home. More on this later.

Your most important interests this year will be finance; communication and intellectual interests (until May 16 and from November 6 onwards); home and family (from May 16 to November 6); career (until November 8); friends, groups and group activities (from November 8 onwards); and spirituality.

Your paths of greatest fulfilment this year will be career (until November 8); friends, groups and group activities (from November 8 onwards); love and romance (until November 17); and health and work (from November 17 onwards).

Health

(Please note that this is an astrological perspective on health and not a medical one. In days of yore there was no difference, both of these perspectives were identical. But now there could be quite a difference. For a medical perspective, please consult your doctor or health practitioner.)

Health should be good this year. You begin your year with only one long-term planet in stressful aspect with you – Jupiter. From May 16 to November 6 Uranus will also be in stressful alignment, but this will mostly impact those of you born very early in the sign of Aquarius – January 19 to January 23. Those of you born later in the sign will hardly feel this – though you will certainly feel it in the coming years as Uranus starts to establish himself in Taurus. From November 8 onwards there will be no long-term planets in stressful alignment with you.

Two Lunar Eclipses in the coming year indicate changes in the health regime. Since this regularly happens twice a year (the Moon being your health planet) these seem more like 'course corrections' rather than anything serious.

A Solar Eclipse in your 6th house of health could produce more change in the health regime and perhaps a health scare. But your health is basically good as we have said, and it is not likely to be more than that.

Good though your health is, it can be made even better. Let there be more attention given to the following – the vulnerable areas of your chart:

- The ankles and calves. These are always important for Aquarius, since your sign rules these areas. Regular ankle and calf massage should be a part of your regular health regime. It won't hurt to massage along the shin bone as well. Feel for any tender spots and massage them away. Give the ankles more support when you exercise.
- The stomach is another important area (the reflexes points are shown in the chart above). Diet is always an important issue for you. What you should eat should be checked by a professional as your dietary needs can change from year to year and even month to

Important foot reflexology points for the year ahead

Try to massage all of the foot on a regular basis – the top of the foot as well as the bottom – but pay extra attention to the points highlighted on the chart. When you massage, be aware of 'sore spots' as these need special attention. It's also a very good idea to massage the ankles.

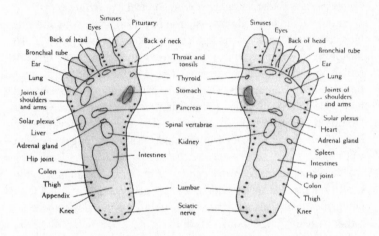

month. So frequent checks are necessary. But just as important as what you eat is *how* you eat. We have discussed this many times over the years. The act of eating needs to be elevated from mere animal appetite to an act of worship. The energy vibrations of the act need elevation. Thus, meals should be taken in a calm and peaceful way (not so easy in our frenetic world, but do your best). If you can have nice soothing music playing as you eat, all the better. Chew your food well. Bless the food and express gratitude for it. Do your best to 'ritualize' the act of eating. This will not only raise the energy vibrations of the food you eat but it will raise the vibrations of the body and digestive system. The ancient mystics and masters understood this very well and almost every religion has rituals for eating.

- The breasts. This applies more to women than men (and especially to Aquarian women). Regular check-ups are a good idea. It would also be beneficial to massage the top part of the foot, as the reflex points to the breasts are located here.

Your health planet, the Moon, is the fastest of the fast-moving planets. Thus there are many short-term health trends that depend on where the Moon is and the aspects she receives. Because the Moon moves so quickly a symptom or discomfort can appear briefly and disappear quickly as well. The Moon was just not in the right place when the discomfort happened – nothing more than that. These short-term trends are best discussed in the monthly reports.

Home and Family

Home and family has not been a big issue for you for many years, but this is now about to change. Uranus, the ruler of your Horoscope, and a very powerful planet, is starting to move into your 4th house. This year it is a short visit (by the standards of Uranus) – only about six months. But next year, from March 7 onwards, he will move into your 4th house for the long term. Big and sudden changes are on the cards in the home and the family circle.

For a start, you are going to be paying much more attention here. Career is important this year and you can't ignore it. But family is becoming equally important and by next year will be even more important than career.

You seem more personally involved here. You're more devoted to the family and especially to a parent or parent figure. You're being very innovative and creative in the home. You will be upgrading the home almost routinely. Year to year – and perhaps even month to month – the physical home will be changing. There can be multiple moves or renovations in the coming years. This year, though, most likely only one.

Uranus in the 4th house shows that you are working to create a team spirit in the family. You're working to make it more egalitarian. Family hierarchy is frowned upon. There are no bosses, only teammates and (perhaps) a coach. Everyone is equal to everyone else. Everyone does what is most comfortable for them.

The home will be modernized this year (and even more so in coming years). You will be installing all the latest technical gadgetry. Some of these gadgets are not yet even invented – but they will be over the coming years.

Though you're successful careerwise this year, you are going to identify more as a 'family person' – more so than with your 'professional identity'.

Moves and renovations can happen from May 16 to November 6. But if you're interested in beautifying the home – repainting it or rearranging furniture – April 1 to May 20 seems best. This is also a good time to buy objects of beauty for the home.

A parent or parent figure in your life becomes more restless from May 16 to November 6. There is a need for more personal freedom, a need to lighten up on responsibilities. He or she seems more restless and is probably living in different places for long periods of time. The marriage of this parent or parent figure is being tested (and this will get stronger in coming years). The good news is that the spouse is trying very hard to keep things together. Will it be enough? An open question.

A sibling or sibling figure has family dramas too, but these seem more short term. A move isn't seen here. Children and children figures are also having a stable family year. If they are of appropriate age, there is romance in store from November 8 onwards. For younger children this shows a more active social life, new friends coming into the picture. Grandchildren (if you have them) are better off not moving.

Finance and Career

As we mentioned, you can look forward to a prosperous and successful year. This is a strong finance and career year. In many cases, depending on your age, it is the best of your life. But even for older Aquarians, the year should be among the best.

Jupiter, as we have said, is in your 10th house of career until November 8. This shows promotions and pay rises. You have the financial favour of bosses, parents, parent figures and authority figures. They are supportive of your financial goals. Your good career reputation – which should be guarded zealously – brings higher earnings as well.

Friends and social connections are also unusually supportive, both financially and in the career. You know people in high places and they are giving you a boost. Friends in general are more successful this year.

Your natural networking and high-tech skills are boosting both the career and the finances. Your natural gifts with groups and organizations, likewise. These gifts are getting more recognition this year.

Neptune, as your financial planet, signals good financial intuition – the short cut to wealth. It indicates an affinity for industries involving water – water utilities, shipping, ship-building, the fishing industry, water purifiers and bottlers, and for other 'Neptune' industries – oil, natural gas, pharmaceuticals involved with anaesthesia, mood control or pain relievers. These are interesting as investments, businesses or jobs. People in these industries can be important in your financial life as well – and thus, indirectly, you profit from these industries.

You have been idealistic in your finances for many years now, but this tendency has become stronger of late. You're unusually charitable. When you hear a sob story the wallet or purse opens up. In general you like giving to altruistic or spiritual-type causes. You spend more on spiritual pursuits, but you can also earn from them.

Financial information and guidance will come to you in dreams and visions, through psychics, astrologers, tarot readers and spiritual channels. These would be specific kinds of guidance. This has been so for some years now, but even more so now.

The whole year is going to be good financially, but February 18 to March 20, June 21 to July 23 and October 23 to November 21 will be the most prosperous.

The most stressful financial periods will tend to be from May 21 to June 20, August 23 to September 22 and November 22 to December 21. All this means is that you'll have to work harder for your goals than usual.

Love and Social Life

Your 7th house is not a house of power this year, so love and romance don't seem like a big deal. It does look happy though, with the Moon's North Node occupying this house until November 17. This happiness tends to the status quo: you're happy with things as they are. Those who are married seem happy in their marriages, while singles seem happy being single.

However, as we have mentioned, we do see shakeups and disturbances here – some testing of the current relationship. The spouse,
partner or current love also feels this testing. Two eclipses happen in
your 7th house and two happen in your own sign. These are strong
eclipses. Aside from that, three Solar Eclipses of your love planet, the
Sun, are also signalling drama and turmoil. (Your love life generally
gets tested twice a year; this year it gets shaken up four times.)

Eclipses tend to bring out the hidden, repressed grievances in a relationship. Every relationship has them. No human, mortal, relationship
is perfect. So the dirty laundry gets a good cleansing. Good relationships – the ones that are basically sound – generally survive this and
get even better. The dust settles and corrections are made. Later you
and the beloved can look back and laugh at the incident. But flawed
relationships can easily dissolve under this pounding. Sometimes the
eclipse will not bring up dirty laundry, but will cause life-changing
dramas (either personal ones or in the life of the current love). These
can test the relationship or force adjustments. The relationship needs
to change because of the events. The testing of love is generally not
pleasant, but it is beneficial. This is how we know that love is real. We
always find out in the tough times.

We will cover the eclipses in more depth in the monthly reports.

Since your love planet, the Sun, is a fast-moving planet, in any given
year he moves through every house and sign in your Horoscope. Thus
romantic opportunities can happen in a variety of ways and with a
variety of people, depending on where the Sun is and the aspects he
receives. These short-term trends are best dealt with in the monthly
reports.

Aquarians tend to be better at friendships than at committed love.
They like their freedom and independence. And this area becomes very
happy – very expansive – from November 8 onwards. Jupiter moves
into your 11th house of friends – his own sign and house, the place
where he's most powerful – and expands this whole area. This will
bring new and important friends into the picture. Your career goals are
more or less attained by November 8, and you start to reap the rewards
of career success – a higher and better social circle.

Self-Improvement

Saturn, your spiritual planet, is in his own sign and house for the next two years. This means he will be operating in a more powerful way than usual.

This is emphasizing tendencies that have been going on for some years. Spirituality is important to you. But the message of the Horoscope is, if you want to progress, if you want to succeed here, you need to be very disciplined and orderly about it. You need a daily, disciplined kind of regime. Your spiritual practice must become part of your lifestyle.

You tend to be very experimental about things, you like innovation and change. But in the spiritual life, Saturn is saying, the traditional methods are best. Rather than seek out the new and the trendy, go deeper into the traditional ways. Understand them in a deeper way.

Pluto, your career planet, has been in your spiritual 12th house for many years now and will be there for many more to come. This has various effects. You have been seeking a more spiritual type of career. Something meaningful. Just making money and being successful, good though that is, isn't enough for you. You need something that is 'approved' by Spirit, something that has the support of your Soul. In many cases this leads to a career in ministry or charity or with a not-for-profit organization. In other cases, one will pursue an outer worldly career and do philanthropic work on the side. And in some cases, for those more advanced along the path, it means that the spiritual practice itself is the career. That is the mission these days.

Basically, the Horoscope is saying that you have to approach the spiritual life with the same dedication and discipline (perhaps more) that you would devote to your worldly career. You have been chosen to do something very special in the world. Something no one else can do. Your spiritual practice will lead you there and you'll start to follow it.

Neptune in your money house is also more powerful than usual. Again, he is in his own sign and house and he is expressing his power easily. Thus you're going deeper into the spiritual dimensions of wealth. You've been involved with this for many years, and the trend continues. It is important to keep one thing in mind. When it comes to the spiritual supply, how much you have, how your business is going, economic conditions, etc. are never, never the issue. The issue is how much Spirit has (it has it all) and how much you can receive.

You are learning that wealth is really an interior activity, always happening in the here and now – right where you are. Wealth is not at the office or the shop (that's only the side-effect). It is an inflow from the mind of the Divine into your aura. An inflow of energy and substance into the aura that will eventually become the tangible things that we associate with wealth – money, possessions, etc. It creates the necessary conditions for manifestation. This is why there is often a time lag from the prayer or meditation to the finished, tangible result.

Month-by-month Forecasts

January

Best Days Overall: 8, 9, 17, 18, 19, 27, 28
Most Stressful Days Overall: 3, 4, 10, 11, 25, 26, 31
Best Days for Love: 3, 4, 5, 6, 15, 16, 27, 28, 31
Best Days for Money: 1, 2, 10, 11, 20, 21, 29, 30
Best Days for Career: 5, 6, 10, 11, 15, 16, 25, 26

In general you're in a very independent kind of year, and especially so this month. Very unusually, for half the month *all* the planets will be in the Eastern sector of the self. Only the Moon will visit the social Western sector for some of the month, so you're definitely having things your way these days. Your personal happiness is important to the cosmos. You have the power (and support) to create the conditions of your own happiness. Make yourself happy and the whole world will basically agree to it. This doesn't mean that you harm others or disrespect them; you just go your way if they don't agree.

You begin your year, as you do most years, on a spiritual note. Your 12th house of spirituality is easily the strongest in the Horoscope at the moment. So, this is a month for spiritual study, spiritual practice and getting closer to the Divine within. The inner life, your inner growth, is the main focus.

Your love planet, the Sun, will be in your 12th house until the 20th. Pluto, your career planet, has been here for many years. So, the message here is get right spiritually and love and career will fall into place.

You're in a strong career month too – this will be a very successful month in a successful year. Pluto receives wonderful aspects from the 8th to the 10th and on the 24th and 25th. This brings both success and opportunity to you.

A Lunar Eclipse on the 31st brings some excitement and change to you. Reduce your schedule around that period as the eclipse seems to affect you strongly. It occurs in your 7th house of love and will test a current relationship. It need not dissolve it – only test it – bring up repressed grievances. Sometimes there are dramas in the life of the beloved that stress the relationship. Good relationships survive these things, but they change. Corrections are made. The eclipsed planet, the Moon, is your health and work planet, so every Lunar Eclipse impacts on the health and the job situation and this one is no different. So, job changes are afoot. The conditions of work change. You will need to make important changes to your health regime. Often this kind of eclipse brings health scares, but your health looks good and it's probably no more than a scare. The spouse, partner or current love has changes in his or her spiritual life – changes of practice, teachings and perhaps teachers. There are important changes in his or her spiritual attitudes.

February

Best Days Overall: 4, 5, 14, 15, 23, 24
Most Stressful Days Overall: 6, 7, 21, 22, 27, 28
Best Days for Love: 4, 5, 14, 15, 16, 25, 26, 27, 28
Best Days for Money: 6, 7, 16, 17, 25, 26
Best Days for Career: 2, 3, 6, 7, 11, 12, 21, 22

Another eclipse – the Solar Eclipse of the 15th – tests the love life and a current relationship. As we mentioned last month, a basically sound relationship will easily survive. It is the flawed ones that are in danger. In the case of singles, two eclipses one after the other involving love often shows a desire to change the marital status. Often it signals a marriage. This eclipse occurs in your own sign. All of you will feel it, but those of you born later in the sign of Aquarius (February 14–18) will feel it strongest. It isn't only love relationships that get tested here. Jupiter, your planet of friends, is also impacted. So friendships in general are shaken up. The good ones will survive. The flawed ones are in danger. The 11th house also rules your high-tech equipment and gadgetry, so these things get tested too, and if there are any hidden flaws there you find out about them. A parent or parent figure can be having a financial crisis and needs to make course corrections in their financial thinking and strategy. Often people change banks, brokers, financial planners or accountants under these kinds of eclipses. Children and children figures in your life are affected here too. They should take things easy and avoid dangerous type situations. Some of these changes are normal – they reach puberty, have a sexual awakening, go off to school, etc. – but still they are disruptive.

Though the eclipse shakes things up, the month ahead is basically happy and prosperous. You're still in a period of great personal independence and are able to have things your way. You have life on your terms. You have been in the midst of one of your yearly personal pleasure periods since January 20. In spite of all the testings, love is good. You look great and the spouse, partner or current love is eager to please – he or she is very devoted to you, at your beck and call. Singles don't have to do anything to attract love – it finds them.

This is a great period for buying clothing or personal accessories. Your taste is spot on.

On the 18th, both the Sun and Mercury enter the money house and you begin a yearly financial peak. The financial intuition is always good, but especially so this period. The 20th to the 22nd and the 25th and 26th bring nice paydays (although the entire period will be prosperous).

March

Best Days Overall: 3, 4, 13, 14, 22, 23, 31
Most Stressful Days Overall: 6, 7, 20, 21, 26, 27
Best Days for Love: 6, 7, 8, 16, 17, 18, 19, 26, 27
Best Days for Money: 6, 7, 15, 16, 17, 24, 25
Best Days for Career: 1, 2, 6, 7, 10, 11, 12, 20, 21, 29, 30

The planetary power is now mostly on the night side of your chart, and has been since last month. You're a night person these days, engaged in the activities of the night: rest, inner orientation, getting into emotional harmony, handling the home and family. Your career is still important (and successful) but now is the time to gather the energy – to build up the force – for your next major career push, which will begin in the summer. You're not yet in the midnight hour of your year (this will happen next month) but are getting close. It is late evening.

Night is for dreaming, visualizing, getting in the right mood for what you want to achieve. Live in the feeling – in the mood – of your goal and just stay there. Your psychological state must eventually express outwardly by the spiritual law.

Prosperity is still very strong. You have the financial support of the spouse, partner or current love. Your social contacts are important. The 3rd to the 5th is a strong financial period.

For singles, love opportunities happen as you pursue your financial goals or with people involved in your finances. Wealth, material support and material gifts are romantic turn-ons. This is how you show love, this is how you feel loved. You look to the good provider. This changes after the 20th as your love planet moves into your 3rd house of communication. For singles this shows that love is found close to home in your neighbourhood and perhaps with neighbours. You're attracted to people who are rich in mind, not necessarily monetarily rich. You like people who are easy to talk to – who have the gift of the gab. Conversation is a form of foreplay these days. There are romantic opportunities in educational settings – at lectures, seminars, the library or book shop.

Health and energy are still good – they have been all year. However, you can enhance the health even further in the ways mentioned in the yearly report.

From the 20th onwards is a good time to take courses in subjects that interest you. A good time both for studying and teaching others. The mind is much sharper. Information is more easily retained. Students below college level should be successful this period.

April

Best Days Overall: 1, 9, 10, 11, 18, 19, 27, 28
Most Stressful Days Overall: 2, 3, 16, 17, 23, 24, 29
Best Days for Love: 4, 5, 7, 8, 14, 15, 16, 17, 23, 24, 25, 27
Best Days for Money: 2, 3, 12, 13, 21, 22, 29, 30
Best Days for Career: 2, 3, 7, 8, 16, 17, 25, 26, 29

Many positive career developments are happening these days, but behind the scenes. Not much you can do about it except to let events play out. The two planets involved in your career – Pluto and Jupiter – are retrograde. In the meantime focus on getting the home and family in right order. With so much power in your 4th house this month, it is good to build the foundation – the infrastructure – that will enable future career success to happen. You'll do more to foster your career by interior methods – meditation, visualization and prayer – than by external methods.

Your 3rd house of communication and intellectual interests is powerful all month. So, like last month, this is a good period for students. There is focus and success in their studies. Good to study, read and take courses in subjects that interest you. Good to catch up on the phone calls, letters, emails or texts that you owe people. Aquarians always have the gift of the gab and this month more so than ever. Overstimulation of the mind – overdoing a good thing – is probably the main danger now. The mind is set into motion easily, and if it is not controlled it will churn and churn and churn. This can cause insomnia and other nervous problems. Use the mind when necessary and turn it off when not in use.

Power in the 4th house (from the 20th onwards) is also good for psychological therapy. Those of you undergoing formal therapy will see much progress. But even those of you not in any kind of formal therapy will have psychological breakthroughs this month (and next month). The memory body is highly stimulated now. Old memories will spontaneously arise to be dealt with and reinterpreted. These memories are not 'random', though it seems that way to the conscious mind. They are revelatory. They show the origins – the whys and the wherefores – of your present condition. Look at them from your present state of consciousness and they will lose their power over you.

Finances are good all year, and good this month too. I would say they are better after the 20th than before though.

Love is close to home this month. There will be no need to travel far and wide in search of it.

May

Best Days Overall: 7, 8, 16, 17, 24, 25
Most Stressful Days Overall: 14, 15, 20, 21, 26, 27, 28
Best Days for Love: 4, 5, 7, 8, 14, 15, 17, 20, 21, 24, 26
Best Days for Money: 9, 10, 18, 19, 26, 27
Best Days for Career: 4, 5, 14, 15, 22, 23, 26, 27, 28

Your love planet the Sun has been in your 4th house since April 20 and he will remain there until the 21st of this month. So, there is more socializing from home and with the family; the family like to play Cupid and make introductions. You're attracted to people with whom you can have emotional intimacy – people you can share feelings with. Emotional intimacy is a form of foreplay these days. Often there are encounters with old flames under this transit. Sometimes it's not the actual person, but someone who embodies his or her personality traits. This too tends to be therapeutic (although sometimes it works out). Old issues get resolved. This is the purpose.

On the 21st, your love planet moves into your 5th house, bringing another change in the love attitudes. Now it is all about fun. Love is a form of entertainment now, rather than anything serious. You're attracted to people who can show you a good time – people who are 'happy go lucky' and easy to have fun with. This is not an aspect that's conducive for marriage or serious relationships. Romantic opportunities happen at resorts, the theatre, parties – places of entertainment.

Entertainment – fun – becomes a major focus after the 21st. Too much involvement with family and the emotional life can make a person too serious. It is time to have some fun. Personal creativity is much enhanced too. You're in one of your yearly personal pleasure peaks and you should give the urge to play full rein. The time for work will come next month when you'll be more in the mood for it, and therefore more productive.

Your health needs watching until the 21st. There are no major disasters here, but your energy is not up to its usual standards. Make sure to get enough rest. (This is easy to say but not always easy to do – especially in our frenetic world.) Enhance the health in the ways mentioned in the yearly report. On the 19th Venus enters your 6th house of health, so give more attention to the kidneys and hips. Hip massage will be more effective than usual. Good emotional health is also more important than usual.

Finances are better before the 21st than after. They are OK after the 21st but require more work.

June

Best Days Overall: 3, 4, 12, 13, 20, 21, 22, 30
Most Stressful Days Overall: 10, 11, 16, 17, 23, 24
Best Days for Love: 3, 4, 6, 7, 12, 13, 16, 17, 23, 24
Best Days for Money: 5, 6, 7, 14, 15, 23, 24
Best Days for Career: 1, 2, 10, 11, 18, 19, 23, 24, 28, 29

Last month, on the 16th, Uranus entered your 4th house. This shows various things: for a start, you're paying more attention to the home and family. There is more focus here. There also seems to be more emotional volatility in family members. They seem more rebellious and unpredictable, and a parent or parent figure longs for more personal freedom.

Home is important, but don't forget to have some fun. You're still in the midst of a yearly personal pleasure peak until the 22nd. Like last month you don't seem too serious about love. You just want to have some fun. Those of you who are in relationships should schedule more leisure with the beloved. A troubled relationship can be healed through more fun activities this month.

On the 22nd your 6th house of health and work becomes powerful. Now, you're in the mood for work. You want to work. Work is good for its own sake. Work is a form of therapy now. This is a good transit for job seekers and there are at least three opportunities here. It is also good for those of you who employ others. Even those of you already employed will have opportunities for overtime or side jobs.

The love attitudes also change after the 22nd. You seem more serious now. More practical. You're attracted to people who serve you and your interests. The workplace is not just a workplace but a social centre as well. Singles will have opportunities for office romances with co-workers. There is also an attraction to health professionals or those who are involved in your health.

Finances are a bit rocky on the 6th and the 7th, but the month ahead is prosperous. Your financial planet, Neptune, is involved in a Grand Trine in the water signs all month. (This is a rare aspect and a positive one.) This shows good fortune in finance – an easy flow of energy. The only issue is Neptune's retrograde on the 18th, which complicates things and perhaps introduces delays and indecision. But it won't stop earnings, only slow things down somewhat. Important financial decisions or investments should be made before the 18th. After that date, things will need more research. Make only necessary purchases and delay big expenditure until you have some clarity on the matter. Due diligence is always important, but especially after the 18th.

July

Best Days Overall: 1, 10, 11, 18, 19, 27, 28, 29
Most Stressful Days Overall: 7, 8, 14, 15, 20, 21
Best Days for Love: 3, 4, 5, 6, 12, 13, 14, 15, 16, 21, 22, 25, 26
Best Days for Money: 1, 3, 4, 12, 13, 20, 21, 27, 28, 29, 30, 31
Best Days for Career: 7, 8, 16, 17, 20, 21, 25, 26

Mars has been in your sign since May 16 and will be there all of this month. This has both good and bad points. The good points are that it gives energy and courage. You get things done quickly. You have a 'can do' spirit. On the other hand, it can make a person more combative and impatient. You don't suffer fools gladly these days. Rush and hurry can lead to injury or accident. So make haste, but in a mindful kind of way.

We have two eclipses this month. One, a Solar Eclipse on the 13th and the second, a Lunar Eclipse on the 27th. Both eclipses are powerful, but the Lunar Eclipse affects you most as it occurs in your own sign. Make sure you reduce your schedule then.

The Solar Eclipse of 13th occurs in your 6th house and thus announces job changes – either within your present company or with another one. There are disruptions in the workplace. The conditions of work are changing (perhaps there are new rules and regulations). You will also be making important changes in the diet and health regime in the coming months. Children and children figures in your life have their finances disrupted and are forced to make financial course corrections. This is not an especially great time for speculations. Once again love will get tested. (You've gone through these things many times.) Be more patient with the beloved this period. Pluto, your career planet, is hit by this eclipse – pretty directly – and this would indicate career changes. There are shakeups in your company or industry. Perhaps the government changes the law. The rules of the game are changed. With the way your chart is, this eclipse will help the career. Obstructions to your progress get blasted away.

The Lunar Eclipse of the 27th is, as we mentioned, stronger on you. Not only does it occur in your own sign, but it impacts on Uranus, the ruler of your Horoscope. So take it nice and easy during this time. Avoid unnecessary driving (Mars is also affected), and if you must drive, be more mindful and defensive. This eclipse will test the social life of the spouse, partner or current love. Once again there are changes in your health regime, job changes and perhaps a health scare. Your health looks good, so it probably won't be anything more than a scare. You will need to start re-evaluating yourself – your image and self-concept. A healthy thing to do. This will cause you to change and update your wardrobe, and change the way you present yourself to others.

August

Best Days Overall: 6, 7, 14, 15, 24, 25
Most Stressful Days Overall: 4, 5, 10, 11, 16, 17, 31
Best Days for Love: 2, 3, 5, 10, 11, 14, 15, 20, 24, 25, 31
Best Days for Money: 8, 9, 16, 17, 26, 27
Best Days for Career: 4, 5, 12, 13, 16, 17, 21, 22, 31

Another Solar Eclipse, on the 11th (the third one this year), will test your current marriage or relationship. It looks like a current relationship is getting a severe 'stress test' to see how well it holds up. Be more patient with the beloved this period – he or she seems under duress. Only the really good relationships are likely to stand up under this relentless pounding. That's the good news. If you can make it through this, you can probably make it through anything.

The planetary power is now on the day side of your chart. You are a day person now, achieving your goals through action – the methods of day. You are beginning a new career push now. It is becoming ever more important. Keep in mind, though, that Uranus is still in your 4th house, so home and family are still very important and a major interest. Your challenge will be to have a successful career along with a successful home and family life. This is a classic challenge that many people face. There are no rules for this. Sometimes you swing to the career, sometimes to the home. You just have to work it out case by case.

Your health has needed more attention since July 22. You, or the spouse, partner or current love, seem involved in some major, major project. (Children or children figures also seem involved.) These things are always stressful and delicate. Enhance the health in the ways mentioned in the yearly report. You're going to be busy, but don't forget to schedule some rest periods into your diary.

Health will start to improve later in the month. On the 18th Mars moves out of your sign, and on the 22nd the Sun will leave his stressful aspect.

Finances get more stressful from the 22nd onwards. These are not major problems – you're still in a cycle of prosperity – but the finances do become more challenging. You have to work harder for earnings.

You're in the midst of a yearly love and social peak until the 22nd. The eclipse of the 11th is testing love however, and probably friendships too. The 25th and 26th bring happy romantic opportunities for singles. For those in troubled relationships, these days bring an opportunity for reconciliation.

September

Best Days Overall: 2, 3, 11, 12, 20, 21, 29, 30
Most Stressful Days Overall: 1, 7, 13, 14, 27, 28
Best Days for Love: 1, 2, 3, 7, 9, 13, 18, 19, 22, 23, 29
Best Days for Money: 4, 5, 13, 14, 22, 23, 24
Best Days for Career: 1, 9, 10, 13, 14, 18, 19, 27, 28

Health and energy are good this month and you're going to need it. You look very busy these days. Mars moves back into your sign on the 11th, bringing courage and enhanced energy. (Over-activity can be a problem.) You excel in athletics and workout programmes. You get things done quickly. But, again it can make you combative and overly impatient. Watch the temper. Avoid rush and haste – sometimes the fast way in the short term is really the slow way in the long run. Drive within the speed limits.

Career is becoming ever more prominent. You haven't reached your career peak yet, but you're getting close. It's still necessary to balance the career and the home life, but the good news is that the family seems supportive of the career. On the 9th, Venus, your family planet, moves into your 10th house. Your success seems like a 'family project' rather than a solo affair.

The two planets that rule foreign travel in your chart – Jupiter, the generic ruler and Venus, the actual ruler – both occupy the career house from the 9th onwards. So there is travel this month and it is probably business travel – travel related to the career. Your willingness to travel is a big plus these days. Your social skills also seem important. Jupiter rules friends and Venus rules the social life generically. Your professional skills are important, but so are the social ones. Often in business, where there are people with equivalent professional skills, the one that has the better social skills is the one who is hired or promoted.

The love life is good this month, and will get even better after the 22nd. Your love planet in Virgo until the 22nd can make you too critical and too much a perfectionist in love. If you guard against this, things can work out. Until the 22nd it is the sexual magnetism that matters most. After the 22nd, with your love planet in romantic Libra, romance becomes more important – all the niceties of it, not just the sex. You're attracted by foreigners and exotic types. Romantic opportunities can happen in your place of worship or at religious or educational functions. You find mentor types alluring. The sexual magnetism still matters, but other things also matter.

If a current relationship is problematic, a foreign trip can make things better. It might also be beneficial to worship together or attend Bible or scripture classes together as a couple.

October

Best Days Overall: 1, 8, 9, 17, 18, 19, 27, 28
Most Stressful Days Overall: 4, 5, 10, 11, 25, 26, 31
Best Days for Love: 1, 2, 3, 4, 5, 8, 9, 10, 11, 18, 19, 20, 21, 29, 30, 31
Best Days for Money: 2, 3, 10, 11, 20, 21, 29, 30
Best Days for Career: 6, 7, 10, 11, 15, 16, 25, 26

There is beautiful cosmic timing happening in your career. Just as the career is becoming most prominent, Pluto, your career planet, starts moving forward. This happens early in the month – on the 2nd. So there is clarity about the career and, just as important, there is drive and ambition. A successful month ahead.

Though your yearly career peak begins on the 23rd, your career house is powerful all month. Jupiter and Venus (the two beneficent planets of the zodiac) are in your 10th house all month. Mercury, another beneficent planet (he rules your 5th house of fun and creativity) enters on the 10th while the Sun will enter it on the 23rd.

Career, then, is the main headline of the month and it is excellent. You have much cosmic support. You have friends in high places who are helping. Family and children are helping, and after the 23rd the spouse, partner or current love is also helping. You are elevated and recognized. Honours are likely to come. It is important to understand that the cosmos wills your success.

The health does need more watching from the 23rd onwards. The main issue seems to be over-work. The downside of all this success is that more demands are made on you. Mars, still in your sign all month, can make you overly optimistic about the body – the tendency would be to push it beyond its limits. It great to be successful but not at the expense of your health. So, work hard but schedule more rest periods. Enhance the health in the ways mentioned in the yearly report.

The love life becomes very prominent this month too. The Sun's move into your 10th house shows its importance. It is high on your priorities and this tends to success. The current love is also succeeding. You are attracted to successful people and will tend to socialize with them. You'll be meeting these kinds of people this month. The love planet in your 10th house often indicates romantic opportunities with people of high status and position – bosses, elders and authority figures. You gravitate to people who can help you careerwise.

Finances are super all month. There is luck in speculations. You have the financial favour of bosses, elders, friends and the current love. Pay rises (official or unofficial) are likely. Though this is not a yearly financial peak – it is close.

November

Best Days Overall: 4, 5, 14, 15, 23, 24
Most Stressful Days Overall: 1, 6, 7, 8, 21, 22, 27, 28
Best Days for Love: 1, 4, 5, 6, 7, 8, 14, 15, 16, 17, 23, 24, 27, 28
Best Days for Money: 6, 7, 8, 16, 17, 19, 25, 26, 27
Best Days for Career: 2, 3, 6, 7, 8, 11, 12, 21, 22, 29, 30

The career is still prominent this month, but it is winding down. By the end of the month, your 10th house will be empty. This I read as a good thing. You've achieved your short-term career goals and now you want to focus on other things.

Jupiter leaves the 10th house on the 8th and enters your 11th house of friends – your favourite house. Mercury will spend the entire month in your 11th house and the Sun will enter there on the 22nd. So the month ahead will become ever more social.

Aquarius is the 'natural' ruler of the 11th house so these movements are comfortable for you. They play to your natural strengths. You will be more involved (more so than usual) with friends, groups and group activities. You always have good technological expertise and now it will become even stronger. With Jupiter in your 11th house you will be getting all kinds of new high-tech equipment.

Aquarians have a natural love for astrology. (I would wager that most of the readers of these books are either strong Aquarians or strong in the 11th house.) Now (and over the next twelve months) your knowledge increases. My experience has been that many people get their first Horoscopes done when the 11th house becomes prominent.

Health and energy are improving steadily. You still need to be mindful of your health until the 22nd, but the stresses are much weaker than last month. On the 6th Uranus moves away from his stressful aspect. Mars leaves your sign on the 16th. Jupiter leaves his stressful aspect on the 8th and the Sun on the 22nd. By the end of the month there are *no* planets in stressful alignment with you. It will be like magic – from frenzy and fatigue, to health and energy. Perhaps some therapist, pill or potion will get the credit for this but astrologers know that it is merely the universe turning in your favour.

Last month the financial life was great. This month there are more challenges to deal with. Earnings will happen but through more work and effort. You will have to go the 'extra mile' for earnings.

December

Best Days Overall: 2, 3, 11, 12, 21, 22, 29, 30
Most Stressful Days Overall: 4, 5, 18, 19, 25, 26, 31
Best Days for Love: 2, 3, 6, 7, 14, 15, 17, 23, 24, 25, 26, 27
Best Days for Money: 4, 5, 6, 14, 15, 16, 23, 24, 26, 31
Best Days for Career: 4, 5, 9, 10, 18, 19, 27, 28, 31

Your 11th house of friends is still very strong until the 21st, so you are in your natural milieu. Your online activity is increased; social media activity likewise. The month ahead is not so much about romance, but more about friendship and group activities. Last month you were attracted to power and position. Now you want friendship in a lover – a relationship of peers. Often with the love planet in the 11th house someone who has always been 'just a friend' now becomes more than that. Sometimes, romantic encounters are engineered by friends or through social media. This is not a position of marriage or commitment. It is more like 'friendship with benefits' as the saying goes.

On the 21st, as the love planet moves into your spiritual 12th house, the love attitudes shift again. Now spiritual compatibility becomes important. With spiritual compatibility almost every problem in a relationship can be worked out. Without it, very few things can be worked out – and not for long either. This is not a time to look for love out clubbing or at night spots. Love happens as you attend spiritual lectures or seminars, at meditation sessions or while singing kirtans, at charity events. Love is much more idealistic now. Nothing matters – not money, not position, not service – only the feeling of love, the feeling that the relationship is sanctioned by a Higher Power. If there are problems in existing relationships the chart is counselling the surrender of your love issues to the Divine. If one does this sincerely miraculous things start to happen. The most complicated situation will straighten out.

Finances still require more work. If you put in the effort, there is prosperity. Mars spends the month in the money house, signalling earning from sales, marketing, advertising and good use of the media. Siblings and sibling figures are playing a role in finance (especially from the 5th to the 7th). Neighbours can also be playing a role. A parent or parent figure is prospering greatly this month. He or she will have twelve more months of prosperity, but this month seems especially strong.

Health and energy are excellent all month. You can enhance your health further in the ways mentioned in the yearly report.

Career is active this month and seems successful. It is not your major focus, but it is active. Venus moves into your 10th house on the 2nd and spends the rest of the month there. This shows family support for your career. It shows the elevation of the family as a whole.

Pisces

THE FISH

Birthdays from
19th February to
20th March

Personality Profile

PISCES AT A GLANCE

Element – Water

Ruling Planet – Neptune
  Career Planet – Jupiter
  Love Planet – Mercury
  Money Planet – Mars
  Planet of Health and Work – Sun
  Planet of Home and Family Life – Mercury
  Planet of Love Affairs, Creativity and Children – Moon

Colours – aqua, blue-green

Colours that promote love, romance and social harmony – earth tones,
  yellow, yellow-orange

Colours that promote earning power – red, scarlet

Gem – white diamond

Metal – tin

Scent – lotus

Quality – mutable (= flexibility)

Qualities most needed for balance – structure and the ability to handle form

Strongest virtues – psychic power, sensitivity, self-sacrifice, altruism

Deepest needs – spiritual illumination, liberation

Characteristics to avoid – escapism, keeping bad company, negative moods

Signs of greatest overall compatibility – Cancer, Scorpio

Signs of greatest overall incompatibility – Gemini, Virgo, Sagittarius

Sign most helpful to career – Sagittarius

Sign most helpful for emotional support – Gemini

Sign most helpful financially – Aries

Sign best for marriage and/or partnerships – Virgo

Sign most helpful for creative projects – Cancer

Best Sign to have fun with – Cancer

Signs most helpful in spiritual matters – Scorpio, Aquarius

Best day of the week – Thursday

Understanding a Pisces

If Pisces have one outstanding quality it is their belief in the invisible, spiritual and psychic side of things. This side of things is as real to them as the hard earth beneath their feet – so real, in fact, that they will often ignore the visible, tangible aspects of reality in order to focus on the invisible and so-called intangible ones.

Of all the signs of the zodiac, the intuitive and emotional faculties of the Pisces are the most highly developed. They are committed to living by their intuition and this can at times be infuriating to other people – especially those who are materially, scientifically or technically orientated. If you think that money, status and worldly success are the only goals in life, then you will never understand a Pisces.

Pisces have intellect, but to them intellect is only a means by which they can rationalize what they know intuitively. To an Aquarius or a Gemini the intellect is a tool with which to gain knowledge. To a well-developed Pisces it is a tool by which to express knowledge.

Pisces feel like fish in an infinite ocean of thought and feeling. This ocean has many depths, currents and undercurrents. They long for purer waters where the denizens are good, true and beautiful, but they are sometimes pulled to the lower, murkier depths. Pisces know that they do not generate thoughts but only tune in to thoughts that already exist; this is why they seek the purer waters. This ability to tune in to higher thoughts inspires them artistically and musically.

Since Pisces is so spiritually orientated – though many Pisces in the corporate world may hide this fact – we will deal with this aspect in greater detail, for otherwise it is difficult to understand the true Pisces personality.

There are four basic attitudes of the spirit. One is outright scepticism – the attitude of secular humanists. The second is an intellectual or emotional belief, where one worships a far-distant God-figure – the attitude of most modern church-going people. The third is not only belief but direct personal spiritual experience – this is the attitude of some 'born-again' religious people. The fourth is actual unity with the divinity, an intermingling with the spiritual world – this is the attitude of yoga. This fourth attitude is the deepest urge of a

Pisces, and a Pisces is uniquely qualified to pursue and perform this work.

Consciously or unconsciously, Pisces seek this union with the spiritual world. The belief in a greater reality makes Pisces very tolerant and understanding of others – perhaps even too tolerant. There are instances in their lives when they should say 'enough is enough' and be ready to defend their position and put up a fight. However, because of their qualities it takes a good deal to get them into that frame of mind.

Pisces basically want and aspire to be 'saints'. They do so in their own way and according to their own rules. Others should not try to impose their concept of saintliness on a Pisces, because he or she always tries to find it for him- or herself.

Finance

Money is generally not that important to Pisces. Of course they need it as much as anyone else, and many of them attain great wealth. But money is not generally a primary objective. Doing good, feeling good about oneself, peace of mind, the relief of pain and suffering – these are the things that matter most to a Pisces.

Pisces earn money intuitively and instinctively. They follow their hunches rather than their logic. They tend to be generous and perhaps overly charitable. Almost any kind of misfortune is enough to move a Pisces to give. Although this is one of their greatest virtues, Pisces should be more careful with their finances. They should try to be more choosy about the people to whom they lend money, so that they are not being taken advantage of. If they give money to charities they should follow it up to see that their contributions are put to good use. Even when Pisces are not rich, they still like to spend money on helping others. In this case they should really be careful, however: they must learn to say no sometimes and help themselves first.

Perhaps the biggest financial stumbling block for the Pisces is general passivity – a *laissez faire* attitude. In general Pisces like to go with the flow of events. When it comes to financial matters, especially, they need to be more aggressive. They need to make things happen, to create their own wealth. A passive attitude will only cause loss and missed opportunity. Worrying about financial security will not provide that security. Pisces need to go after what they want tenaciously.

Career and Public Image

Pisces like to be perceived by the public as people of spiritual or material wealth, of generosity and philanthropy. They look up to big-hearted, philanthropic types. They admire people engaged in large-scale undertakings and eventually would like to head up these big enterprises themselves. In short, they like to be connected with big organizations that are doing things in a big way.

If Pisces are to realize their full career and professional potential they need to travel more, educate themselves more and learn more about the actual world. In other words, they need some of the unflagging optimism of Sagittarius in order to reach the top.

Because of all their caring and generous characteristics, Pisces often choose professions through which they can help and touch the lives of other people. That is why many Pisces become doctors, nurses, social workers or teachers. Sometimes it takes a while before Pisces realize what they really want to do in their professional lives, but once they find a career that lets them manifest their interests and virtues they will excel at it.

Love and Relationships

It is not surprising that someone as 'otherworldly' as the Pisces would like a partner who is practical and down to earth. Pisces prefer a partner who is on top of all the details of life, because they dislike details. Pisces seek this quality in both their romantic and professional partners. More than anything else this gives Pisces a feeling of being grounded, of being in touch with reality.

As expected, these kinds of relationships – though necessary – are sure to have many ups and downs. Misunderstandings will take place because the two attitudes are poles apart. If you are in love with a Pisces you will experience these fluctuations and will need a lot of patience to see things stabilize. Pisces are moody, intuitive, affectionate and difficult to get to know. Only time and the right attitude will yield Pisces' deepest secrets. However, when in love with a Pisces you will find that riding the waves is worth it because they are good, sensitive people who need and like to give love and affection.

When in love, Pisces like to fantasize. For them fantasy is 90 per cent of the fun of a relationship. They tend to idealize their partner, which can be good and bad at the same time. It is bad in that it is difficult for anyone to live up to the high ideals their Pisces lover sets.

Home and Domestic Life

In their family and domestic life Pisces have to resist the tendency to relate only by feelings and moods. It is unrealistic to expect that your partner and other family members will be as intuitive as you are. There is a need for more verbal communication between a Pisces and his or her family. A cool, unemotional exchange of ideas and opinions will benefit everyone.

Some Pisces tend to like mobility and moving around. For them too much stability feels like a restriction on their freedom. They hate to be locked in one location for ever.

The sign of Gemini sits on the cusp of Pisces' 4th solar house of home and family. This shows that Pisces likes and needs a home environment that promotes intellectual and mental interests. They tend to treat their neighbours as family – or extended family. Some Pisceans can have a dual attitude towards the home and family – on the one hand they like the emotional support of the family, but on the other they dislike the obligations, restrictions and duties involved with it. For Pisces, finding a balance is the key to a happy family life.

Horoscope for 2018

Major Trends

A happy and prosperous year ahead. A highly successful year as well. For the past two years, Saturn has been in your 10th house of career. You have had to work very hard. Your bosses were probably very demanding and never satisfied. You were 'stretched' in ways that you never imagined. But now, since late last month, Saturn has moved out of your 10th house and into the 11th and the stress has eased. You'll see the results of your hard work this year. More on this later.

Jupiter, since October of last year, has been in your 9th house and he will remain there almost all year – until November 8. This signals foreign travel and career opportunities in foreign lands. Travel is likely to be career related. This is an excellent position for college students and for those who are college bound. It shows success in their studies and efforts. All of you will have happy educational opportunities in the year ahead – and if they are career related, you should take them.

For the past seven years, as Uranus has been in your money house, you have had to deal with much financial insecurity. Earnings were never stable; sometimes they were very high, sometimes ultra-low. It was very difficult to stick to a financial plan, as financial changes kept happening. Much of this will quieten down this year – and especially next year onwards. Uranus makes a major move out of your money house on May 16 and enters your 3rd house of communication. He is there until November 6. Most of the financial lessons that you needed to learn have been learned. You will start to experience more stability and security. More on this later.

Pluto has been in your 11th house of friends for many years now and will be there for many more to come. He is a fixture in this house for a while. This year he is joined by Saturn, who will be there for the next two years. Friendships have been tested for many years. In many cases, friends have died, quite literally. But most often this testing resulted in near-death experiences or surgery. Perhaps friendships – the relationship itself – have also had near-death kinds of experiences. Saturn in this house is going to further test your friendships. More details later.

Neptune has been in your own sign for some years now and he will be there for many more years. He, too, is a fixture in your sign. Always spiritual, this makes you even more so. Always idealistic, this transit enhances it. The good news is that it brings great glamour and 'mystique' to your image. More on this later.

Your most important areas of interest this year are the body, image and personal pleasure; finance (until May 16 and from November 6 onwards); communication and intellectual interests (from May 16 to November 6); foreign travel, higher education, religion and philosophy (until November 8); career (from November 8 onwards); and friends, groups and group activities.

Your paths of greatest fulfilment this year are foreign travel, higher education, religion and philosophy (until November 8); career (from November 8 onwards); health and work (until November 17); and children, fun and creativity (from November 17 onwards).

Health

(Please note that this is an astrological perspective on health and not a medical one. In days of yore there was no difference, both of these perspectives were identical. But now there could be quite a difference. For a medical perspective, please consult your doctor or health practitioner.)

We have noted a steady increase in health and energy over the past few years: 2016 was especially challenging; 2017 was challenging, but less so. This year, health should be excellent. Now that Saturn has moved out of Sagittarius (late last year) *all* the long-term planets are either in harmonious aspect with you or leaving you alone. Only towards the end of the year, from November 8 onwards, is there a challenging long-term planet stressing you – Jupiter. And, Jupiter's impact tends to be mild.

So health is good this year. You seem to have grown in your understanding of health matters, and you seem to enjoy your current regime – the Moon's North Node spends most of the year in your 6th health house. You have learned many health lessons in the last two years and you will learn more this year. Your health regime is pleasurable now. However, we see a need to make many changes this year. Things that were necessary in the past few years are no longer needed. The dynamic is different, and thus the health regime should be different.

We have five eclipses this year (usually there are four). Of the five, four impact on health. So course corrections are necessary this year. (We will discuss these in more detail in the monthly reports.)

Your health is good but you can make it even better. Give more attention, more focus, to the following – the vulnerable areas of your Horoscope:

Important foot reflexology points for the year ahead

Try to massage all of the foot on a regular basis – the top of the foot as well as the bottom – but pay extra attention to the points highlighted on the chart. When you massage, be aware of 'sore spots' as these need special attention. It's also a good idea to massage the ankles and below them.

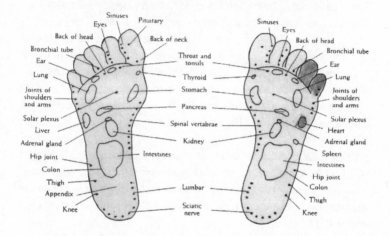

- The feet are always important for Pisces. Foot massage or foot reflexology – see our chart above – should be a part of your normal health regime. Shoes should fit correctly and not unbalance you. Keep the feet warm in the winter. There are all kinds of gadgets – which are not expensive – that massage the feet. Some even give foot whirlpool treatments. These are good investments for you, Pisces. You can have your feet treated while watching TV or at your computer.
- The heart. This, too, is always important, as the Sun, your health planet, rules the heart. (The reflex point is shown above.) It is very important to let go of worry and anxiety, the two emotions that stress the heart. Replace worry with faith. Meditation will help you.

Your health planet, the Sun, is a fast-moving planet, as our regular readers know. In any given year he will move through all the signs and houses of your Horoscope so there are many short-term health trends that depend on where the Sun is and the aspects he receives. These are best dealt with in the monthly reports.

Home and Family

Your 4th house of home and family is not a house of power this year. Thus it is not a major focus. There's nothing against making changes here – nothing against a move – but nothing that especially supports it. This tends to the status quo. It shows a basic satisfaction with things as they are and you have no pressing need to make changes. (You have more pressing interests in the year ahead.)

What we see with you we also see with parents or parent figures, and siblings or sibling figures in your life. A stable, quiet kind of year.

Children and children figures in your life are having many changes and dramas, but the family situation also seems stable. Grandchildren, if you have them, are prospering and travelling this year, but the family situation tends to the status quo. If they are of appropriate age they are very fertile this year.

With a chart like this, no news should be considered good news. It means there are no major disasters either.

A parent or parent figure is successful at work and has many wonderful job opportunities. He or she is successful this year and is helpful in your career too. He or she seems experimental in health matters and gravitates to alternative, untried kinds of therapies.

Siblings or sibling figures are experiencing strong urges for freedom this year, and these urges will just get stronger in the years to come. If they are of appropriate age, their marriages or love relationships will get tested. They will probably travel a lot, live in different places for long periods of time, but probably will not formally move.

Your family planet, Mercury, is a fast-moving planet, and over the course of a year he will move through all the signs and houses of your Horoscope and receive all kinds of different aspects. Sometimes he will move quickly, sometimes slowly and sometimes he will go backwards. This describes your family situation: fluid and constantly changing. Thus there are many short-term trends with family that are best discussed in the monthly reports.

If you're planning to repair and redecorate your home – in a cosmetic kind of way – April 22 to May 19 is a good time. It is also good for buying art objects for the home. If you're planning serious renovations or construction, May 20 to June 21 is a good time.

Finance and Career

As we mentioned earlier, the big news this year is Uranus's move out of your money house and into the 3rd house of communication. He will spend approximately half the year in the money house and half in the 3rd house. The full-blown transit will begin next year, but you're seeing the beginnings of it now.

Many of the trends we've discussed in past years are still in effect, but they are beginning to change. Uranus favours the technology – computers, software, robotics, driverless cars and the whole online world. He favours the electronic media, and radio and TV as well. All these areas are still interesting as investments or businesses. Whatever work you're actually doing, these activities are important. You will spend more on technology but will also earn from it.

Uranus in the sign of Aries favours start-ups – and this is a burgeoning field. Every day we read of some new start-up that has a new technological handle on an old problem. These things are also interesting as investments or businesses.

People in the high-tech world can be playing an important role in your finances. However, gradually over the coming years, the high-tech, online world will become less important for you

Your financial planet is Mars and he is a relatively fast-moving planet. He won't move through all your houses this year – but he does go through five of them. (Some years he moves through seven or eight houses.) So there are many short-term financial trends that are best discussed in the monthly reports.

This year Mars will spend an unusual amount of time (approximately four months) in your 11th house – in the sign of Capricorn. (Usually he spends approximately a month and a half in a house.) This reinforces what we have said above. It favours the high-tech world, the online world, and electronic media.

Mars will make one of his rare retrogrades this year, from June 26 to

August 27. (They only happen once every two years.) This will be a time to put your finances under review. A time to see where improvements can be made. A time to gain mental clarity on your financial life. It is not a time for major purchases or investments.

It seems to me that you will prosper this year. Jupiter in Scorpio makes beautiful aspects to you and tends to improve finances.

The year ahead is going to be a strong career year – but later on. You're basically preparing for Jupiter's move into your 10th house of career on November 8, where he will be in his own sign and house. This is a very powerful position. He is home. He exerts his beneficence with great power. So the career is going to be successful. You will be elevated, recognized and perhaps even receive honours. In the meantime you can enhance your career by a willingness to travel – this seems important. You have wonderful relations with your bosses and superiors. You have their favour. It would also be good to take advantage of any educational opportunities related to the career. Mentoring others will also be helpful. The bosses and authority figures appreciate this.

Love and Social Life

Your 7th house of love and social activities wasn't strong last year and is not strong in the year ahead either. Love and romance don't seem big issues. Now, there's nothing in the chart that's against romance. But there's nothing special supporting it either. This tends to the status quo. Those who are married will tend to stay married, and singles will tend to stay single. There is a basic satisfaction with things as they are.

In truth, the year ahead is not very social. Saturn will be in your 11th house of friends all year, which tends to restrict friendships. Oh, you will still have friends, but the ones you have will be good ones. This is not a year for having hordes of lukewarm friends.

Saturn is a genius at reorganizing things. He will put existing friendships through a 'stress test' and this will go on for the next two years. (A Saturn transit is not really an event, but a process.) Only through the stresses that he engineers will you know who is a real friend and who isn't. It might not be pleasant at times, but it is ultimately good.

In general your most active love period will be from August 23 to September 22.

Your love planet, Mercury, is a fast-moving – and erratic – kind of planet. And this tends to mirror your love life and your love attitudes and needs. Sometimes he moves quickly (at times he moves through three signs and houses in a given month), sometimes he moves slowly, sometimes he stands still, and sometimes he goes backwards. In any given year, he will move through all the signs and houses of your Horoscope, and he will make every possible aspect with every planet in your chart – good aspects and sometimes challenging ones. Thus there are many short-term trends in love that depend on where Mercury is and the kind of aspects he receives. These short-term trends are best discussed in the monthly reports.

A parent or parent figure in your life has an excellent love year towards the end of the year. If he or she is single, a marriage or serious relationship is happening. Siblings and sibling figures are also having an excellent social year. They have love this year. The only question is the stability of it. It seems rocky. Children and children figures (of appropriate age) are better off not marrying. If they are in a marriage or serious relationship it is getting tested over the next two years. Grandchildren (if you have them) of appropriate age are better off not marrying. They seem to gravitate to serial love affairs.

If friends want to improve their love lives they need to lighten up a bit. They seem much too stern and serious.

Self-Improvement

Pisces people are natural psychics. It is a gift that can bless or destroy. It needs to be understood and handled properly. Most of the ills that befall the Piscean come from uncontrolled psychic activity. They absorb energy vibrations that are toxic – often without knowing or understanding what is happening.

With Neptune in your own sign for the past few years (and for many more years to come), these tendencies are greatly magnified. It is always important to be around positive, uplifting kinds of people. Being around the wrong people, negative people – regardless of their wealth or status – can be a very painful thing. But even if one is not with the wrong people, the vibrations of the world at large can be very harmful to a sensitive person.

There is a need to learn how to shield the aura – to block out destructive energies – and to create an aura of health, love and happiness. There is a need to learn the basics of psychic hygiene and to apply these principles. For a Pisces, psychic hygiene is perhaps even more important than physical hygiene. This is a big subject and beyond our scope here. But you should read all you can on the subject.*

Your physical body, as we mentioned, is becoming spiritualized and refined. There's a tendency now to feel psychic vibrations right inside the physical body. It actually feels like a physical sensation. If you're not careful you can 'take it on' and then other problems will ensue. Thus – and we have written of this in past years – if you're around someone with a heart condition, you can feel your own heart constricting or palpitating. Or if someone close to you has a knee problem, your own knee can feel painful. These things are not you – but they feel like you. You're just picking up outside vibrations.

A few years ago I was at the doctor's and as I was waiting I started to feel chest pains – something I never get. It felt physical. I understood what it was – the vibrations of the office and the people – and when the doctor came in to examine me I said nothing. When I got home, I did half an hour of meditation and the pains left. They've never come back. I shudder to think what might have happened had I mentioned the pains to the doctor – I'd have probably been whisked into hospital for surgery for something that was never physical in the first place!

This is the kind of thing we're talking about. You sort of have to be in your body, but detached from it emotionally. Look at it as 'registering device' – a bio meter – registering vibrations and sensations. But these things are not you. This attitude and understanding will prevent many a needless adventure.

You Pisceans will understand what's being said here.

---

* *My book A Technique for Meditation is a good place to start, but there are other books on this too.*

Month-by-month Forecasts

January

> Best Days Overall: 1, 2, 10, 11, 20, 21, 29, 30
> Most Stressful Days Overall: 5, 6, 12, 13, 14, 27, 28
> Best Days for Love: 3, 4, 5, 6, 15, 16, 25, 26, 27, 28
> Best Days for Money: 1, 2, 10, 11, 20, 21, 22, 23, 29, 30
> Best Days for Career: 1, 2, 10, 11, 12, 13, 14, 20, 21, 29, 30

You begin your year with most of the planets in the day side (upper half) of your Horoscope. Even your family planet, Mercury, is above the horizon and in your 10th house of career (until the 11th). Thus your outer goals – your career – are very important. You can downplay home and family issues for a while and focus on your outer goals. The family is supportive of your career, which is also good. Less of a conflict.

You had your career peak period last month, but the career still seems successful. Mercury in your 10th house shows the favour of friends and social connections (who also seem successful) – they are playing a positive role in your career. On the 27th, Mars, your financial planet, enters your 10th house. This often indicates pay rises (official or unofficial), the financial favour of bosses, parents, parent figures and authority figures in your life. Success is measured in hard cash at this time, not status or prestige.

Health is good this month, yet a Lunar Eclipse on the 31st brings changes to the health regime. This eclipse occurs in your 6th house of health and work and announces job changes and shakeups in your place of employment. If you employ others, there are dramas in the lives of employees, and perhaps employee turnover. Children and children figures are having personal and financial dramas. Events caused by the eclipse force them to redefine themselves in a better way. People are getting the wrong impression of them and it needs to be changed. These changes will happen over the next six months. They also need to make course corrections in the financial life.

Health, as we mentioned, is good. You can enhance it further through back and knee massage until the 20th. After the 20th you respond very well to spiritual healing techniques. If you feel under the weather, see a spiritual healer.

This is a prosperous month. Your financial planet Mars is making nice aspects to you almost the entire month. From the 4th to the 9th Mars travels with Jupiter, bringing a nice payday – financial increase and/or opportunity. On the 27th, he crosses the Mid-heaven and enters your 10th house of career. This makes finance a major focus – which is good. We get what we focus on, by the spiritual law.

February

Best Days Overall: 6, 7, 16, 17, 25, 26
Most Stressful Days Overall: 2, 3, 9, 10, 23, 24
Best Days for Love: 2, 3, 4, 5, 14, 15, 16, 25, 26
Best Days for Money: 6, 7, 9, 10, 16, 17, 19, 20, 25, 26, 27, 28
Best Days for Career: 6, 7, 9, 10, 16, 17, 25, 26

A Solar Eclipse on the 15th brings many changes and disruptions. It impacts on many areas of your chart, although its affects are basically benign for you. The eclipse occurs in your spiritual 12th house, signalling important spiritual changes – changes in practice, teachings and teachers. Spiritual attitudes get changed as well. It tends to bring shakeups and disruptions in spiritual or charitable organizations you're involved with. A guru figure in your life has personal dramas. Every Solar Eclipse affects the job and the health regime (the eclipsed planet, the Sun, is your health and work planet), so, like last month, there are job changes, disruptions in the workplace and employee instability. Children and children figures in your life need to make more financial changes – the changes they made last month are not enough. The financial thinking has certainly been unrealistic. This is not a good period for speculations. Mercury and Jupiter are both impacted by this eclipse. So, there are family dramas, career changes, dramas in the lives of bosses, parents or parent figures, and changes in the career path and thinking. Since Mercury is also your love planet, this eclipse will test a current relationship. Perhaps the spouse, partner or current love has a health issue or needs to change the health regime too. As we mentioned, you're personally not very affected by the eclipse – the changes are happening all around you.

This a very spiritual month. Your 12th house is where the action is, until the 18th. The spiritual changes that you make seem due to spiritual breakthroughs, and thus would be natural and normal.

Spiritual healing techniques are still very powerful all month. Until the 18th it would be beneficial to enhance the health through ankle and calf massage. On the 18th, as your health planet moves into your sign, foot massage (which is always good for you) is even more effective.

Once the excitement of the eclipse dies down, the month ahead is happy. On the 18th you enter one of your yearly personal pleasure peaks. A good time to reward your body for its yeoman service to you all these years. Be kind to it. Pamper it a little.

March

Best Days Overall: 6, 7, 15, 16, 17, 24, 25
Most Stressful Days Overall: 1, 2, 8, 9, 22, 23, 29, 30
Best Days for Love: 1, 2, 8, 18, 19, 26, 27, 29, 30
Best Days for Money: 6, 7, 8, 9, 15, 16, 17, 18, 19, 20, 24, 25, 29, 30
Best Days for Career: 6, 7, 8, 9, 15, 16, 17, 24, 25

A happy and prosperous month. The planetary power is at its maximum Eastern position now (this is the sector of the self), and thus you have maximum independence these days. (Last month was also an independent kind of month.) This is a time to have life on your terms. If conditions irk you, you have the power to change them to what you would like. With this power comes responsibility, though. If your creations are amiss, you will pay the price later on. This 'me first' attitude might be considered 'selfish' by others, but it is merely the cycle you're in right now. The cosmos wants you to be happy, wants you to look good, wants you to have your way. If you are happy the world becomes that much happier.

The month begins with only one planet in stressful alignment with you – Mars. On the 17th he will leave this stressful alignment and start making harmonious aspects to you. So health and energy are excellent this month. (Only the Moon – and temporarily at that – will make stressful aspects at various times.) With good health (another form of wealth) and energy, all kinds of things become possible that weren't before. Depression can be defined as 'lack of energy'. When energy is high there is no depression. The horizons expand. The future looks rosy.

Your financial planet, Mars, is still in the 10th house of career, as he was last month. This shows that you still have the financial favour of bosses, elders, parents, parent figures and the authorities in your life. You tend to measure success in monetary terms rather than in status or prestige. Your good professional reputation is like money in the bank and leads to earnings and earnings opportunities. On the 17th Mars moves into your 11th house. This shows that social contacts – especially friends – are helpful in your financial life. This aspect favours the high-tech world and online kinds of activities. On the 20th, as the Sun enters your 2nd money house, you begin a yearly financial peak. Earnings can come in many ways (the money house is chock-full of planets this month). Job opportunities come – opportunities for over-time or second jobs as well. There is good family and spousal support. A business partnership or joint venture can happen. There are financial opportunities close by in your neighbourhood – perhaps actually through your neighbours.

April

Best Days Overall: 2, 3, 12, 13, 21, 22, 29
Most Stressful Days Overall: 4, 5, 6, 18, 19, 25, 26
Best Days for Love: 4, 5, 6, 7, 8, 14, 15, 16, 17, 23, 24, 25, 26, 27
Best Days for Money: 2, 3, 7, 8, 12, 13, 14, 15, 16, 17, 21, 22, 25, 26, 29, 30
Best Days for Career: 2, 3, 4, 5, 6, 12, 13, 21, 22, 29, 30

On February 18 the planetary power began to shift to the night side of your chart. And this will be the case for the next few months. You're a night person now, engaged in the activities of night. It's the time for rest and recuperation, for dealing with home, family and your emotional wellness. A time to build up the forces for the next day – your next career push, which will begin later in August. Your career planet, Jupiter, started to travel backwards on March 8 and will be in retrograde motion for a few months. It is a time to gain clarity on your career. Many career issues won't be solved just yet – only time will resolve them. So, you may as well focus on the family.

The career is going to be great this year, but now work on it through the methods of night – through meditation, creative dreaming and visualization, through putting yourself in the 'emotional state' of where you want to be. Shoot for the Moon now. You're free to think and visualize as you choose. As the saying goes, 'think big'.

You're still in a prosperous month. You're in the midst of a yearly financial peak. The cosmic power is conspiring to prosper you. The cosmos cares about these things. Like last month there are job opportunities for those of you who are unemployed. Those already employed have opportunities for overtime or side jobs. Mercury, your love and family planet, spends the month in your money house. Like last month this shows family support and the involvement of family connections in finance. Again it can show a business-type partnership or a joint venture. But there are delays with this.

Health and energy are still good. Until the 24th there are no planets in stressful alignment with you (only the Moon aligns so, on occasion). You seem more concerned with your financial health than with your physical health. Perhaps you are spending more on health products this month, but you can also earn from this area. You can enhance the health even further through scalp, face and head massage until the 20th. Spiritual therapies are always good for you, but especially from between the 17th and the 19th. (There can be some disturbances at the job from the 17th to the 19th too.) After the 20th enhance the health through neck massage.

May

Best Days Overall: 9, 10, 18, 19, 26, 27, 28
Most Stressful Days Overall: 2, 3, 16, 17, 22, 23, 29, 30
Best Days for Love: 2, 3, 7, 8, 13, 14, 17, 22, 23, 26, 31
Best Days for Money: 4, 5, 9, 10, 11, 12, 13, 15, 16, 18, 19, 24, 26, 27
Best Days for Career: 2, 3, 9, 10, 18, 19, 26, 27, 29, 30

Finances are becoming less important, less of a focus this month. On the 13th Mercury will leave the money house, and on the 16th Uranus will make a major move out of the 2nd house, where he's been for over seven years. This, I feel, is a good sign. Your short-term financial goals have been achieved and you're ready to put your attention elsewhere. Your 3rd house became powerful on April 20, and remains powerful this month until the 21st, so the focus now is on communication and intellectual interests. Reading a good book by a good writer is one of the great pleasures of life. Yet, people are so busy that they rarely have this opportunity. Now is the time for this. It is a great month for students below college level. There is focus on their studies and this tends to success. Teachers, writers, journalists and media people also have a good month. Their work flows more easily. The mind is sharper. Sales and marketing people should also do well.

Though Uranus leaves the money house, technology and online activities still seem very important financially. Mars will be in your 11th house until the 16th and then in the sign of Aquarius for the rest of the month. Both the 11th house and the sign of Aquarius relate to technology. You've been more experimental in financial matters for some years now, and the trend continues in the month ahead. Social connections also seem important.

Mars, your financial planet, in your 12th house of spirituality from the 16th onwards signals the importance of the financial intuition. And, though you already understand much about spiritual wealth, you will go deeper into it. It is a period for 'miracle' money rather than 'natural' money.

Your career planet Jupiter is still retrograde all month, and your 4th house of home and family becomes very powerful after the 21st. So, as we mentioned last month, let career issues slide (or work on them in interior ways, where there are no obstructions) and focus on building the infrastructure for future career success.

Health needs more watching this month – especially after the 21st. There are no major problems here though, only lowered energy levels (the primal disease). As always, make sure to get enough rest. You can enhance the health through neck massage until the 21st, and through arm and shoulder massage afterwards. Good emotional health also becomes important after the 21st.

June

Best Days Overall: 5, 6, 7, 14, 15, 23, 24
Most Stressful Days Overall: 12, 13, 18, 19, 25, 26
Best Days for Love: 3, 4, 6, 7, 14, 16, 18, 19, 23, 24
Best Days for Money: 3, 4, 5, 6, 7, 8, 9, 12, 13, 14, 15, 20, 21, 22, 23, 24, 30
Best Days for Career: 5, 6, 7, 14, 15, 23, 24

Like last month, your 4th house of home and family is powerful, the 10th house of career is empty, and your career planet is retrograde. You're in the midnight hour of your year – the deepest part of the night. A magical time. The 4th house is often called the 'house of endings': an old day ends and a new one begins. In a Natal chart it shows the conditions at the end of the life. In your chart, it shows the conditions at the conclusion of your year – how it will end up. This is because the night sets the tone for the day. The interior condition tends to manifest externally by the spiritual law. You're a star in your family. There is love. You have much psychological illumination and insight.

So, like last month, focus on your interior condition and let career matters go. Only time will resolve certain issues anyway.

Health still needs attention until the 21st. Right diet seems important this month (usually it is not such a big deal), so make sure you're eating correctly. Emotional health will be important all month. Avoid depression like the plague. Use the tools of meditation to keep the moods positive and constructive. Arm and shoulder massage is effective until the 21st, after that abdominal massage will be beneficial.

Finance doesn't seem a big issue this month. The money house is basically empty (only the Moon moves through there on the 8th and 9th), and your financial planet Mars spends the month in your 12th house of spirituality. Thus the financial intuition is ultra-important. The high-tech and online world (and electronic media) seem important in finances. Your financial planet starts to retrograde on the 26th, so do your best to make any major purchases or investments before then. After the 26th it is best to put the financial life under review and work to attain mental clarity here. Trends are not what they seem.

Love is close to home this month. Until the 12th there is more entertaining from home and socializing with family members. There is a tendency to live in the past when the 4th house is strong. Memories start to surface. We remember the 'good old days' – which may, or may not, have been that good but seem that way. In love the tendency is to recreate old happy experiences. However, in love you need to be open to the *now* which, if fully experienced, could be better than the past. There is also a tendency to be more moody in love. People involved with Pisces romantically need to understand this.

July

Best Days Overall: 3, 4, 12, 13, 20, 21, 30, 31
Most Stressful Days Overall: 10, 11, 16, 17, 22, 23, 24
Best Days for Love: 5, 6, 14, 15, 16, 17, 22, 23, 24, 25, 26
Best Days for Money: 1, 5, 6, 10, 11, 12, 13, 18, 19, 20, 21, 27, 28, 29
Best Days for Career: 1, 12, 13, 20, 21, 22, 23, 24, 27, 28, 29

Though this is a year for travel, with the two planets that rule travel in your chart retrograde, this is not a great month for it. Also there's a Solar Eclipse on the 13th that impacts on Pluto, your travel planet. If you must travel – if it's a necessity – allow more time to get to your destination and avoid the eclipse period.

The Solar Eclipse this month is basically benign in its effects on you, but it occurs in your 6th house of health and work and the eclipsed planet, the Sun, is also the ruler of this house. So this area of life is very much affected now. Thus there are job changes, disruptions or dramas in the workplace and changes in the conditions of work. Job changes can be within your present company or with another one. If you are an employer there is instability among employees and likely staff turnover. (Some of this might not be your fault – it can happen because of dramas in the lives of your employees and have nothing to do with you.) The financial thinking of children and children figures in your life is shown to be unrealistic and requires changes. There can be dramas in the lives of aunts and uncles (or those who play this role in your life). The spouse, partner or current love experiences spiritual changes – changes in the inner life, the teachings and perhaps teachers. The guru figures in his or her life are experiencing life-changing dramas.

The Lunar Eclipse of the 27th occurs in your spiritual 12th house and impacts on your spiritual planet. So this area of life is very much affected. This generally produces events 'behind the scenes' that change your spiritual life, teachings, teachers and practice. The earlier eclipse this month brought these changes for the current love; this eclipse brings them for you. A charity or spiritual organization you're involved with seems chaotic – with shakeups and disruptions happening. Guru figures in your life are having life-changing kinds of dramas. Parents or parent figures should be more careful driving during this period. If possible they should stay off the roads. If they must drive, it should be done more mindfully. The eclipsed planet, the Moon, rules children and children figures. So they are having personal dramas. The events of the eclipse will once again force them to redefine themselves in a better way. They will need to create a better image of themselves.

August

Best Days Overall: 8, 9, 16, 17, 26, 27
Most Stressful Days Overall: 6, 7, 12, 13, 19, 20
Best Days for Love: 1, 2, 3, 5, 10, 11, 12, 13, 14, 15, 19, 20, 24, 25, 29, 30
Best Days for Money: 1, 2, 3, 6, 8, 9, 13, 16, 17, 22, 26, 27, 29, 30
Best Days for Career: 8, 9, 16, 17, 19, 20, 26, 27

More job and health changes happening this month. Anything not settled by last month's Solar Eclipse gets settled this month when we have the third Solar Eclipse of the year on the 11th, again occurring in your 6th house of health and work. As before, this area is especially affected as the Sun is also the ruler of this house. So, there are more dramas at work and in the workplace. There is more employee turn-over for those of you who hire others. Children and children figures need to make more course corrections in their finances. There are dramas in the lives of aunts and uncles (or those who play that role in your life).

On the 23rd dawn begins to break in your year. It is time to be up and about. Time to pay attention to your career and outer goals. Time to work on things by the methods of day - through overt action. Adding to this - with perfect timing - is the resumed forward motion of your career planet, Jupiter, which began on July 10. The way is being cleared for your next career push.

There is much power in your 6th house this month. This shows that you're in the mood for work. You work because you want to, not because you have to. This makes you a more productive kind of worker. It is also a good time to achieve all those boring, detailed jobs that you keep putting off. Job seekers have good fortune all month. Those already employed have opportunities for overtime work or second jobs.

Finances are tricky this month. They will be better after the 13th than before, but still they'll not be what they should be or will be later on. Your financial planet is retrograde. So, the financial judgement is not at its best. Add to this that Mars will be 'out of bounds' all month. The urge for earnings is taking you outside your normal sphere. This can make you feel insecure. On the other hand, you seem to have no choice. There are no traditional financial solutions available to you – you have to think 'outside the box'.

Though you're making changes to the health regime, health looks basically good. Even if the eclipse brings some kind of scare, that's all it is likely to be. But after the 22nd your health will need more watching. There's no disasters here, only lower than usual energy levels.

September

Best Days Overall: 4, 5, 13, 14, 22, 23, 24
Most Stressful Days Overall: 2, 3, 9, 15, 16, 29, 30
Best Days for Love: 2, 3, 9, 13, 18, 19, 22, 23, 29
Best Days for Money: 1, 4, 5, 10, 11, 13, 14, 20, 21, 22, 23, 24, 25, 26, 29, 30
Best Days for Career: 4, 5, 13, 14, 15, 16, 22, 23, 24

Last month on the 22nd, as the Sun entered your 7th house of love, you began a yearly love and social peak. Also, shortly before that – on August 19 – your love planet Mercury started to move forward. These are all positives for love.

Last month, Mercury spent the whole time in your 6th house. So the workplace was more than just a workplace, it was your social centre. Mercury is still in your 6th house until the 6th of this month, and with the Sun, your health and work planet, in your 7th house of love since August 22, the workplace is still a social centre this month. There are romantic opportunities with co-workers – the office romance. Sometimes it is the co-worker who plays Cupid and makes introductions. There is also an attraction to health professionals and to people involved in your health.

The health planet in the house of love can make it challenging in love. There is a tendency – like a good doctor – to search for pathologies or imperfections in a relationship. The motives are good – you search for problems in order to cure or assuage them, but this can make a person overly critical – a sure killer for romance. If you can avoid these traps, love can go well. The problems in a relationship will come up – there is no way to hide them – but make sure to look at the good points too. Keep a balanced perspective.

The love life is more active, and singles will date more and attend more parties, but marriage is not likely this month. There's nothing special supporting it.

Finances are improving this month. Mars started moving forward on August 28. He is still 'out of bounds' until the 24th of this month, but you're more secure in your new environment. Financial judgement is better. Mars will be helped by positive aspects from the 22nd onwards and the month ahead should be prosperous. The high-tech and online world still seems very important in your finances. People from these kinds of industries can play an important role too. And, from the 11th onwards, pay attention to the intuition. Financial guidance will often come in dreams or through psychics, astrologers, tarot readers or spiritual channels. The Divine wants you to be rich, but you have to do things its way.

October

Best Days Overall: 2, 3, 10, 11, 20, 21, 29, 30
Most Stressful Days Overall: 1, 6, 7, 12, 13, 14, 27, 28
Best Days for Love: 1, 2, 3, 6, 7, 9, 10, 11, 17, 18, 19, 20, 21, 27, 28, 29, 30
Best Days for Money: 1, 2, 3, 8, 9, 10, 11, 17, 18, 19, 20, 21, 22, 23, 27, 28, 29, 30
Best Days for Career: 2, 3, 10, 11, 12, 13, 14, 20, 21, 29, 30

A happy month. Health and energy are excellent. Many planets in Scorpio this month make very nice aspects to you. Detox regimes will enhance the health all month. Good health is not about adding things to the body, but about getting rid of what doesn't belong there. Surgery could be recommended to some of you, but explore detoxification as an option first. The month ahead is a sexually active kind of month, but try not to overdo it. Listen to the body. It will let you know when enough is enough.

Your 9th house of religion, philosophy, foreign travel and higher education has been prominent all year – but especially in the month ahead. Foreign travel is very likely – it could be job or career related.

This is a great period for college students – they are successful in their studies.

Love will go better after the 10th as your love planet moves into your 9th house. Love opportunities happen at college or college functions, at religious functions, in foreign lands or with foreigners. The 19th and the 20th and the 28th to the 30th are very good romantic days. I don't think marriage will happen, but it's good for romance.

Mars, your financial planet, spends the month in Aquarius, your 12th house. This merely continues a trend we have seen of late. It favours intuition over reason – although intuition is not anti-reason, but a higher form of it. Finances will be better before the 23rd than after. After the 23rd more work, more effort, is needed.

The financial planet in the 12th house shows someone who is charitable. And as we have mentioned in previous months, it favours 'miracle money' over 'natural' money. It favours drawing upon the supernatural supply rather than the natural supply.

There is only one planet in the bottom half (the night side) of your chart this month. The overwhelming dominance is on the day side. So this is the time to focus on your career and outer goals. Doing right will lead to feeling right. This is a time where you serve your family best by succeeding in the world.

November

Best Days Overall: 6, 7, 8, 16, 17, 25, 26
Most Stressful Days Overall: 2, 3, 9, 10, 23, 24, 29, 30
Best Days for Love: 1, 2, 3, 4, 5, 9, 10, 14, 15, 19, 20, 23, 24, 27, 28, 29, 30
Best Days for Money: 4, 5, 8, 15, 16, 19, 20, 25, 26, 27
Best Days for Career: 8, 9, 10, 19, 27

Although you need to watch your health and energy this month, the month ahead is successful and prosperous.

Jupiter moves out of your 9th house on the 8th and into your 10th house of career. The Sun will follow suit on the 22nd, and Mercury will spend the entire month in your 10th house. So there is elevation, recognition and honours. A promotion wouldn't be a surprise either.

Jupiter in his own sign and house from the 8th onwards is more powerful on your behalf than he's been all year. He is in his rightful place. At home. His energy is expressed without impediment. The next twelve months – not just the month ahead – will be successful. Jupiter rules publishing, foreign travel, academia and religion. All these fields seem very interesting in the coming year. And even if you are not in these fields, people in these fields can be important careerwise.

Mars, your financial planet, will move into your own sign on the 16th. A wonderful financial transit. It brings windfalls, expensive personal items, and the feeling and image of wealth. People will see you this way. Financial opportunities will be pursuing you, rather than the other way around.

The Sun travels with Jupiter from the 24th to the 28th. This brings happy job opportunities and success at the job.

The love life also seems more prominent and active this month. Mercury, your love planet, will spend the month in your 10th house of career. This gives many messages. You're attracted to power people these days – to the high and mighty. And you will be meeting these kinds of people. You find love and social opportunities as you pursue your career goals and with people involved in your career. There is a happy romantic or social experience on the 27th or 28th – but because Mercury is retrograde, there can be a delayed reaction. Mercury will be retrograde from the 17th onwards. This doesn't stop the social life, but it does slow things down. No need to make major love decisions while Mercury is travelling backwards.

December

Best Days Overall: 4, 5, 14, 15, 23, 24, 31
Most Stressful Days Overall: 6, 7, 21, 22, 27, 28
Best Days for Love: 2, 3, 4, 5, 13, 14, 15, 23, 24, 27, 28
Best Days for Money: 4, 5, 6, 13, 16, 17, 23, 24, 26
Best Days for Career: 6, 7, 16, 26

You're still very much in a yearly career peak until the 21st. For some of you this will be a lifetime career peak. You're very much a day person now, so focus on your career and outer goals. Home and family issues can take a back seat for a while.

Health still needs watching this month. There will be improvement after the 21st. The most important thing is to get enough rest. Enhance the health through thigh massage until the 21st. This will strengthen the lower back, which will become important after that date. A herbal liver cleanse might also be good until the 21st.

Mars in your sign this month is not only good for prosperity (especially from the 5th to the 7th) but gives courage, energy and a 'can do' spirit. You excel in sports and exercise regimes (you achieve 'personal bests'). You get things done in a hurry. The only problem with this is that one can push the body further than it was designed to handle. Burn out is the main danger this month.

Love looks happy this month. On the 6th Mercury starts to move forward (he went retrograde on November 17). So the social judgement is much improved, as is the social confidence. Mercury will be in your 9th house until the 13th. This favours foreigners, religious people and highly educated people. You gravitate to people you can learn from. On the 13th Mercury enters your 10th house of career and stays there for the rest of month ahead. This tends to bring success to the social life. Mercury is at the top of your Horoscope – indicating that this is high on your agenda. Once again, like last month, you are mixing with powerful people in your life – people of authority and prestige. A lot of your socializing is career related – especially from the 20th to the 22nd. This brings a strong romantic opportunity for singles. This can be with someone with authority in your company, or the authority figure is the instrument through which this happens.

This aspect also shows the importance of social contacts in the career. Your likeability is perhaps as important as your professional skills. You advance the career through social means (and hard work). It will be beneficial to attend (or even to host) the right kind of parties or gatherings.